Confessions of an Ethical Drug Dealer

A psychedelic travelogue and memoir

Jimi Fritz

Published by SmallFry Press, Victoria, BC
Email: jimifritz20@gmail.com
Cover Art: Veronica Fritz

FIRST EDITION
Title: Confessions of an Ethical Drug Dealer
ISBN Number: 978-0-9685721-1-5
Registered with Library and Archives Canada
Printed in Toronto, Canada by Marquis

This may, or may not be, a work of fiction.

1

First things first.

An explanation is needed to address the provocative and seemingly oxymoronic title of this eponymous tome.

Drug dealer is a loaded and problematic term, both over-generalised and imprecise. It conjures images of addiction, broken lives, unethical behaviour, violence, lawlessness and the seedy soft-underbelly of desperate and lost souls. Drug dealers are dishonest, depraved monsters who have no concern for the pain and suffering they inevitably cause. They hang around school yards preying on the innocence of children. They are heartless scoundrels who inevitably come to sticky ends.

But there's another brand of drug dealer, one with a completely different agenda and modus operandi, one who deals a different class of drug to a distinct and specialised clientele. It is in this second category that I placed myself and have always preferred to consider myself a purveyor of fine psychedelics for the discriminating and responsible psychonaut.

The human brain is a bubbling caldron of chemical soup. The slightest tinkering with its biochemical balance can produce profound and surprising effects. Psychedelic drugs are one of the most powerful and effective ways to alter our brain chemistry and therefore our consciousness. We are currently in the midst of a revolution to understand what these substances do, what they are good for, and in doing so, discover their full potential.

Here's the thing: there's a clear distinction between drugs that get you *into it* and drugs that get you *out of it*.

There are smart drugs and dumb drugs. Smart drugs increase your perception and awareness of yourself and the world around you and therefore improve and enhance the quality of your life. Dumb drugs decrease awareness and perception of yourself and the world around you and consequently deteriorate and decrease the quality of your life. People do smart drugs because they want to embrace and experience the world more fully. People do dumb drugs because they hate themselves, hate their lives and want to escape from an intolerable reality. Smart people do smart drugs to improve their lives. Dumb people do dumb drugs and end up destroying their lives. If dumb people do smart drugs it can help them to become more aware, more perceptive and therefore smarter. If dumb people do smart drugs responsibly and for long enough they can end up becoming smart people doing smart drugs. Smart people can do some dumb drugs and get away with it for a while, but if smart people do too many dumb drugs for too long they become dumb people doing dumb drugs.

While this analysis may seem somewhat simplistic, there is wisdom in these musings, a modicum of merit in their madness.

Which drugs are dumb and which ones are smart?

Try this for starters:

The dumb drugs are cocaine, crack, crystal meth, heroin, opiates, benzodiazepines, and the heavy-weight champion, the Obergruppenführer of self-medication and the most addictive and harmful drug of all: alcohol.

Smart drugs are psychedelics and empathogens. They include cannabis, LSD, MDMA, DMT, 2CB, psilocybin, ayahuasca, peyote, and mescaline. These two categories are diametrically opposed, have opposite effects, and are consumed for completely different reasons.

The term, 'Psychedelic' was first coined by the British psychiatrist Humphrey Osmond at a meeting of the New York Academy of Sciences in 1957, the same year the Space Age began and the first Soviet atomic bomb was detonated.

Osmond had been researching mescaline as a cure for alcoholism with remarkable results. At the time, he corresponded with Aldous Huxley, the author of the dystopian novel, *Brave New World*, who was also interested in the potential of mescaline as a tool to explore human consciousness. At the time, Huxley was using mescaline regularly and writing about his experiences.

In discussing what this new class of drugs might be called, Huxley proposed the unpronounceable, phanerothymes. In a rhyming couplet he sent to Osmond, he wrote, "To make this trivial world sublime, take half a gram of phanerothyme." Osmond replied with a couplet of his own, "To fathom hell or soar angelic, just take a pinch of psychedelic."

From its Greek roots, psyche (soul) and dēloun (to make visible), the term appropriately translates to 'mind-manifesting'.

Empathogens, a term coined by the American psychologist Ralph Metzner, are a class of drug which engender a feeling of empathy or emotional connection. Empathogens are best exemplified by MDMA and its chemical family of phenethylamines. Osmond's phrase, "To fathom hell or soar angelic," is revealing in that it points to the potential of the mind to manifest what is 'in the mind.'

Psychedelics do not plant ideas or visions in our minds; they merely amplify our inner psyche to a far greater degree. Manifesting a troubled mind can be troubling, or even terrifying. Psychedelics are not for everyone, and those prone to psychosis or other mental disorders would be wise to steer clear altogether. But for those with an inquiring and relatively stable psychology, the rewards can be substantial and often life-changing. We are only now beginning to discover their full potential.

So-called, 'bad trips' are both rare and easily avoidable. It's what Timothy Leary, that impish, Irish rabble-rouser and renowned Harvard psychologist referred to as 'set and setting.' This cannot be emphasised enough. 'Set' is your state of mind, 'Setting,' is the environment in which you have the experience. Both are equally critical.

Leary was once described by US President Richard Nixon, as the most dangerous man in America. Tim took it as a compliment. For years, Nixon harboured a personal vendetta against Leary whom he saw as a threat to the status quo. There is no greater threat to a controlling bureaucracy than an enquiring, free, and open mind. Nixon and Leary epitomized the chasm that exists between those who cling to a rigid, immutable worldview and those who are open to new ideas and experiences. Psychedelic drug users enthusiastically leap with both feet into the latter camp.

Leary was hounded by the authorities for years and finally taken down on trumped-up possession charges. At one point he ended up in solitary confinement in the next cell to Charlie Manson.

Despite his reputation as an irresponsible agent-provocateur, Leary was a dedicated scientist who conducted thousands of LSD research sessions, kept meticulous notes, and saw the potential of psychedelics to raise the consciousness of a generation. Somewhere in the New York Public Library is a massive cache of his research papers and notes. His autobiography, *Flashbacks*, is an extraordinary account of an amazing and improbable life. Do yourself a favour and read it.

Aldous Huxley also experimented extensively with psychedelics and ended up writing, *The Doors of Perception*. You should read that too. The worlds of art and science are filled with innovators and original thinkers who have drawn valuable inspiration from psychedelic drug use.

It is with this perspective in mind that I begin my musings of a life inextricably linked to the pursuit of altered consciousness. Insofar as we can trust our memories, I have strived to be as accurate and truthful as possible, while resisting the urge to exaggerate or embellish. Names have been changed to protect the guilty.

This account of my journeys, both geographical and psychological, is by no means comprehensive or complete, but it's my hope that a vicarious experience of my explorations will leave you with a more realistic perspective on our collective relationship with these substances.

For my part, I can report nothing but positive consequences and outcomes from my fifty-year experiment with consuming, purchasing and selling psychedelic drugs.

2

Like most people, I began my foray into consciousness-altering substances with alcohol, the emperor of gateway drugs.

One sunny afternoon, as a naive thirteen-year-old, I found myself sitting in the beer garden of an English country pub with my father and grandfather. My grandfather's name was Albert, but everyone, including his wife, called him, 'Pop.' A few of his older friends called him Bert, a contraction of Albert. My father's name was Bertram Albert, both of which contracted to Bert. Some people thought it a grand joke to call him Bert Bert.

Generally, when ordering drinks, I was automatically given a Coke or a Pepsi or a cherry flavoured abomination called Tizer. This was invariably accompanied by a packet of cheese and onion crisps. On this day, however, Bert Bert and Bert had cooked up a plan to introduce me to the great British pint. My father went to get drinks from the bar and returned to the table with three pints of bitter. He plonked one down in front of me and with great aplomb commanded, "Get that down ya." Pop nodded his approval.

Contrary to its name, 'bitter' is a synonym for English ale and, despite the dictionary definition, has no connection to its flavour. In England, a pint of bitter simply refers to a pint of ale or beer. Decades later, I would discover that this concept is impossible for North Americans to grasp. The word bitter is inherently abhorrent to them and is the reason English ale is so hard to find in America and Canada. They wince at the mention of Extra Special Bitter or Best Bitter, imagining a sharp or disagreeable flavour, and no amount of explanation or education is sufficient to shift their intractable position. North Americans also insist on pluralising the word bitter to bitters. This is another inexcusable gaffe, and another habit that is impossible to break. So be it. Like the complete inability of North Americans to make a decent cup of tea, I have had to serenely accept the things I cannot change. So, while two generations of beer-sodden patriarchs looked on in quivering anticipation, I took my first sip of fine English ale.

I'd imagined by the fervour and ubiquitous fashion with which this beverage was consumed by every single male adult I had ever known, it had to be something wholly spectacular. I mentally prepared myself for an earth-shattering epiphany. I raised the glass and tentatively took the first sip.

I was underwhelmed initially. It tasted earthy, and yeasty, and flat, nothing like the sweet, fizzy drinks I was used to. But encouraged to persevere by the enthusiastic, multi-generational peer pressure of my father and grandfather, I forged ahead and took a few more swigs. By the half-way point I was beginning to acquire a taste for it, and by the time I drained the last few drops from the pint glass, I was a confirmed and life-long beer drinker.

Soon after my initiation, and driven on by the unrestrained and indiscriminate nature of the teenage brain, I set about testing the limits of this new intoxicant.

English pubs often had a takeout service called an Off Licence. They had a separate entrance to the main pub and alcohol could be purchased to drink off the premises. Soon after I had acquired my taste for alcohol, a few like-minded school friends and I hung around near our local Off Licence and waited for a likely suspect willing to buy us booze. Our mission was to get as drunk as possible, as quickly as possible, and as cheaply as possible. To this end, we pooled our lunch money and bought a bottle of sherry and a bottle of cider. This fit our limited budget and provided a variety of flavours with which to thrill our taste buds. Retiring to some nearby woods, we stood in a circle and passed the bottles around, swigging alternating mouthfuls of sherry and cider. I don't recommend this as a mixed drink but there was something about the combination that really did the trick.

Fifteen minutes later, the bottles were empty, leaving us all staggering around laughing and joking and marvelling at the disorienting effects of the booze. Shortly after that, the puking began. One by one, we were heaving and vomiting into the bushes. But we had accomplished the mission and victory was ours. Vomiting was an illustrious badge of courage and the measure of success. The next day at school we claimed our bragging rights and took great pride in regaling our friends with heroic tales of alcohol poisoning.

It wasn't long before I discovered new ways to alter my brain chemistry and my journey on the psychedelic superhighway began in earnest.

3

It all started with a conversation in the summer of 1969. This was the year that humans landed on the moon, The Beatles performed their last concert, and Charlie Manson went berserk.

I was born and raised on Pondwood Road in Crawley, Sussex. It was a green and pleasant land until the pond was filled in and the wood chopped down. Both were replaced with an endless array of row housing.

The town of Crawley was an urban planning disaster perpetrated by a demonic cabal of evil bureaucrats in the early fifties. As a solution to overcrowding and housing shortages in London, a series of 'new towns' were proposed to alleviate the problem. Six of these towns were planned, circling the City of London in a star pattern. Crawley New Town was the southernmost outpost, exactly halfway between London and Brighton.

The master plan for Crawley probably looked like a good idea on paper, neatly arranged and colour coded in geometric patterns. The plan might have gotten a B minus in drafting school. But an ugly reality was about to be foisted upon thousands of unsuspecting victims desperate for a new beginning. Londoners were promised a better life and a steady job in this new modern suburb, a place where all their dreams could come true. Many people, including my parents, jumped at the chance.

The town center and main shopping area of Crawley was

surrounded by a dozen neighbourhoods each with identical row houses, each with a school and a shopping plaza, complete with a butcher, a baker, and a candlestick maker. A massive industrial estate nearby, packed with factories, provided menial labour for generations of workers who toiled until they dropped dead from exhaustion or boredom. The problems inherent in the design and planning of this misguided, modern experiment later became obvious and manifested as a rat's nest of malcontents, civil unrest, mental disorders, rampant racism, and violence, eventually resulting in the highest number of registered heroin addicts in the British Isles.

During my formative years, I attended a special school for backward teachers. These undertrained and under-motivated educators are best described as inept demagogues, bullies, tyrants, pederasts and bicycle-seat sniffers.

Hazelwick Secondary Modern Comprehensive was the biggest school in Sussex and a colossal failed experiment in education. Apart from basic reading and writing skills, I cannot think of a single useful thing I ever learned there, except perhaps a deep-seated resentment and distrust of unearned authority.

You will sometimes hear successful people extol the virtues of influential, dedicated teachers who helped form their character or offered their inspiration at critical times in their lives. They fondly remember mentors who encouraged and motivated. As hard as I try, I cannot think of a single one.

The most common educational tools employed by the teachers of Hazelwick were primarily, the cane (three whacks on each open palm), a wooden ruler (rapped across the back of the knuckles), the rubber (a heavy, wooden, blackboard eraser thrown at the head from across the room), and the slipper (six of the best with a rubber-soled shoe).

Children were beaten and verbally abused on a daily basis. Students sometimes fought back, resulting in very exciting, full-on fist fights. The teachers usually won, but not always. We celebrated our infrequent victories.

Other folks cherish fond memories of their halcyon school days. Mine are best described as a forced death march though the dystopian and dysfunctional bowels of Hell.

I remember a front page story in the local newspaper about our school's headmaster, Mr. Keytes, who had recently imported canes from India. The article was accompanied by a photo of Mr. Keytes proudly bending a bamboo cane between his fists in a not-so subtle warning to all of us wretched, rule breakers. The crooked smile on his face gave me the willies.

Several teachers at Hazelwick were notoriously arrested and charged with the sexual abuse of minors. An art teacher was dragged from the school one day, kicking and screaming, while a crowd of students watched and cheered from the playground. He was thrown into the back of a police van and carted off to a mental asylum.

Of all the malevolent and incompetent staff at Hazelwick, Mr. Keytes was by far the most terrifying. He was, as my mother Hazel once remarked, a particularly 'nasty piece of work.' He was a tall, gaunt man with a sallow face, hooked nose and black heart. He haunted the halls like the Angel of Death. His sadistic propensity was the stuff of legend.

He cornered me in the playground one day. He liked to tower over his victims with his head bent forward like a great emaciated vulture. His voice was measured and ominous. On this particular occasion, he was concerned about my footwear. "What's wrong with your shoes, Boy?" he asked in a menacing tone. It was a trick question. There was no way to give a correct answer. It was a game of cat and mouse and there was no doubt as to who was the mouse. "What colour are they, boy?" This was an easier question. I looked down at my feet and said, "Brown?"

"And what colour *should* they be?" He was referring to a school rule stipulating that all shoes had to be black. I knew about the rule but played dumb and pretended to make a lucky guess, "Is it black, Sir?"

"And do you know *why*, Boy?!" he bellowed.

This was another trick question and I couldn't for the life of me come up with a reasonable explanation for such an arbitrary and pointless rule. I decided to play it safe, "No, sir," I said.

Mr. Keytes bent closer and put his mouth right next to my ear. I got a close-up view of his oily, scaly skin and an unmistakable whiff of sulphur. He lowered his tone to a rumbling growl made up of subsonic frequencies detectable only to elephants and blue whales. "Because," he snarled, "Brown-shoed boys are liars and cheats. They are hooligans and reprobates. Brown-shoed boys amount to nothing. They are doomed to failure. They are miserable worms." He rolled the letter r in worms to great effect.

On the day I left school for the last time, Mr. Keytes stopped me in the hallway and reiterated in great detail why I would amount to nothing. He called me lazy and stupid and said that if he had the misfortune to run into me five years hence, I would have been fired from every job I ever had and was surely condemned to a lifetime on the dole. It was amid the horrors of Hazelwick that the seminal conversation ensued.

At lunchtime one day, myself and a group of boys, as well as one very attractive blond girl, were standing in a circle behind the bike sheds smoking cigarettes. One of the boys was slightly older and the blond was his girlfriend. They fancied themselves as rockers and were trying to impress us with their anti-establishment attitude. They told us that the Woodstock music festival was taking place in a couple of weeks and took a poll as to who among us would take drugs to enhance the musical experience. He didn't specify which drugs but the girl immediately piped up with great bravado and enthusiastically said she would. If it would improve her enjoyment of the music, she was definitely in. The rocker nodded in agreement and approval. Most of the other boys my age looked coy or were vehemently opposed to the idea, citing the slippery slope of addiction. When it came to my turn, I hedged by bets. After a thoughtful pause, I found myself saying, "Probably."

Of course, none of us ended up at Woodstock because it was 3,452 miles away and we were fourteen-year-old school kids. But a few weeks later, while Joe Cocker was getting high with a little help from his friends and Jimi Hendrix was reimagining "The Star-Spangled Banner," I smoked my first joint.

4

In the sixties, no one was particularly concerned about underage drinking and every weekend, the pubs were filled with teenagers. Me and my fourteen-year-old pals were already regulars at our local pub.

On weekday evenings, the pubs opened at six o'clock and closed at ten. On Fridays and Saturdays, they stayed open until eleven. This gave us only four or five hours of drinking time but on any given weekend, with the type of dedicated practice known only to Olympians, we consistently chugged back twelve to fourteen pints in a single evening.

One auspicious Saturday night, I was ushered out of the pub by my good buddy, Fitzroy Trinidad. He looked like Jimi Hendrix and could play guitar like him too. We walked down a muddy path to the River Mole, a trickle of a stream that ran behind the pub. Fitzroy pulled out some rolling papers and a matchbox containing a couple of grams of Moroccan hashish. It was the first time I had ever seen hashish. Fascinated, I watched as he feverishly scraped away at the oily lump with a pocket knife, crumbled it into a small pile and rolled it up with tobacco into a joint. Without a second thought, I lit up and puffed away. Everything became hilarious and unreal. We cracked up at nothing and instantly became best friends. We shared a Mars Bar and as we munched away, we imagined all our teeth were falling out. This we found particularly amusing. Our long walk back to Fitzroy's house, normally a routine trek, became a grand adventure, a magical mystery tour; a tiptoe through the tulips. For the first time in my life I was experiencing a completely new state of mind. After years of oppressive subjugation under the sledge hammer of secondary modern comprehensive education, I was finally liberated. It was just what I needed.

There are some pivotal moments in one's life that dictate and colour all future events. The importance of these influential events is only visible in retrospect. With the warm glow of hashish flooding my veins, I experienced another dimension to my psychology, another perspective heretofore undiscovered. My mind had been changed, my brain chemistry inexorably altered, my cerebral rudder irrevocably tipped to chart a new course as I set sail towards a destiny less ordinary. One thing was certain; I would need a steady supply of this miraculous substance, and a way to pay for it.

The going price for a quarter ounce of hash at that time was five pounds, also known as a fiver, or five quid. The British monetary system at the time went like this: two farthings were a halfpenny, two halfpennies made a penny and truppence, or a thuppenny bit was three pennies. Two thuppenny bits made a tanner which was sixpence. Two sixpenny bits were a shilling. There were twelve pennies to one shilling and twenty shillings to a pound. A florin was two shillings or twenty-four pennies. A pound was two-hundred and forty pennies. Two-and-six was two shillings and sixpence, or half a crown. A crown was five shillings or five bob. Two crowns were ten bob which was half a pound. Twenty-one shillings was one pound and one shilling which was a guinea. A pound was a quid and a quarter ounce of hashish was five quid.

All through my school years, when adding amounts of money, we made three columns: one for pounds, one for shillings and one for pennies. The symbols used at the head of each column read: L.S.D.

In 1971, the currency in England switched to a decimal system. It couldn't have been simpler. There was only one thing to remember: there were one hundred pennies to one pound. It literally took years for people to figure this out. They complained that the new system was way too complicated.

I figured out I could buy a quarter ounce (seven grams) sell four, make back my 'nut' and smoke or sell the rest. This way I could smoke for free and make some money as well. And herein lies the first rule of drug dealing: the cost of goods sold, to coin an accounting term, is your 'nut'. This is not your money to spend, lend, or otherwise appropriate. Not until you have recouped your initial expenses are you free to allocate the 'profits.' After you have recovered the initial cost, you are then at liberty to smoke, sell, consume, or share the revenue.

Follow this simple rule and you will never lose money.

5

In England, throughout the seventies, we smoked mostly hashish. By far the most common type came from Morocco. It was available in several qualities. Zero-Zero was the best. It got its name from the size of fine mesh through which the plant matter was rubbed. Zero-Zero was a black, sticky resin the consistency of chewing gum and was relatively rare. The next grade down was Premier, the most common Moroccan hash available. After that were First Quality and Second Quality.

No one wanted Second Quality.

Also on offer, though much less common, were several other types of hash including Red Leb, from Lebanon, with its crumbly texture and rosy hue, Paki Black, dense black hash from Pakistan, and Afghani Black, which not surprisingly came from Afghanistan. I'll let you guess where Nepalese Temple Balls came from.

Grass or pot was extremely rare. If we did see some, it was usually from the Congo or Malawi or Durban Poison from South Africa. It looked awful by today's standards. It was almost totally black, full of sticks and stems and squashed flat like it had been run over by a steamroller.

Contrary to the popular belief that pot was less potent back then, some of the African varieties really packed a punch. We'd use it just like hash. We'd roll a standard three-paper joint, two wide and one perpendicular, load in one and a half cigarettes and sprinkle the pot down the middle, exactly like we did with hashish. A record album cover was used to separate the stems and seeds by crumbling the pot on one upturned end and letting the heavier stems and seeds roll down the cover and fall off the edge. You can't do that with an MP3.

My first encounter with the mighty Durban Poison was hitchhiking from Crawley to Brighton. I was picked up by a long-haired, pseudo-hipster-granola-head, who was pumping Led Zeppelin through an overblown sound system. He immediately lit a joint and passed it to me. Five minutes later, I was getting very stoned. Ten minutes, after we finished the joint, I felt like I'd ingested sixty micrograms of LSD.

The music was pounding away as he yelled at me above the din. He was speaking English, a language with which I was usually familiar, but as time passed he became more and more incomprehensible and seemed to be lapsing into an unknown dialect of Urdu. I attempted to lip read but this proved even more confusing.

The car felt as though it was speeding faster and faster. On the bends, I began to experience what I imagined to be g-force seven. I braced myself on the dashboard and prepared myself emotionally and physically for a crash that seemed inevitable. The whole car was vibrating. The music became deafening. Convinced of my imminent death, I decided to abandon the mission and yelled over the music for him to stop the car. Instead, my driver, grinning from ear to ear, began to recount a terribly amusing anecdote in ancient Aramaic. I resorted to sign language, frantically pointing downward (here) followed by the thumbs-up sign (will do) Confused and somewhat disappointed, my distracted driver finally got the message. The car came to a stop and I got the hell out of there.

This was an important lesson in dosage. Every drug has

an optimal dosage, dependent on the individual's state of mind, brain chemistry and environment. This is the essence of Leary's 'set and setting.' Decisions on dosage should be made before ingesting any substance. The golden rule is, start low and increase dosage or frequency accordingly. This is often a question of body weight. A standard dose of MDMA is 100mg. For a two-hundred-pound man, this is a moderate dose. For a one-hundred-pound raver chick, it's a double dose.

It's possible to do too much of anything. Correct dosage and frequency are essential to safe and responsible drug use. It's always a balance between maximum benefits vs. minimal side effects. As the dosage increases, less of the beneficial effects are felt and more of the less desirable side effects begin to manifest. Sometimes less is more. As the fifteenth century Swiss proto-chemist, Paracelsus, once put it, "The difference between a medicine and a poison is dosage."

Dosage can be massaged and modified in order to produce the best possible outcome. This can vary greatly between individuals. Your brain is a bio-chemical machine, a finely tuned molecular hot-rod. The trick is to learn how to drive it.

6

By the time the sixties were winding down, Crawley New Town had become a cesspool of social ills. Unemployment was rampant. Soccer hooligans battled for supremacy in the streets. Gangs of working-class skinheads prowled the night Paki-bashing and gay-bashing. These two groups were routinely singled out and beaten up as a form of entertainment. A Paki was anyone who looked remotely foreign. A gay was anyone who didn't look like a soccer hooligan or a skinhead or a Paki.

Everybody was broke and angry and ignorant. Everyone I knew was either unemployed or toiled at menial jobs in factories for subsistence wages. They complained about everything and blamed everyone else for their miserable lives. Their only respite was drinking or drugging themselves into oblivion. Alcoholism and heroin addiction were rampant. Fourteen-year-olds were shooting up in the Laundromats, parks, and pubs.

Heroin addicts get addicted to the needle rush. When they can't get a fix, they'll shoot up almost anything. I've seen addicts shoot up aspirin and whisky. One time, a friend of mine, desperate for a needle rush, sucked up some lager with a syringe from a pint mug and shot it up, right there in the pub.

Here's something I've learned from having known dozens of heroin addicts in Crawley. Contrary to the prevalent perception of addicts as drug-crazed fiends, the truth is that they are generally sensitive, fragile people who cannot deal with the struggles and vicissitudes of daily life. Everyday life for the addict is overwhelming, oppressive and fraught with insurmountable problems. They simply can't hack it. Heroin provides a safe haven and welcome relief from their emotional pain and trauma. It's an escape from a hostile and bellicose world. Heroin makes you feel safe and calm and warm, like being wrapped up in a cotton-wool blanket.

Another myth about heroin is that if you use it, you become instantly addicted. Fact is, you have to do a lot of heroin for a significant amount of time to get a habit. I've known people who tried to get hooked and failed. Once you do, of course, it's a long, hard road back. It's best not to go there in the first place.

The situation in Crawley New Town eventually became untenable. Addiction rates shot up, crime was rife, overdoses all too common, and the prisons were filling up. In the midst of this crisis, The National Health Service decided to do something about it. What did they do? They decided to treat addiction as a public health issue instead of a criminal matter. They gave every addict a prescription of pure pharmaceutical heroin, free of charge. This meant that addicts no longer had to spend every waking moment hustling for a hit. During the day, junkies lay around in government funded bedsits, watched television, listened to music and read science fiction novels. At night, they ventured out, strolling around town wearing dark glasses.

Emergency calls and overdoses nose-dived and the crime rate plummeted. They no longer had to break into cars and houses to service their habits. This gave them time to think; a lot of time to think. It was a cure by boredom.

Eventually, almost all of the addicts I knew in Crawley kicked the habit and went on to live productive lives. Fifty years later, we have yet to learn this lesson.

At the age of ten, my ambition was to become a dustbin man. I was fascinated by their exciting lifestyle, the way they hung on to the side of moving garbage trucks, jumping on and off, noisily crashing the metal cans about. There seemed to be no limit to the amount of noise they were allowed to make. I was especially drawn to the large, leather work gloves worn by dustbin men. It looked like they led a thrilling life of carefree abandon. Dustbin men were rugged and free; masters of their own destiny. They were the English equivalent of cowboys, and I longed for a life on the rubbish range.

By the age of thirteen, my new ambition was to travel the world and play the bongos. That dream came true.

In England, the earliest legal age at which students were allowed to drop out of school was fifteen years and three months. I couldn't wait. I bought a calendar and crossed off the days, one by one, like a prisoner counting down to a release date.

As the fateful day approached, I went to see a career councillor whose function was to ship students off to the factory estate for a life of low-paid servitude and drudgery. Off the cuff, I suggested a career as a chef.

My mother's idea of cooking was opening a can, or adding boiling water to a packet of unidentifiable, powdered chemicals. As a child, the choice was simple: learn to cook or starve to death. My interest in cooking increased at the same rate as my hunger. Besides, I rather fancied wearing one of those tall, puffy white hats. The career councillor shuffled some files and my fate was sealed. I was placed as an apprentice chef in a Brighton hotel. That was on a Friday afternoon. Three days later, on Monday morning, I left school, home, and town.

There was a widely used expression in Crawley which conveyed an emphatic rejection and condemnation. It was generally said with an attitude of contempt, resignation and unequivocal denunciation. I used it for the last time on the day I left that awful town. The expression was, "Good riddance to bad rubbish."

7

I turned fifteen years and three months old in January 1971. This was the year the microprocessor was invented, Disney World opened its doors for the first time, and Charlie Manson received the death sentence.

My mother drove me to the Crawley train station and bought me a one-way ticket to the sea-side town of Brighton. Carrying a single battered suitcase, I boarded the train and waved goodbye to my mother who I left crying and waving on the platform.

Brighton is on the south coast of Sussex, twenty-five miles from Crawley. Unbeknownst to me or my mother, it enjoyed the reputation of being the epicenter of British drug culture. It was also a vibrant, cosmopolitan town full of foreign language students, hippies and alternative culture. In the summer, the beaches were packed with beleaguered working-class proletariats sitting in rows of deck chairs with knotted handkerchiefs on their heads, determined against all odds to have a good time. Their grim faces epitomised the unwavering resolve that served to protect them from any pesky thoughts that might challenge their ridged determination to never change their minds about anything.

Brighton was also the gay capitol of England.

I was housed in a staff annex next to the Sackville Hotel, a four-star establishment featuring French cuisine where I would serve my apprenticeship for the next three years. I was promptly assigned a shared room with an Italian gay waiter named Alberto.

For the first few months, Alberto was my first and only friend in this strange new land. He instantly recognised me as an uncorrupted innocent and took me into his care. For entertainment, we exclusively frequented gay pubs, gay restaurants and gay clubs with the other hotel staff. Most of the other waiters were also gay. The Maître d' was gay. The assistant manager was gay.

For a fifteen-year-old straight kid from the most homophobic place on earth, it was a real eye opener. There were only two kinds of sexuality in Crawley, you were either heterosexual, or you got beaten up.

In retrospect, it amazes me how perfectly normal it all seemed. Although I had never even met a gay person before, I had no problem fitting in. I admired the flamboyant nature of the queer community and their unrepentant individualism which would later become the hallmark of all my future associations. They were welcoming, fun-loving and really knew how to have a good time. They were pretty, witty and well, gay.

They had their own language called, 'Polari,' with which I quickly became fluent. 'Boner' was a common expression for very good, as in, "Simply boner, ducky." 'NAFF,' an acronym for Not Available for Fucking and therefore useless, meant worthless. Men and women were 'omees' and 'palones,' and 'Nada to vada in the larder,' was an insult for someone with a small penis. I rarely used that one.

Alberto always made a point of introducing me as his, 'straight friend.' Despite my devilish good looks, my boyish charm and wavy locks, in all the time I spent in the gay scene in Brighton, no one ever made a pass or came on to me. I couldn't decide whether to be flattered or disappointed.

After a while, I made new friends, dope-smoking friends,

weirdos and ne'er-do-wells. As the hilarious American comic, Gary Gullman once asked, "How often did they do well? Ne'er."

My new friends were folks who lived on the fringes of society, they were corrupters of convention and what John Locke, the seventeenth century philosopher and father of the Enlightenment would term, free-thinkers. They were the creative types, artists, musicians, writers, raconteurs, roustabouts and trick cyclists extraordinaire. They were people who went with the flow, were open-minded and free-spirited. They were the rut-less, rootless and rudderless. These would be my people from here on in.

With my connections back in Crawley, I continued to deal hashish. I had graduated from selling grams to buying ounces and selling quarters and had begun to experiment with various other pills and potions. At the Kings Head pub in Brighton, you could find almost anything.

One night, while out with my straight pal, John Royston Oxley, we were approached by a local deviant who offered us some 'trips.' John was a dim-witted but good-natured fellow, dumb as a stick but happy as a lark. Devoid of ambition or volition, John thought carpe diem was a brand of fish fingers. But he was game for anything and immediately bought several tiny purple pills the size of rice grains. Judging by their diminutive size, we were not expecting very much. After another pint or two, we headed back to my rooms at the Sackville Hotel. Alberto was home and all three of us swallowed the little purple pills.

Previous to this, I had barely even heard of LSD. I had no idea that we were about to experience the full force of three-hundred and fifty micrograms of the now legendary purple microdots.

What followed was pure mayhem.

The effects came on fast and we all started to feel very

strange. At first, we found the trip amusing and marveled at our warped vision and the flood of new perceptions. We shared our experiences for a while, but as the effects became stronger and stronger, we became isolated in our own altered personal realities, no longer able to communicate with each other. An hour in, John became more and more agitated, restless and emotional. His troubled mind might have been best left un-manifested. He paced the room like a caged animal speaking in tongues. Uncontrolled emotions boiled to the surface and overflowed into the room. At one point he was crying for his mother.

I was hallucinating like a Catholic saint, but rather than a diaphanous vision of the Virgin Mary dressed in a white negligee, the whole room transformed into an underground burrow, complete with tree roots and thick with cobwebs. Spiders and worms lined the walls.

Alberto had apparently gone completely insane. He was cowered in the corner of the room, wrapped in a blanket, hugging his knees and rocking compulsively back and forth. In his heavily Italian-accented English, he was loudly chanting, "I DON BLOODY FEEL NOTHING, I DON BLOODY FEEL NOTHING, I DON BLOODY FEEL NOTHING." He did this continuously for several hours.

I was now convinced that I too had gone completely insane and would likely remain in this state permanently. The prospect was terrifying but I was struggling to somehow accept it as my new reality. Astonishingly, amid all this madness, a sliver of my brain retained the ability to rationalise.

After about three hours, John became violent. His emotions, unchecked and unfettered, erupted from his body like lava from a volcano. He smashed my TV and tore strips of wallpaper off the wall while yelling and moaning like a wounded badger.

I had now lost all references to mundane reality. Solid

matter was a thing of the past. The world was fragmented, fluid and in constant motion. An intense hum pervaded my head and I thought my brain might explode. I touched my neck hoping to find something familiar but found only clumps of loose skin hanging under my chin like the warty dewlap of a lizard. It would be two years before I was able to touch my neck again.

In the maelstrom of distorted hallucinations, I became convinced I was dead. I desperately tried to come to terms with the fact that I was now living in a permanent, chaotic afterlife that might last forever. Nothing was tangible or concrete. I reasoned that if I could find something solid it might bring me back to reality. I thought about my shoulder. I was certain that two bones intersected there. At the point they connected, there had to be something solid. I reached up, placed a hand on my shoulder and gave a tentative squeeze. My hand closed and my shoulder oozed out like jelly between my fingers. I was in hell and there was not a single hand basket to be found.

John Royston Oxley had now thoroughly demolished my room. He had punched a hole in the TV screen, pulled down my shelves and flipped over the bed. With nothing left to destroy, he lumbered out the door and made his way upstairs to where the hotel's chambermaids were housed. Several vacuum cleaners were stored on the landing and John began to swing them around by their chords, smashing them into the walls. Later, we learned why the women had not called the police. The only phone in the entire house was mounted on a wall on the upstairs landing and they were too terrified to venture out.

Meanwhile, Alberto had assumed the fetal position in the corner of the room, tangled in a blanket and talking gibberish. His body vibrated like a giant, high-powered dildo. I was barely hanging on, lost in a frenzy of scrambled visual and audio hallucinations. The barn doors of perception had been thoroughly and totally blown off.

The madness continued for over ten hours.

Eventually, the storm subsided and daylight pierced through the curtains. A white mist hung in the air, illuminated by shafts of morning sunlight. The nightmare was finally over. John was sleeping in a crumpled heap beneath the upturned bed, his face mashed and distorted against the wall. Alberto was also finally at peace. I walked a block down to the pebbled beach in front of the hotel and sat in the morning sunshine, glad to be both alive and sane. It would be two years before I tried acid again.

The next time was a different story, but more on that later.

Again, the three important lessons to take away from this story are dosage, dosage and dosage. Twenty micrograms of LSD will put you in a good mood, brighten up your day and put a spring in your step. Three hundred and fifty micrograms with the wrong set and setting can seriously fuck up your day.

8

With my apprenticeship completed and my papers in hand, the idea of working in a kitchen for the rest of my life seemed a dim prospect. I'd enjoyed my time at the Sackville Hotel but the hours were long, the conditions arduous and the job required getting up early every morning.

I wanted to travel the world and play the bongos.

So, in the summer of '73, as the Vietnam War ended and Pink Floyd's seminal album, *The Dark Side of the Moon* was released, I packed my ruck-sack and left Brighton to hitch-hike around Europe. My three years at the Sackville Hotel would be the last regular, permanent employment I would ever have. From here on in, I would be one scam ahead of a job.

Stanley Cartesian, an old Hazelwick school buddy, decided to join me. With slim hips and long golden, flowing hair, he was a dead ringer for Robert Plant from Led Zeppelin. Like Robert, he wore low-slung, skin-tight jeans and preferred his chest only partially covered.

Under a grey sky, in the merry month of May, Stanley and I took the Folkestone ferry across the English Channel to Dieppe on the northern coast of France. From there, we made a beeline to Paris.

The French have a reputation for snobbery. Apparently there are historical precedents for the deep-seated animosity between the English and the French. Not being a history buff, I didn't get the memo but soon uncovered evidence of that pernicious missive.

I had successfully managed to completely ignore four years of French language classes at school. I remembered mindlessly reciting verbs but they meant nothing to me. I was barely aware that it was another language. I learnt to speak French like a parrot learns about crackers. My view of French people was limited to a romantic vision of beret-wearing, striped-shirted mimes riding around on bicycles with baguettes under their arms.

That myth was soon exploded.

Hitchhiking in France was more difficult than in other European countries. Cars sailed by and Stanley and I often waited several hours for a ride. Passing drivers avoided eye contact. Noses were pointed skyward. We were refused drinking water in gas stations and denied access to wash-rooms in restaurants. Older Parisians were especially aloof and indifferent. Fortunately, our guileless innocence and complete ignorance of this centuries-long, international feud left us largely immune to its effects.

The Bois Du Boulogne is a large park in the center of the city. We pitched our tent in the camping site there, smoked some dope and struck out to explore Paris.

In the Quartier Pigalle, the red-light district, we were repeatedly propositioned but were too nervous to accept. Some of the women were terrifying. One night, Stanley was approached by a Rubenesque, black hooker who wouldn't take no for an answer. At what point Rubenesque becomes obese is open for discussion but weighing in at over three-hundred pounds, a five-foot six woman might be approaching that threshold. Her face was caked with thick, garish make-up accented with an oversized red slash around her mouth. She lowered her price repeatedly and then offered to do him for free. Who wouldn't want to sleep with Robert

Plant? Stanley was polite but firm and we made a tactical retreat back to our tent.

After a couple of weeks exploring La Ville des Lumières, we hitchhiked south to the French Riviera. In a campsite in Cannes, we befriended an English folk-singer. He taught me to play some chords and three weeks later in Florence, Italy, I bought my first guitar. Two weeks after that I had learned three songs. By the time I got to Rome a week later, I was busking every day and making a living. Stanley collected the money in a hat as we went from café to café and town to town. For me, this would become a reliable source of supplemental income for the next ten years.

After France and Italy, we hitched down to Spain and worked for a month as waiters on the Costa del Sol, famous for its drunken English louts, fish and chip shops and Watneys Red Barrel. The Monty Python sketch where Eric Idle rants about being herded into endless Hotel Miramars with swimming pools full of fat German businessmen forming pyramids, pretending to be acrobats and frightening the children, and audio-typists from Birmingham with flabby white legs and diarrhea trying to pick up hairy-legged wop waiters called Manuel, turned out to be more of a documentary than a social satire.

After a month or so, we picked up our pesetas, hitchhiked south to Malaga and took the ferry to Ceuta on the North African Coast. From there we took a bus to Tetouan in Morocco and on to the beach at Martil.

Morocco was like travelling back in history to biblical times. Men walked the smoky streets shrouded in hooded djellabas. They spent their days in cafes smoking *kif* from wooden pipes called *sibsis* and drank bottomless pots of mint tea. A regular cup of English tea was nowhere to be found.

Packs of mangy, feral dogs prowled the streets begging for scraps. Occasionally they were clubbed to death by irate restaurateurs. Moroccan women were conspicuously absent, relegated to the home and a life of subjugation and servitude, allowed out only when accompanied by a male relative and covered head to toe in a black bag.

We were completely oblivious to this unfamiliar way of life and our cluelessness served to suspend our judgement. We assumed there must have been ancient and valid reasons for the inequitable and sometimes brutal customs we witnessed. We took it all in our stride. This was a long way from Crawley and we soaked up the exotic culture with relish.

Hash is made from rubbing the resin off mature marijuana plants. The leftover plant matter is compressed into small bricks and referred to as *kif*. Young Moroccans smoked hashish but the old men smoked only *kif*. We spent a lot of time hanging around in cafes smoking *kif* with old men. This was done with a great deal of ritual. First, a pipe in three pieces called a *sibsi* was produced from a leather pouch. Two wooden pieces screwed together to form the shaft and a clay bowl, or *shkaff*, was fitted to one end. The owner of the pipe, filled it, lit the bowl and took one hit. He passed the pipe to the first person in the circle who was expected to finish the bowl and pass it back to the owner. It was then refilled, lit and passed to the next person in the circle. This was repeated until the pouch of *kif* was consumed. After a short pause and another round of mint tea, someone else would take out their pipe and repeat the ritual. Any deviation from this formal procedure was frowned upon.

The *kif* came in cone-shaped paper packages and contained one third black tobacco and two thirds *kif*. The two substances were mixed together according to personal taste. Interestingly, the *kif* was legal but the black tobacco was not.

Mint tea was similarly ritualised. A handful of fresh mint was placed in a pot of hot black tea and a ludicrous amount of sugar was added and stirred in. The tea was then poured, from a great height into tiny cups. The cups were emptied back into the pot and then re-poured. This procedure was repeated three times. This was a far cry from the great British cuppa which was now a distant but fond memory. Any expectation I may have had of revising a thousand years of Moroccan tea-making traditions seemed futile.

Hashish was illegal but plentiful and every other Moroccan we met offered to sell us some. We decided to send some back to friends in England. An accommodating local named Mohamed sold us a couple of hundred grams of Zero-Zero and we returned to our tent to package it for mailing. Using a wine bottle as a rolling pin, we flattened out the hashish on a smooth stone into thin, one-ounce slivers. Sandwiched between two postcards and placed in an envelope, they could be mailed like a letter.

In the middle of this operation, someone suddenly grabbed Stanley's leg and pulled him backwards out of the tent. I quickly scrambled to conceal the evidence. Two men in khaki sweaters and black berets were hassling Stanley as I exited the tent. One of them brandished a truncheon and was waving it about menacingly. The other quickly searched the tent and produced a few crumbs of hash left on the floor. As if having discovered the Holy Grail, he held it up in the air and triumphantly declared, "HASHISH!"

The two men yelled in broken English about the illegality of hashish possession and the severe consequences we might face. The chaotic scene went on and on. We pretended we didn't understand a word, which only made them angrier. One of them threatened us with a fifteen-year prison sentence. He went on to describe the appalling conditions in Moroccan correctional facilities.

We squabbled for some time until I suggested we might settle out of court. Perhaps we could pay a fine? The mood instantly changed and we began to haggle over the price.

They suggested the equivalent of two-hundred dollars. We offered ten. They consulted and came back with a hundred. We claimed extreme poverty and handed them ten dollars in dirhams. They took it and left.

Later, we discovered they were not police at all but two enterprising local entrepreneurs who made their living fleecing unsuspecting tourists. This was a national sport in Morocco. Subsequently, when we saw them about town, they'd wink and smile at us. Apparently, it was all in good fun.

The next day, we headed to the post office to mail our 'letters.' The clerk took the first one and tossed it on to the scales. "Ah, *kif*," he guessed.

"No, no, no," we insisted. He took another and weighed it.

"Ah ha, hashish." Again, we denied it.

"No, no, no, postcards."

Nonplussed, he casually threw the packages into a crumpled cardboard box in the corner of the tiny room. We paid up and hoped for the best but were not surprised when none of our packages arrived at their destinations.

9

One sunny day in Tangiers, a young Moroccan guy rushed up and asked us if we'd bought hashish from Mohamed the night before. We had. Everybody we bought hashish from in Morocco was named Mohamed.

The guy was frantic and told us that Mohamed had been arrested, his teeth had been knocked out and the police were now looking for us. We had to leave town fast and he offered to escort us to the bus station and help us escape. Terrified, we hurriedly packed up our gear and followed him. He told us that the police were cracking down on tourists and several had already been arrested and sent to jail for lengthy sentences. He impressed on us that the conditions in Moroccan prisons were decidedly substandard.

When we arrived at the bus station it was time for the rub. He explained that in exchange for saving our lives, he would require a hefty reward. He could have been nominated for an Oscar. We gave him two dollars for effort and told him to fuck off. It was another scam and the last we would ever fall for.

These swindles were widespread in Morocco but only worked on novices. We were now seasoned travellers. In the future, when approached by hysterical Moroccans with outrageous tales about someone named Mohamed, we'd smile knowingly and inform them that we were well aware of this routine. This was invariably met with a good-natured smile and an instant retreat. As fierce and aggressive as these shakedowns could be, I never once saw any of these hostile confrontations end in physical violence. It was all bluster, blow, and blather.

After a week or two in Tangiers, we took the bus south to Fez, the second largest city in Morocco and the name of a famous hat. The medina, or marketplace, looked like a set from Cecil B. DeMille's, *The Ten Commandments*. I could have sworn I saw Charlton Heston and Yul Brynner sitting in a café drinking mint tea, but it turned out to be two German tourists. At one point, Stanley spotted Jesus on his donkey but he was gone before we could ask any pertinent questions. We checked into a cheap riad, a small hotel in the old town and set off to explore another century.

In Morocco, one is constantly propositioned with exciting deals at bargain prices. Here's a classic: "Sure, man, why not? You buy ten kilos hashish, maybe you buy car and we ship to England, all student prices. Good deal for you, good deal for me, everybody happy." And to give themselves more credibility, they often claimed to be good friends with George Harrison. Apparently, George had made a lot of friends in Morocco. On the street, you could buy and sell student cards, traveller's cheques, passports, a driver's license, gemstones, a kilo of hashish, or Uncle Tom Cobley's kitchen sink.

Some Swedish travellers informed us that hashish in the north of Morocco was worth twice the price in the south. We could double our money. We hunted around for a good deal and finally settled on an enterprising young fellow named Mohamed. He led us through a labyrinth of narrow alleyways to a shabby storefront. After much whispering and clandestine negotiations with the store owner, Mohamed beckoned us inside. The room was dimly lit by a bare, forty-watt light bulb and smelled of camel dung. Even if you've never smelled camel dung, it is instantly recognisable.

The storekeeper was an old man whose face looked like a relief map of the moon. He looked us over with a sardonic gaze, as if deciding whether or not to cut our throats. We were keen to conclude our business and leave, but ancient rituals had to be observed. Out came the mint tea and *kif* pipe. An hour later, we had negotiated a fair price and were presented with a kilo and a half of premiere quality hashish. It was the most hash either of us had ever seen. Pleased with our purchase, we headed back through the maze of narrow streets to our hotel room.

We'd been warned there were sometimes police road blocks on the highways to the south to deter the very activity we were engaging in. I don't remember giving it a second thought. Back in our hotel room, we taped fifteen, one-hundred gram slabs to our bodies and caught a bus to Marrakesh.

Yes, this was the acclaimed Marrakesh Express taking us to Marrakesh, and all the hippies on board were singing that famous David Crosby song.

The bus did get stopped twice at road blocks. The police got on board, asked a few people for passports and checked a few bags, but luckily there were no pat downs. The hash was securely taped under our arms, on the insides of our legs and in the smalls of our backs.

Marrakesh was even further back in time than Tangiers with its ancient souks, sword-carrying Berbers and real snake charmers with real snakes. After shacking up at a hippie hotel in the center of town, we set about sampling the hash and quickly made a lot of new friends. That golden rule about covering your nut before recouping your costs went completely out the window, along with great billowing clouds of hashish smoke.

We rolled jumbo joints, packed chillums and built pipes made from carburetors filled with red wine. We spent hours constructing devices from plastic tubing and glass bottles, each more elaborate than the last. We creamed up five-gram lumps and sprinkled it on noodles for breakfast. We smoked off hot knives and did Mexican hat tricks. We mixed in *kif* and opium to spice things up. We had competitions for who could roll the most complex joints, combining multiple three-paper spliffs into windmill shapes. And we learned an important lesson about building up tolerance to drugs.

This type of unbridled, indiscriminate consumption eventually yields diminishing returns. When you smoke dope from morning to night, day after day, week after week, you barely catch a buzz. What can I say? We were eighteen-years-old, full of derring-do and devil-may-care. Sometimes you have to go to the limit to figure out where the limit is. As far back as the fifteenth century, the English poet and painter, William Blake shed light on this time-worn, enigmatic problem. Most are familiar with the first half of his famous quote, "The road of excess leads to the palace of wisdom." The next line is often left out but is equally pertinent, "You never know what enough is until you know what is more than enough."

Needless to say, our get-rich-quick scheme fell somewhat short of being a total success. We did make a few sales, but in the end, and with a little help from a lot of friends, we managed to smoke up the entire stash in less than three months.

From Marrakesh, we headed north to Casablanca. I loved the movie, but the modern city lacked the romance and intrigue of Bogart and Bergman. I was also disappointed to discover the movie wasn't filmed in Casablanca, or even in Morocco. It was filmed in a Hollywood studio six-thousand miles away. I felt cheated. So with the tip of our metaphorical hats and a, "Here's looking at you, Kid," we boarded a bus and headed south again, to Taghazout, also known as Banana Beach.

Taghazout, pronounced as if a wad of figs is stuck in the back of your throat, had a reputation as a hippie haven. The town, if you could call it that, consisted of a couple of dozen one-story concrete sheds with tin roofs. These were mostly shops and bargain hotels. Most travellers pitched tents on the beach and so did we.

The beach had beautiful fine white sand and was surrounded by a semi-circle of tall palm trees. There were about a hundred tents strewn about and most of the residents looked like rejects from a Woodstock refugee camp. Some had built elaborate shacks from driftwood and palm leaves. Some of them had been there for years.

We pitched our tent and had just enough hash left to make proper introductions to the locals. After the bustle and turmoil of the big cities, Banana Beach was a welcome break, peaceful and quiet. We settled in, slowed down, turned on, tuned in and dropped out. A month drifted by and life was a series of social escapades and spontaneous buffoonery. Time not only flew, it did back flips, barrel-rolls and loop-the-loops.

A German doctor wandered by our tent one day. We chatted for a while and he told us he'd been touring Moroccan prisons researching a book about tourists who were serving lengthy sentences for hashish possession. He described the conditions. They sounded appalling. We were glad to not be part of that project. Then the subject turned to psychedelics and to our surprise, the doctor suggested a prescription of LSD.

It had been over two years since my first disastrous experience in Brighton, but since then I had undergone a thorough education on the subject of expanded consciousness and mind-manifesting. While on the road, I'd read Leary and Huxley and Lilly and Hunter S. Thompson. I'd studied Zen and read Alan Watts and Burroughs and the Beats. I was good to go. Set? Check. Setting? Check. Clear runway; ready for blast-off.

My second LSD trip was the antithesis of the first. My set was sound, my setting perfect. This time the experience was expansive, immersive and connected. I saw the world anew, bathed in iridescent, golden light. I synchronised my breathing with the palm trees and the surf. I felt a deep connection with everything and everyone. The ocean breeze passed effortlessly through my diaphanous body like a ghostly nebula. Time stood still, and then speeded up. What was Time? What, or who, was I? My body dissolved into an ephemeral soup as I frolicked in the endless white sand. Epiphanies came and went with the tide. I was consumed by Oneness, awash in a vortex of infinite possibility and revealed truth.

You get the idea.

When psychologists ask people to rate their experience with LSD, they often describe it as one of the most meaningful of their lives. It consistently scores on a par with a firstborn child, or a first love. Even if they never try it again, they will credit the experience with lasting and profound effects.

The transformative power of LSD cannot be underestimated. Leary once claimed that with conventional counseling, or psychotherapy; a third of patients benefited, another third received no benefit and a third got worse. People who received no therapy at all achieved identical results. That's why he was so fired up about the therapeutic potential of LSD. After only one or two LSD sessions, Leary saw deepseated behaviors transformed and the lives of his patients improve. This motivated him to dedicate his life to bringing this powerful tool to the masses. Where did it get him? Booted out of Harvard and thrown into jail.

After ten hours or so, the acid wore off. Exhausted but exhilarated, I crawled into my tent and slept deeply. When I awoke, I felt drained and lethargic. I attempted to get up and found I hadn't the strength. I thought I had caught a bad case of the flu. Stanley went to find the German doctor who returned and poked his head into the tent. He immediately noticed the whites of my eyes had turned bright yellow. He suspected hepatitis and suggested I go straight to the nearest hospital in Agadir. I was too weak to walk, so Stanley and the doc helped to load me into the back of a van. At the hospital, the waiting room was filled with the participants of a recent axe fight. Young men held gaping wounds together while pools of blood crept across the floor. Despite the desperate situation, everyone remained remarkably calm as they patiently waited for attention.

After a good while, I finally saw a doctor who, after a quick glance, confirmed that I had hepatitis and told me to go home.

With the last of my money, I boarded a plane back to England where I was quarantined at my parents' house for the next three months. What happened to Stanley? He went on to the Canary Islands and joined a hippie commune.

10

Hepatitis A is a viral liver disease caused by the ingestion of fecal matter. I'll spare you the scatological humour. It is most often spread due to poor hygiene and inadequate hand-washing. A lot of Moroccans carry the virus without knowing it. As hashish is made by rubbing the resin off the buds with the palms of the hands, I surmised the most likely suspect was all that fresh, raw hash we had eaten. Live and learn.

There is no treatment or cure for Hepatitis A. Just rest, and because it is highly infectious, quarantine. Also, because my liver was no longer producing enough bile to process fats, I was placed on a bland diet of boiled rice and veggies. My parents, as usual, were good natured about the ordeal and nursed me back to health over the next three months. They were getting used to my unorthodox lifestyle and vicariously enjoyed my exploits.

My parents, Hazel and Bert, were not model parents. The only Dr. Spock they were aware of was on Star Trek. They were working class folks with broad backs, thick skin, and stiff upper lips. They did their best and got on with it. I was probably always a bit of a mystery to them but nevertheless, they always accepted me for who I was.

Their relationship was one of convenience and the tragic result of a lack of imagination. Their marriage ran out of gas long before I left home and never recovered but, to their credit, they never resorted to overt conflict. Theirs was a silent and secret war of attrition. Bert learned to keep his head down and his mouth shut. If he did something, it was invariably wrong. If he didn't do the same thing, he was equally wrong for not doing it. But true to their marriage vows, they played out this stubborn game of catch 22 until death did part them.

After my liver had deflated back to its normal size, I received a clean bill of health and returned to Brighton. I rented an apartment with the recently returned Stanley Cartesian, as well as Royston Trinidad, and Byron Thomas, another old chum from Hazelwick. Byron held the all-time record for both school detentions and canings. His aversion to authority was legendary and even greater than my own.

Once, in an attempt to get himself expelled, he refused the cane from Mr. Keytes, something no one had ever before dared to do. He informed us of his audacious plan and a group of us huddled in the bushes outside the head-master's office to watch the show. Keytes performed his usual terrifying prelude, shouting and pacing up and down, whipping the cane around like a rapier. When he was good and worked up, he ordered Byron to hold out his hand. Byron, our hero, stood his ground and defiantly stuffed his hands in his pockets. Keytes went ballistic, slashing the cane wildly about Byron's body and legs and yelling at the top of his lungs. This unbridled onslaught was too much to bear, even for the courageous Byron. His resolve wavered and he reluctantly stuck out his palms. Keytes caned him so hard it left deep, red welts across both hands which lasted for weeks. He failed in his bid for expulsion, but had earned my lifelong respect and friendship.

We were a merry band of misfits and life in the Brighton apartment was one long party. I made money busking around town and selling hashish. We played Joni Mitchel's, *Blue* and Van Morrison's, *Astral Weeks* over and over and over. We all dropped acid, and while lying on our backs on the floor with our eyes closed, Royston played electric guitar like Jimi Hendrix in extended jams that could last for hours.

On the extremely rare occasions that we ran out of hash, we'd vacuum the carpet, spread out the contents on the kitchen table and sort through the debris, finding tiny crumbs of various types of hash until we had enough for a joint. There was always just enough.

It was 1974, the year Nixon quit, Muhammad Ali reclaimed his world title, and I discovered amphetamine sulphate.

Amphetamines come in many forms, both legal and illegal. Call them what you will, they are all speed and they are all addictive. Black Bombers or Black Mollies were a prescription medication. Just one could keep you going for twelve hours. Benzedrine, or bennies, could amp you up all night and induce super-human powers of concentration and focus. Jack Kerouac popped copious amounts of Benzedrine which enabled him to write *On the Road* in three weeks and *The Subterraneans* in only three days. Not wanting to waste any time changing sheets of paper, Kerouac adapted his typewriter to take large rolls of printer's paper so he could type uninterrupted. His road to excess finally caught up with his palace of wisdom in 1969, when he died of esophageal hemorrhaging due to cirrhosis of the liver. He was forty-seven years old.

In Brighton, amphetamine sulphate was a street drug readily available on the black market. I once took some and played guitar for eight hours straight, until my fingers were bleeding. In the words of the great American songwriter, David Bromberg, "You gotta suffer if you wanna sing the blues."

Nowadays, the most common form of street speed is methamphetamine, also known as crank, crystal, ice, whizz, meth or zip. This is a particularly nasty and highly addictive form of speed that is presently wreaking havoc in urban centers around the world.

Here's the thing about speed, or any addictive drug, which you won't hear on the six o'clock news. It's possible for any substance to be used responsibly but you have to be informed, aware *and* responsible when using it. In fifty years of experimentation with recreational drugs, I have never experienced anything close to addiction. Even in those heady, teenage days in Brighton, after scarfing down amphetamine sulphate for several months, none of us got hooked. This is not to say that addiction is benign. Clearly, some people have addictive personalities and should stay away from anything remotely habit-forming. But it should also be noted that these individuals invariably have underlying problems of trauma, abuse and mental illness and so on. They use drugs to self-medicate, as an escape from underlying causes. Like taking a pain killer; the pain is the problem, the pain killer is a solution. It's not a drug problem; it's a mental health problem. Drug addiction is a symptom and not a cause. Granted, it's a misguided solution, but it does provide a temporary respite from deep-seated, psychological distress.

The best thing in a junkie's life is junk.

As for psychedelics, if you have an unstable psychology, mental illness or any propensity for psychosis, you should avoid them.

Even alcohol, which ruins more lives than any other drug is mostly used responsibly. As with most drugs, the majority of those who consume alcohol never have a problem. If it's a problem, it's a problem. If it's not, it's not. It's always about striking a balance, making responsible choices, planning ahead and knowing your dosage and frequency. And if you happen find yourself being chased through the jungle by a marauding band of murderous militants, your best bet might just be twenty milligrams of crystal meth to put some pep in your step and get you out of trouble.

After a memorable summer, the apartment in Brighton had become a doss-house with a constant parade of sketchy characters coming and going. Joni and Van had been replaced with heavy metal and hard rock. Royston had replaced hashish with heroin.

The day I saw Stanley shoot up his first hit of heroin, I knew it was time to move on.

11

The next three years were spent in perpetual motion touring Europe. From Valencia on the western coast of Spain up to the French Riviera and across to the Italian Riviera, there are twelve-hundred kilometers of coastline packed with bars and restaurants. It's a busker's paradise.

Playing guitar and a harmonica mounted on a neck brace, I started at one end of town, moving from café to café collecting wads of Spanish pesetas, Italian lira and French francs. It was a liberating lifestyle. The streets represented a vibrant sub-culture buzzing with life and colourful characters. My days were spent with local street sellers, musicians and travelers. In the evenings I worked the cafes and bars, and at night slept on the beach where there was always a party.

Italy was one of my favorite countries in which to travel and busk. I found the Italians vibrant, fun and excitable. The young women looked like Sofia Loren or fashion runway models with jet black hair, push-up bras and tight skirts. Later in life, possibly due to their high caloric diet, they became shorter and fatter and dressed exclusively in black.

Italians are obsessed with food, and on many occasions, I was invited by locals for lunch or dinner. This sometimes involved driving out into the country to secluded restaurants or family homes for extended meals that could last for several hours. Italians approach meals with all the fervour and tradition of a religious pageant. Generations of family members gathered around the table for course after course of delicious, home-cooked food. Lunch can last all afternoon. I loved these chaotic scenes filled with lively conversation and familial warmth. To this day, there are few activities that give me more pleasure than a big, crazy dinner party.

On one of my expeditions around Europe, I discovered a busking hotspot in Freiburg. In Brighton, I had met a foreign language student named Emil. His mother, sister and older brother Hans lived in Freiburg and he invited me to join him for a family visit.

Freiburg is a picturesque, market town located in the Black Forest in the south of Germany. The cobblestoned main square held a bustling market every weekend. The people of Freiburg had a unique appreciation of street performers. Audiences gathered around, listened attentively, and tossed generous amounts of deutschmarks into my open guitar case. And I had a free place to stay.

This was only twenty-five years after the Second World War had ended. The younger Germans were largely progressive, broad-minded liberals but there remained an undercurrent of animosity among the older generation, particularly towards the British. Even with my inadequate knowledge and interest in history, I quickly figured out that it was best not to mention the war or, more importantly, who had won.

At a café in Freiburg one afternoon, a couple of old Nazis at a nearby table were making disparaging remarks about the Jews. Something about not finishing them off while they had the chance. Emil overhead the comments and on our way out he swiped one of them across the back of the head, knocking off his hat and glasses. That night at dinner, he related the incident to his older brother, Hans who then explained what he called the 'German dilemma.' There comes a time in every young Germans' life when they first discover the hard truth about their country's history and the horrors of the Holocaust. For Hans, this moment came in the form of a small, hardcover book.

The book sat high atop a bookshelf, out of reach for most of Hans' young life. At thirteen, his curiosity got the better of him. He stood on a chair, reached up, retrieved the book and read it. It was called *The Yellow Star* and it outlined, in graphic terms, Germany's persecution of the Jews and Hitler's Final Solution.

Like many young Germans, his first question was, "Who knew?" He was hoping the question would provide a way out of an uncomfortable, philosophical conundrum. If most ordinary Germans were unaware of the atrocities their fathers and grandfathers had committed, they could find consolation and claim the innocence of ignorance. Hans questioned both his parents and his grandparents and asked them, "Who knew?"

Their answer gave him no peace. They told him simply, "Everyone knew."

The next summer, at the end of the busking season, I finished up in Genoa and then hitched across to Rimini on the Adriatic coast of Italy. This was Federico Fellini's home town and the location of his autobiographical masterpiece, *Amarcord*. I'd seen the film many times and it was a thrill to wander the streets where so many memorable scenes had been shot. If you haven't seen it, you should.

After a short visit to Venice, I found myself close to the Yugoslavian border and, on a whim, decided to head down to Greece and on to the Middle East.

There was no great master plan to my itinerary. I was driven by an intense curiosity to see new places and to experience different cultures. Rather than a means of getting from one place to another, travelling became a lifestyle. I found the feeling of leaving one place, coupled with the anticipation of discovering another, exhilarating. I was powered by an engine of curiosity.

Yugoslavia was something altogether different. It lacked the cosmopolitan flavour of Western Europe and at the time was still considered to be behind the imaginary Iron Curtain. Later, it would become six different countries. Crossing the border, the world went from colour to black and white and grey. The Yugoslavian people looked stern and resigned, like characters from a Kafka novel. Apparently they had all purchased their dark, heavy overcoats from the same store. In restaurants, they ate goulash standing up. I didn't even think about ordering a cup of tea. I decided not to linger and continued down the coast road to Greece.

I had heard something about the Greeks at Hazelwick but due to my total lack of interest, couldn't remember what it was? Upon arrival in Athens, I smoked a joint at the Parthenon which sat on top of the Acropolis and contemplated its significance. It looked like a bombed-out building, much smaller than I imagined, and in a shocking state of disrepair. A renovation was out of the question. It was clearly a demo job.

While I failed to grasp the importance of Ancient Greece at the time, my subsequent exposure to Greek philosophy and to the Stoics in particular, revealed a fascinating and pragmatic worldview.

The Stoics, I later discovered, predated Christianity by a thousand years. The Ancient Greeks invented geography, the theatre, showers, streets, central heating, levers and water wheels, analogue computers and vending machines, democracy and the winch. And although they had also dreamt up a pantheon of fantastical deities worthy of an inspired team of Marvel comic-book writers, they were the first civilisation to give up their gods in favour of reason and logic.

Good for them.

At a critical juncture in human history, two-thousand years ago, the Romans had a choice to make between Christianity and the reasoned philosophy of the Greeks. They chose Christianity and we've been paying a heavy price ever since.

If you want a few tips on how to live a moral life, forget the Bible and instead read the Stoics. Their central message is this: take personal responsibility for what you do, or say, or feel, or think. You are not responsible for whatever anyone else does, or says, or feels, or thinks. To make decisions, use your head rather than your heart, and lead an examined life ruled by virtue. If you want to know more, read *The Meditations* by Marcus Aurelius, *The Moral Letters* by Seneca, and *The Discourses and Handbook* by Epictetus. You'll be amazed at how well these texts have held up after thousands of years.

Apart from inventing almost everything worthwhile, the Greeks are also credited with some of the earliest uses of psychedelics. The Eleusinian Mysteries were ritualistic, drug-fuelled, all-night parties. It was a tradition that carried on for hundreds of years. Initiates consumed a potent secret brew called kykeon, thought to have psychedelic properties. It would appear that the Greeks also invented raves.

In Athens, I loitered around the Port of Piraeus for several days trying to get a job on one of the ships that carried cargo to various ports in the Middle East. I had heard this would be easy. It was not. I abandoned the mission and travelled north towards Turkey.

On my way out of Athens, I pitched my tent in a park and awoke the next morning to a circus being set up all around me. Despite the name, El Circo Española, most of the acts were Italian. With my newly-acquired half-assed Italian, I chatted with some of the performers and asked for a job.

I was hired on the spot as a general hand and travelled with the circus for the next three stops, from Athens in the south to Thessaloniki in the north. It was the hardest work I'd ever done. Working from dawn to late at night, the job entailed setting up the big top, assembling bleachers, assisting performers, and generally humping heavy objects from one place to another. Circus folk hail from a distant planet. They are idiosyncratic bohemians, uncompromisingly independent and indefatigable. The people of El Circo were as fascinating as the work was relentless. I remember going into town one day with a troupe of Italian acrobats. I walked while they tumbled, cartwheeled, walked on their hands, and did back-flips. One morning I had breakfast with an Austrian animal trainer and three chimpanzees. Their table manners were atrocious.

Ultimately, my youth and vigour proved no match for the gruelling and unrelenting work-load. By the time we finished packing up in Thessaloniki, I collapsed with exhaustion and had to quit. After pitching my tent in an olive grove and sleeping for two days, I hitchhiked east, to Istanbul. My intention was to continue down to the Middle East but the capricious and flighty finger of fate had other plans.

12

In Istanbul there's an area called Sultanahmet, named after the Blue Mosque at its center. It's a well-known meeting place for travellers en route to India.

Near the mosque was a famous hippie hang-out called, The Pudding Shop. Throngs of international itinerants gathered there to change money, exchange information, buy hashish, drink Turkish coffee and arrange rides to the East. Turkish coffee is a thick, black sludge served in an egg cup. It's an acquired taste but still preferable to Turkish tea which is too strong, too sweet, over-stewed, and served without a trace of milk.

I bought a quarter ounce of Nepali hash and quickly made some new friends who invited me back to a nearby hotel room. Everyone was buzzing with the news that an American named, Billy Hayes, had just escaped from a Turkish prison where he'd been serving a four-year sentence. Billy had been busted with two kilos of hash taped to his body. Later, his story became the Alan Parker movie, *Midnight Express*. This led to a discussion of penalties for hash possession in Turkey. The general formula was two years per gram. I looked down at the lump I was rolling into a joint and calculated it could get me fourteen years. Undeterred by the prospect, I finished rolling the joint, took a toke and passed it around. After completing the circle, it came back to me. As I was puffing away, there was a mighty hullabaloo at the door and three Turkish police officers burst into the room.

I was sitting on a bench by an open window. As the officers entered, I carefully placed the joint, still lit, behind me on the outside ledge. Next, I concealed the lump of hashish under my right foot. Like most police incidents in third world countries there was a lot of posturing, loud accusatory tones and gnashing of teeth. They performed the standard routine; stomping around the room, shouting and waving truncheons. I imagined there must be a school somewhere that taught this particular technique. These guys had obviously come top of their class.

Due to the considerable language barriers, we never quite figured out what they wanted. Perhaps they were looking for someone? Perhaps they got a kick out of terrifying tourists? Luckily, a punchy and indignant German got in their faces and distracted most of their attention. I laid low, sat back and watched the show.

The German demanded to see the chief of police and threatened legal action. He claimed his father was a lawyer who would make short work of these incompetents. After a while, the cops ran out of gas. Frustrated, defeated, and no match for stalwart German determination and resolve, they left the room and slammed the door behind them. I casually retrieved the joint from the window ledge behind me and took a puff. It was still lit.

Istanbul is the only city in the world that is spread over two continents with the Bosphorus strait forming the dividing line between Europe and Asia. After a week or so my feet began to itch, so I walked across the bridge to the Asian side and stuck out my thumb. Hitchhiking in Europe is relatively easy; sooner or later someone will pick you up. Not so in Asia. The Turks failed to fully grasp the meaning of the international, standardised symbol of the raised thumb.

They took it as a friendly gesture and often gave me the thumbs-up back as they sailed merrily past.

Hitchhiking is a fine art. To the uninitiated, it looks simple and straightforward enough. You stand on the side of the road, stick out your thumb and hope for the best. But this is a gross and uninformed simplification of what is a finely calibrated, poetic dance between man and machine. There are many subtle forces at play and one can greatly increase the odds of a ride by honing one's technique. As with the restaurant business, location is of the essence. You must be visible from a good way off to give the driver ample time to contemplate stopping. Picking up a complete stranger is a decision that requires careful consideration. Standing on a corner or next to a heavily trafficked area will get you nowhere. It's well worth walking to a place that provides maximum visibility.

Next, the driver must have a safe and visible place to pull over. Just before a layby, a hard shoulder or a gas station works well. Now that you can be seen from a long way off, your body language becomes critical. Slumping over a backpack creates a poor first impression. Never sit or—perish the thought—lie down on the side of the road. You must stand erect, confident and poised. Always face the cars head on and try to make eye contact with the driver. Imagine you are an old friend and flash a look of recognition. Keep the face relaxed, calm and self-assured. Avoid smiling too broadly. This can make you look like a weirdo.

Once you have established a solid connection with the driver, use your thumb to reel them in. Your thumb is a magic wand. A stiff thumb denotes tension and this can transfer to the driver, sending a negative subconscious signal. Keep the thumb relaxed but purposeful. Thumb technique is a skill akin to fly fishing. Your thumb is used as a rod to guide the car towards a safe place to stop. Think of the tip of your thumb as a dancing fly that serves to both attract and mesmerise. After making full eye contact, take a step back as if making room for the vehicle to slow, and stop. With a gentle swooping motion, use your thumb to guide them in. This will serve you well in most places, but not in Turkey.

Despite years of experience and superior technique, I stood on the side of the road for over six hours with no luck. As night fell, I gave up and looked for a place to sleep. A nearby bridge looked promising so I climbed down a steep embankment and found a spot on a concrete pad under the abutment. The concrete floor prevented the use of tent poles or pegs, so I put them to one side, spread out the collapsed tent on the hard ground and crawled inside.

For safety, I carried my passport and money in a cloth pouch hung around my neck. In the collapsed tent, I relocated my neck pouch and put it in my backpack which I placed under my feet along with my boots. I then tucked the entrance of the tent under the whole package and tried to sleep. The concrete pad was hard and cold and I slept fitfully, tossing and turning and waking up frequently. In the morning I awoke and found my legs hanging out of the tent. Everything was gone. My passport, money, backpack, boots and everything I owned had been stolen in the night. I was left barefooted, standing in my jeans and T-shirt with nothing in my pockets. My sole remaining possessions were a trashed sleeping bag and a poleless tent, limp and damp, and as worthless as a used condom.

I walked five kilometers back to Istanbul in bare feet and told my tale of woe to a group of travellers at The Pudding Shop. They were sympathetic and gave me a little money, a morsel of hash and several pairs of socks. I traded what was left of my tent and sleeping bag for a hairy, Afghan jacket. For shoes, I fabricated crude sandals from two strips of old car tire and tied them to my feet with nylon rope.

The next day, I headed for the British Embassy. They were less sympathetic than the travellers at The Pudding Shop. In Istanbul it was common practice for people to sell their passports or travellers cheques, claiming them stolen. The embassy staff had heard it all before. They took my information and told me to come back in a week.

Back in Sultanahmet I was forced to rely on the generosity of strangers. I slept on the roof of a hostel and ate the cheapest food available. I could buy a plate of beans for thruppence. In retrospect, it seems like a fairly desperate situation but, at the time, through the eyes of a fearless and naive nineteen-year-old, it was all a grand adventure; a bit of a lark.

I got the brush off from the embassy several more times but was eventually issued a train ticket to Thessaloniki and an emergency passport valid for the seven countries I would have to cross en route back to England. The day I left Istanbul it snowed for the first time in twenty-five years. Had I given astrology even the faintest spec of credence, I might have blamed my luck on a retrograde Mercury.

In Thessaloniki, I checked into a youth hostel, a dull, drab building near the city centre. There were about a dozen other travellers at the hostel from various European countries. Some had just arrived from Athens, where they described martial law and brutal killings. The country was undergoing a violent military coup. The dictator, Papadopoulos, who took power with a violent military coup in 1967, was now being ousted by another violent military coup. What goes around comes around. It was Greek politics as usual.

A distraught Frenchman at the hostel claimed that two-hundred students had been gunned down in the streets for demonstrating against the government. The country was in turmoil. The next day we learned that military rule had been established over the entire country. A twenty-four hour curfew was imposed and the owners and staff at our hostel abandoned their posts and disappeared.

Left to our own devices, we hunkered down and waited for things to blow over. Several days later, we ran out of food. We drew straws to decide who would venture out on a mission to find something to eat. I got one of the short straws, along with the distraught Frenchman.

The streets were eerily deserted except for a few tanks and military vehicles. Everything was closed but we managed to attract the attention of some locals on their apartment balconies. With crude sign language and a garbled blend of linguistic gymnastics, we managed to communicate hunger. Before long, an older couple appeared at the front door and handed us two bags of groceries. We thanked them profusely and made our way back through the empty streets towards the hostel.

We were prematurely claiming victory when a Greek soldier in full battle gear, abruptly stepped out of an alley and blocked our way. He spread his legs and pointed his submachine gun in our direction. We froze. The Frenchman turned white and had a flashback of the dead students in Athens. I pointed at the bags of food and made the universal gesture for eating. The soldier stiffened, hesitated for a moment, and then shouted, "All days is no ways!" which we took to mean, "Please obey the curfew and return to your residence," which we did.

After another week or so things quieted down and we learned that the train station and the border with Yugoslavia had temporarily opened. We decided to make a run for it. As we were preparing to depart, the nervous-looking Frenchman dumped a bag of weed into the garbage. It was about six ounces of what I would now classify as scragweed, low quality marijuana full of sticks and stems. Whatever possessed me to grab it, I'll never know. It was an instinctive reaction. I cannot stand to see things go to waste. Or as the great Chet Baker once lamented, "Blame it on my youth." I stuffed the pot down the front of my pants and headed for the train station.

The train to Dubrovnik was packed with people frantic to leave the country. My ticket promised reserved seating but my designated carriage was already crammed full of refugees fleeing the coup. Desperate looking families with children and piles of baggage filled every seat. A crate of chickens were squawking in the luggage rack.

I was now travelling with a fellow Englishman I'd met at the hostel. He too was being repatriated. He kindly offered to hide my pot in his backpack as I was luggage free and the bulge in my pants could have attracted the wrong sort of attention. Besides, looking like a dishevelled Afghan refugee in my shaggy jacket, long hair and car-tire sandals, I was likely to attract more attention than my compadre.

As all the carriages were full, we ended up in the corridor for the entire trip. During the night, we slept on the filthy floor, which was strewn with cigarette butts and garbage. Every couple of hours we were woken up by a food cart rattling up and down the corridor and frequently had to stand up to let it pass. It was a long night.

When the train stopped at the Yugoslav border crossing, several heavily armed, jackbooted, leather-clad customs officers boarded and demanded our papers. I produced my emergency passport, which was a single sheet of crumpled paper with my photo stapled onto one corner. One of them pointed to my companion's backpack and demanded to inspect it.

The pot was wrapped in a heavy plastic bag hidden halfway down the bag inside a pair of shorts. The officer started to remove the contents, piece by piece. When he got to the shorts, he paused and gently squeezed. To me, the sound of the plastic bag was deafening. The shorts crackled and crunched like a Mamba dance class for electric eels. I began to plan my new life in a communist forced labour camp. My luck had finally run out. I was surely headed for the Gulag. Mentally, I planned out my future. I would learn Russian, practice meditation, bide my time and eventually, like Billy Hayes, make a daring escape. After what seemed an eternity, he gently put the shorts down to one side and continued his fruitless search.

My travelling companion got thoroughly spooked and immediately withdrew his support. He handed me the bag of grass which I stuck back down the front of my pants. In retrospect, it's easy to interpret this as another reckless and irresponsible action. But we do not live our lives in reverse. At the time, it seemed like the right thing to do.

Over the next three days we passed through five more international borders without incident. I arrived in London and made my way back to Crawley and my beleaguered parents' house. I discovered the embassy in Istanbul had contacted them and demanded money for my travel expenses. Unfortunately, they didn't have any and said so. They had assumed I'd find my own way back. My mother was shocked at my appearance and recoiled in disgust. After nearly a month without changing my clothes or showering, I looked like Rasputin on a bad hair day and stunk like a wild animal. While I was in the shower, my mother quietly burned all my clothes in the back yard.

13

Once again, Brighton became my base of operations but housing was scarce and overpriced so I moved into a squat. This was the golden age of squatting in Brighton.

This is how it worked: identify a house that had been left empty for at least a year, gain entry, change the locks and post a sign on the front door claiming 'squatter's rights.' Next, report and officially register the squat at the police station, then move in and invite all your friends. The issue was now a civil matter and not subject to criminal prosecution. Even if the owners showed up, and they sometimes did, they would have to file a civil suit which could take up to six months before an eviction notice could be served. In some cases, a deal was struck with the owners to allow squatters to stay on for a nominal rent. Some of these squats lasted for years.

Squatting was essentially a political act. It was about reclaiming living spaces for people who'd been squeezed out of the rental market by greed and speculation. During this time, I inadvertently became a squatting activist and ended up liberating several houses to the hapless, hopeless, and homeless.

The Sussex Square squat was a four-storey town-house in an exclusive, affluent mews on the Brighton sea-front. Our neighbours on either side turned out to be Dame Flora Robson and Lawrence Olivier who had just finished filming *The*

Merchant of Venice. They were not amused by our presence. After our house warming party got a little out of hand, Larry was livid and called his lawyers. He demanded a pound of flesh. After receiving a nasty letter threatening legal action, we thought it prudent to move on.

Our next location was chosen with more care. It was a dilapidated, eight-bedroom house in a more modest neighbourhood. I moved in and invited several of my homeless junkie friends from Crawley. What is it with me and junkies? In this case, it was affordable housing.

About the same time, I acquired a library card and developed an insatiable appetite for reading. It was in these damp and dilapidated houses that I gave myself the education that Hazelwick could never hope to offer. How did I choose which books to read? I went to the literature section. Everything worth reading is there, in alphabetical order. I read the complete works of Kurt Vonnegut, Hermann Hesse, John Steinbeck and Charles Bukowski. I read the Russians and the French Existentialists and Kafka and Sartre and Hemingway. I learned more about history and psychology and philosophy from works of literary fiction than I could from any non-fiction.

When you read great works of fiction, you are not just reading a story with characters and events. You are reading the mind of the writer. You are having a vicarious experience of another human psyche while expanding your own. A well written book is a mind expanding drug. Forget the pulp fiction of Stephen King and Michael Crichton and Dan Brown. Do yourself a favour and check out the literature section instead.

After a few weeks, a Canadian junkie named Max showed up at the front door. He was a nice guy with a sensitive disposition. He said he'd heard about the place. Junkies all seem to know each other. If I believed for a nanosecond in telepathy, I might have thought they communicated using some sort of psychic transference amplified by the use of opiates. More likely they just went where the junk was. Max made his case, answered a few perfunctory questions, passed the audition and moved in.

Max had the dubious title of being the longest-running registered heroin addict in the British Isles. He'd been using junk for over thirty years. Contrary to popular belief, heroin doesn't kill you. Junkies die from adulterants and overdoses. With a clean, reliable source of heroin, they can live long and relatively healthy lives. Many hold down regular jobs. Max was over fifty-years-old and in good physical condition. Heroin is the ultimate stress buster. Turns out, stress is more dangerous than heroin.

The jazz musician, Chet Baker, famous for his heroin use, didn't die from his life-long addiction. He was thrown out of a fourth-storey window of a hotel in Amsterdam. Chet was sixty-years old but the coroner reported he had the body of a thirty-five-year-old.

Max's prescription was for fourteen pills of English pharmaceutical heroin a day. This is a massive dose. A fix for a typical addict is one full pill. A casual user or amateur might shoot up half a pill for a decent hit. Max needed four pills just to get out of bed in the morning.

Once a week, Max made a pilgrimage to the local pharmacy to pick up his heroin. One particular day, I discovered him panicking because his prescription had run out and he was beginning to twitch and sweat. If he didn't get a fix soon, he would likely fall into a coma and die. This was his worst fear and you could see the fear in his eyes. I loaded him into a taxi and rushed him to the local chemist. I went in to get his prescription because Max was too weak to get out of the cab and was flaked out on the back seat. After explaining the dire situation, the chemist came out onto the street and placed a bottle of heroin pills and a box of syringes on his chest and we sped back to the squat.

By the time we got back, Max was in a bad state. He desperately jabbed around to find a vein, most of which had long since collapsed. He tried his arms, the back of his hand, his groin, all to no avail. His hands were shaking so much he could barely hold the syringe and was fast approaching full-on panic mode. If he went into a coma, he would likely never come out of it. Eventually I stepped in, held his foot over an electric heater to raise a vein, grabbed the syringe out of his trembling hand and shot him up.

Amazingly, in all the years I knew and lived with junkies, I never once tried it myself. This was not due to any value judgment. It just looked like a bit of a downer. I was more interested in getting into it than getting out of it.

14

After a summer of squatting and busking in Brighton, I once again teamed up with my old mate, Stanley Cartesian. We were up for an adventure and needed to make some money. After considering our options and eliminating the dismal prospect of regular employment, we hatched a plan to fly down to Morocco and bring back some hash oil. We bought one-month round-trip tickets to Tangiers and packed light.

In Tangiers, it took some time to find the right contact but after a few false starts, we finally settled on a friendly young chap named Mohamed. He claimed to have access to a new kind of potent red hash oil. It was made with a chemical process and reacted in sunlight. The process turned the oil a rich, ruby-red colour. It sounded good to us so we purchased three-hundred grams. Back at our hotel room, we set about packaging and preparing the oil which we planned to swallow and transport back to England in our stomachs.

I have no clue where we got the idea for this hare-brained scheme. Neither of us had known anyone who'd attempted such a mission and it proved much more difficult than we had anticipated. We considered various packaging methods and settled on condoms.

We unfurled the condoms one by one and poured approximately five grams into the tip of each one. Twisting the tip into a ball, we pulled the condom inside itself forming a double layer. Next, we twisted the ball and repeated the process until we had a neat package with four or five layers. We finished them off with a tight knot and ended up with fifty-four one-inch balls. We split the batch into two halves and had twenty-seven each to swallow.

Concerned about structural integrity, we put the balls through a number of tests. I threw a couple at the wall as hard as I could, check. I slammed one in a door jamb, all good. Stanley stomped on one, not a scratch. We even stuck a pin in one and watched in amazement as the layers shifted, self-sealing the hole.

Now all we had to do was swallow the bastards.

The first attempts were discouraging. It was near impossible to gag them down. After some experimentation, we found that a mixture of yogurt and over-ripe, slimy banana acted as an effective lubricant. It took a couple of hours to gag them all down.

It was a three-hour flight back to London. With the travel time on each end and the wait time at the airport, the whole trip would be more like seven or eight hours. We had no idea how long we could hold the balls in our stomachs so we swallowed them just before we left for Tangiers airport. We didn't want any nasty accidents on the plane.

Packing the oil had been a messy business. Our hands were covered in red goo and the knots on the end of each package and the balls themselves were laced with oil residue which we had now ingested. By the time we arrived at the airport we were both downright blotto. We were so stoned that we had trouble navigating the airport. Our eyes were blazing, bloodshot red.

We were immediately spotted, pulled aside by security guards and given a thorough search. We both had long hair, mine was brown and wavy and Stanley's was an extravagant cascade of blond curls reaching past his delicate, slender shoulders. As per the fashion dictates of the day, we both wore headbands. It was pretty obvious we were up to something.

While waiting for our flight, we were singled out again, questioned and given another full body search. We watched with rapt attention as they used a long, metal tool to probe inside the frame of our backpacks. Finally, we were ready to board and walked out onto the tarmac towards the plane.

As we prepared to climb the stairs, another two enthusiastic customs officials rushed up and pulled us out of the line. In front of all the other passengers, we were subjected to another full pat down. A wide-screen image of Billy Hayes flashed before my eyes. After this final, unproductive search, we boarded the plane, fastened our seat belts and prepared for take-off.

Looking back, I am once again struck by the capacity of the undeveloped, teenage brain to disregard obvious danger. We had completely failed to consider even a cursory risk/benefit analysis. Although aware of the illegalities and risk involved, we really didn't believe we were doing anything fundamentally wrong. The police and customs officials were wrong for bothering us. The laws were wrong. We were exercising our basic human rights as autonomous, sovereign citizens of the world. We were righteous warriors of freedom, sticking it to the Man.

The flight back to London was thankfully uneventful. High on hash oil, success and the sweet sting of victory, we had a couple of drinks but refused the meal.

Back in Brighton, I stretched some cellophane cling film over the toilet, snapped on some rubber gloves and set about retrieving the booty. I'll spare you the details. After a thorough wash and rinse, I counted twenty-six balls.

One had gotten stuck somewhere.

I called Stanley who claimed total success. I palpated my abdomen and was able to feel the foreign object in my gut. I drank a lot of water and massaged the area repeatedly. I did back-bends, jumped up and down and gyrated my hips like a belly dancer. After a couple of hours, I felt the thing move inside me. Back on the toilet, I was relieved, both physically and psychologically, as I recovered the errant ball.

The following day, Stanley and I rented an apartment in Brighton and invited Royston Trinidad and Byron Thomas to move in with us. We were given a hero's welcome and there was much celebration. After a twenty-four hour victory lap and exhaustive sampling of the product for quality purposes, we packaged the red oil into one-gram batches and put the word out to potential customers.

Hash oil can be difficult to smoke. It's messy and gummy and sticks to everything. Most people smeared it onto a cigarette paper and rolled a joint. It can also be smoked off a pin, sucking up the smoke with a straw or cardboard tube. My preferred method was mixing it with Drum tobacco rolled into cigarettes.

Walking home late one night with Stanley, Royston and Byron, a police car spotted our motley crew. They did a double take and made a quick U-turn in our direction. The cops lined us up in front of the police car and demanded we empty our pockets. I was on the end of the line and realised the baggy I had in my pocket contained a few remnants of oil-soaked tobacco. While the cops worked their way towards me, I palmed the baggy and flipped it under the police car. One of the cops immediately retrieved it and held it up victoriously exclaiming, "Ah ha! This is the stuff?!"

"Yes," I said, "It's the good stuff."

I remember the officer took obvious pleasure when he read this comment of mine out in court. Apparently, someone had tipped them off to our Morocco trip. We were escorted back to our apartment where the police executed a search warrant.

I had put about forty separate one-gram lots on a shelf in the kitchen cupboard. The oil was sandwiched between pieces of clear plastic, lying flat on the top shelf. There were four cops sniffing around and I saw one of them open the kitchen cupboard and rummage inside. The oil packages were a little too high for him to see, so he felt around with his hand and blindly patted the top shelf. He had his hand right on the sachets of oil, but because they were flat and spread out, they remained undetected. The rest of the oil, still in the original condom balls, was stashed in my guitar case. An officer asked who owned the guitar. I confessed it was mine.

A guitar case has a box with a lid in the neck compartment where picks and accessories are stored. The officer sat across from me and slowly opened the case. He removed the guitar and looked inside it with a flashlight. He then placed the guitar to one side and carefully felt around the lining of the case. At one point, he paused and checked me out for a reaction. I remained pokerfaced. The pick box had a tab on it. All he had to do was lift the tab, open the box, and reveal the mother lode. For some inexplicable reason, he didn't do it. To this day, it's a complete mystery. The officers finished their search and left empty-handed.

I found out several days later, the police had also showed up at my parents' house in Crawley and searched their house and backyard with sniffer dogs. My poor mother nearly had a heart attack. Although she was the most law-abiding person on the planet, she was terrified of the police and it took a while for her to forgive me.

What happened? A few meagre, oily strands of Drum tobacco were sent to a lab and came back as 0.02 of a gram. Barely a trace. I was eventually arraigned in court, given a good talking to, and a small fine. This would be my one and only bust in a fifty-year career of illicit shenanigans.

15

I n the summer of 1975, the American gangster Sam Gian-
cana died in a hail of bullets and Jimmy Hoffa mysteri-
ously disappeared forever. I was hitchhiking from Brighton
to Crawley and got picked up by an almost famous Canadian folk singer in a rented car. We'll call him David.

He was travelling around southern England looking up
distant relatives. With nothing better to do, I joined him
for the next two weeks. We became fast friends and before
he left, he invited me to come and visit him in Toronto,
Canada. He promised to show me a good time and give me
a free place to stay. That was good enough for me.

Previously, I had planned on travelling around the States
but my visa application was refused. Even with a relative in
California, I was told to forget it and not bother applying
again. Canada sounded like a reasonable alternative. The
hash oil money had run out so I worked twelve-hour night
shifts at the local Wonder Bread factory and three weeks
later was knocking on David's door in Toronto.

Up to that point, all I'd heard about Canada was The
Lumberjack Sketch from Monty Python's Flying Circus.
I was looking forward to some good-spirited camaraderie,
group singing and hanging around in bars. I was pleasantly
surprised to find a cosmopolitan city bursting with life and
new possibilities. The streets and cars were twice the size of
those in England. It reminded me of every American TV
cop show I'd ever seen. Canadians are horrified with the

idea that their country is comparable to the U.S., which they view with a highly critical and condescending eye.

David invited me to live with him and his South African girlfriend, Pippa. We all got along famously until Pippa decided that she liked me more than David. After much ballyhoo, he moved out, leaving us the apartment.

I was on a three-month tourist visa and was determined to make the most of it. Live music was everywhere. There were coffee houses with folk singers, live jazz in the clubs, rock bands in the bars, musicians in the street and revolution in the air. I loved the double-wide streets, the green spaces, the relaxed lifestyle and friendly disposition of the multi-cultural Canadians. Toronto was the cleanest city I had ever seen, with thought-provoking public art everywhere.

In Crawley, the streets were full of garbage and the nearest thing to public art was the fountain in the city center which was regularly vandalised and defaced by hooligans and nit-wits. There was only one downside to the country to which I would soon swear allegiance. They had no clue how to make a proper cup of tea. This fact would inspire a lifelong mission to educate coffee-mad North Americans in the fine art of tea making, a mission that has proven to be entirely unsuccessful.

I wrote to Stanley Cartesian and he immediately flew out to join me. My romance with Pippa was much like Pippa herself, short and sweet. She was five-foot three, I was six-foot four. We both knew our vertical challenges could never be resolved so she packed her bags and went back to South Africa.

Stanley and I now shared the Toronto apartment with a jazz guitar player from New York named Kenny McDougal. Kenny spoke with the broadest New York accent I'd ever heard. No one understood a word he said.

In response to dwindling financial resources, we

responded to an ad in the newspaper and we all got jobs as door to door salesmen selling oil paintings. We were told the paintings were original works created by Canadian artists. We later found out they were mass produced in Taiwan and Hong Kong. Unbeknownst to us, our shady employers bought them in bulk and signed them with phony signatures. On weekends and evenings, we were driven out to the Toronto suburbs with rolls of canvases under our arms. We told people we were cutting out the middleman to bring them original Canadian art at discounted prices. It worked remarkably well and we made good money on our commissions. Stanley and I, with our English accents, became the top salesmen of the Toronto Art House. Kenny didn't fare as well and was the first to quit. At first I believed what we were told about the art but when I eventually caught on to the deception, my moral compass twitched to true north and I, too, had to quit.

Stanley Cartesian, that handsome, golden-haired, slim-hipped, silver-backed devil, hooked up with a Canadian girl named Helen. He was as enamored with Canada as I was and wanted to stay. Helen agreed to a passport marriage and they tied the knot with a Justice of the Peace. Things did not end well for Stanley and Helen but their union did serve to plant an idea in my mind that would come to fruition four years later.

When my visitor's visa ran out, I returned to England and filled out a fifteen page application for permanent residency in Canada. The response was swift and decisive. I was told to forget it and not bother applying again.

Not one to give up easily, I returned to Toronto in the spring of 1977, the year the first *Star Wars* movie was released, Roman Polanski got busted and Elvis dropped dead.

I arrived at Toronto airport with two-hundred Canadian

dollars and a one-way ticket. I was eyed with suspicion and given a twelve-day visitor's visa marked by a big black, full-page stamp in my passport. Exactly two years later, I would be apprehended in Vancouver by immigration police and thrown into jail. More on this later.

Meanwhile, I bought false ID from a cab driver in Toronto and began my new life in Canada. For the bargain price of twenty-five dollars, I got a driver's license and a social insurance card which would allow me to work. My new name was Michael Sydney Willan. I was born on November 28th 1958. I was a Sagittarian from Sudbury, though Sagittarians are notoriously contemptuous of astrology.

The busking was excellent in Toronto and the people there were friendly and generous. I played every Friday, Saturday and Sunday evening on Yonge Street and made a good living. I rented an apartment in Kensington Market and settled in to a carefree life, living what I imagined to be the Canadian dream. I also started buying and selling pot.

There were two kinds of pot in Toronto at that time, Mexican and Colombian Gold. By the late seventies, Acapulco Gold, Panama Red and the superior Maui Wowie could also be found. Thai sticks came a little later and consisted of cured cannabis flowers skewered on a bamboo stick, wrapped in fan leaves, and tied together with hemp string. Mexican, also known as 'commercial,' was the cheaper option at twenty-five dollars an ounce. Colombian Gold was superior and went for forty dollars an ounce. Some dealers bought ounces, or 'lids' and sold one-gram dime bags or half-gram nickel bags. This kind of dealing necessitates making a lot of sales, having many customers, and requires a lot of running around. The more customers, the higher the risk. My preferred method was to buy pounds and sell ounces thereby doubling my money. I learned very early on to screen my customers.

Here's a golden rule of drug dealing: choose your customers. If you choose people with integrity, people who are reliable, honest and won't crack under pressure and betray you, you'll never have a problem.

Rochdale College on Bloor Street was an experiment in student-run alternative education and co-operative living. It quickly became the beating heart of drug culture in Toronto. Many of the students, and even some of the teachers, took up dealing all manner of drugs. I knew several dealers there and could always find a pound of pot for a fair price. But during an unusually dry period, a friend suggested another source. He knew some Rastafarians in a nearby apartment building who had pounds of Colombian for four-hundred dollars.

Not all Rastafarians are created equal. The authentic ones are laid back and say things like "yah mon" and "one love" and "cool runnings." Despite their irrational and preposterous religion, they are, for the most part, genial and moralistic. They are primarily interested in listening to reggae music on large sound systems, knitted hats and smoking as much dope as possible. The other type are known as rude boys. They are villains and scoundrels. At first glance, they are indistinguishable from each other.

We strolled over and knocked on their door. A dreadlocked Rasta appeared. We couldn't yet tell what category he fell into. In the room behind him there was three more milling around. We made a preliminary request and waited at the door. Before long, the first Rasta came back, looked at us contemptuously, took our money, and shut the door. Confused, we knocked again. The door reopened and two new Rastas appeared. One of them was holding a hand gun. He casually used the barrel to adjust his woolen hat. It was now clear they fell firmly into the rude boy category. They proceeded to wave the gun around, called us bald heads, batty boys, and dam lagga heads. When they'd finished insulting us, they told us to galang right off and slammed the door shut again. We got the message. Potless and penniless, we made a dignified and tactical retreat.

Back at my apartment, I took stock and related my sad story to my Puerto Rican neighbours. They claimed that they too had guns and pulled one out to show it to me. They wanted to help and kindly offered to go and get my money back. I decided I didn't want to add a gun battle to my already disastrous day and declined their generous offer.

This highlights another myth of the generic drug dealer. In police photos of drug busts, pounds of various controlled substances are often shown next to an array of illegal firearms. This represents a criminal element in the trade concerned only with making money at any cost. The ethical drug dealer has no use for weaponry. He is invariably unarmed and more concerned with quality, service and education than gun play. From that day forward, I would screen my suppliers with as much vigour as my customers. This brief encounter with the pseudo-Rastafarian rude boys would be the only time I ever encountered a gun.

Rochdale had now earned a reputation as the drug dealing capitol of North America and came under intense police scrutiny. The place was consistently in the news, repeatedly raided, and eventually closed down.

My next supplier was Pat, a dealer of pot and hash oil. Pat looked like a bank-teller, wore V-neck cashmere sweaters and was quite possibly the nicest guy in the world. He was a gentleman, a dealer, and a man of the old school tie. He radiated innocent charm, was reliable and honest, and drove around in a 1968 Plymouth Valiant with a trunk full of high-grade marijuana.

The general formula for dealing pot—and it holds true to this day—went like this: a pound is sixteen ounces. Ten ounces should cover your cost so, back in 1975, if a pound cost five-hundred dollars, each ounce sold for fifty. The remaining six ounces were profit. Today, a pound of pot is closer to two grand, so to cover the cost with the first ten ounces, an ounce sells for two-hundred dollars. Amazingly, over the past thirty years, the price of pot has held steady at two-hundred dollars an ounce, making it the most stable commodity on the planet. For a secure and reliable economy, we might want to consider indexing our currencies to cannabis.

Pat was good company and we spent many happy afternoons high on LSD wandering around the aptly named, High Park. One time, we drove up to his parent's cabin in Northern Ontario with some mescaline.

Mescaline is the active ingredient found in the peyote cactus. It is also present in San Pedro and Peruvian Torch. The effects are similar to LSD and magic mushrooms. Mescaline was a favorite tipple of the psychiatrist Humphrey Osmond who, you'll remember, invented the term psychedelic.

We took two hundred milligrams of the drug in the early afternoon and went for a walk in the woods by a lake. In the fall, the colours of the trees in Northern Ontario are a blaze of fluorescent yellow, orange, red and gold. The colours are so vibrant, they appear unnatural. In a normal state of mind, they are spectacular. On mescaline, they become amplified to the extreme, vibrating and melding in variegated patterns like a Van Gogh painting. The swirling sky literally took my breath away. I developed super-hearing and could detect the sounds of small animals moving in the undergrowth hundreds of yards away. At one point, I tuned in to a couple whispering to each other on the far side of the lake. The sound of their voices skipped over the still water like flat stones. I could hear every word. The most notable effect was a complete dissolution of the ego, common to many psychedelics. The boundaries between self and the world become blurred. Feelings of connection are amplified. Objective, intellectual analysis falls away and is superseded by direct experience. This is the mystical here and now touted by Zen Buddhists and other adherents of meditation. It is a state of mind that can take years to achieve with conventional meditation. With psychedelics, you can get there in about forty-five minutes.

After Pat and I became separated, I finished my trip lying spread-eagled on a rock at the side of the lake, staring up at the night sky. The Milky Way was clearly visible and I allowed myself to be sucked up into its vortex, floating up through the stars. There is nothing like a trip round the universe to clarify and focus the mind.

A few weeks later, I went to buy some more pot from Pat. He was nowhere to be found. After a few days, he resurfaced with a tragic story. He told me he'd bought a liter of hash oil from a biker who turned out to be an undercover cop. Like Frankie Howard in *Carry on up the River*, Pat's gast had never been so flabbered. The 'biker' was the dirtiest, greasiest, nastiest, roughest and toughest guy around. He smoked dope, dropped acid, befriended dealers, and then busted them.

Talk about dishonest.

After a full year in Toronto, I was looking down the barrel of another Ontario winter. The last one, like the proverbial snowman, had been abominable. The temperature plummeted to thirty below with six-foot snow drifts. It was impossible to busk outside, so I retreated to the Toronto subway stations and played my guitar with fingerless gloves.

One of the best spots was Union Station which was both a subway stop, and a train station. The subway police patrolled one area and the railway police patrolled the other. There was a white line on the floor delineating the two jurisdictions. I'd first set up on the subway side of the line. When I saw the subway police approaching, I'd push my guitar case over the line, step over to the railway side and continue playing. The same procedure was followed if the railway police approached from the other side.

While busking at Union Station one day at twenty-five below zero, I took a break to collect my loot and leaned my guitar against the wall. The guitar neck had barely touched the tiled wall when I heard a sharp crack and the frozen head stock snapped off. The crunching of the wood was accompanied by a sickening twang as all the strings detuned themselves. It was the sound of a chord that signified an unequivocal ending. The prospect of another winter in Toronto was out of the question.

I had heard that if you tilted the North American continent on its side and shook it, all the loose elements would fall to the West Coast. I was intrigued by the idea and decided to hitchhike the four-thousand, two-hundred and six kilometers to Vancouver, BC.

16

It was 1978, Space Invaders began a world-wide video game craze, Roman Polanski skipped bail and Jim Jones told nine-hundred people to commit suicide, and they did.

I was twenty-three years old; a young man going West.

For the most part, hitchhiking in Canada was relatively easy, but before leaving Toronto, I was warned about a dead spot in Wawa, Ontario. Sure enough, after several good rides, I sat on the side of the road in Wawa and waited with my thumb in the air for almost three days.

The mosquitoes and black flies in Northern Ontario have achieved a well-deserved, mythical status. They are all-pervasive, aggressive, persistent, and the size of dragon-flies. To pass the time, I counted a hundred and fifty-seven bites on my face alone. Eventually, I was picked up by a benevolent truck driver who was shocked by my appearance. My whole face was a swollen, red lump of hot flesh. He joked that I looked like I'd gone fifteen rounds with Muhammad Ali.

We drove across the Prairies which was an endless, flat, featureless wasteland of farmland and wheat fields. Just before the Rocky Mountains, I caught a ride in a Chevy van going all the way to Vancouver. The driver was exhausted and needed a break. He asked if I would take a shift and drive through the night. He asked me if I had a licence. I did not, but said yes. How hard could it be? I took the wheel while my unwitting acquaintance slept in the back seat. For the next ten hours, I learned how to drive while crossing Saskatchewan, Alberta, and the Rocky Mountains.

I had an address in the West End given to me by Stanley Cartesian's girlfriend. She claimed to be a friend of Joni Mitchel and had gone to California to stay with her. This potentially freed up her room for me. I made my way to the address with a note of introduction. It turned out that no one at that address had ever heard of her. Disappointed, I wandered down Barkley Street towards Stanley Park, planning to spend the night in the woods. On my way, I encountered some Québécois guys playing Frisbee in the street. One of them recognised me from busking in Toronto. I joined in the game and by the end of the day was invited to stay in their unfinished basement. French Canadians are a jolly lot and love to drink beer and party. We got along famously.

I had arrived in Vancouver with twenty dollars, a cheap camera, and several subway tokens. I immediately sold the camera, but due to the total lack of subways in Vancouver, discarded the tokens.

Vancouver's West End was a thriving hub of heritage houses, filled with fun-loving bohemian beatniks, underground culture, coffee houses, beaches and parks. Compared to the bustling metropolis of Toronto, Vancouver was more relaxed and laid back, the pace slower. People operated on a temporal scale known as West Coast Time. This turned out to be nothing more than a pathetic excuse for being chronically late. I'd also heard there was a certain British influence in British Columbia and hoped this might extend to tea making. It did not.

During the day, I busked at the zoo next to the pink flamingos. At night I prowled the bars and clubs and enjoyed the live music scene. I saw my first punk rock gig in a bar on Granville Street. It was electrifying. The place went totally ape-shit and the music had an intensity I had never experienced before. Something was definitely going on.

In the mornings I drank tea on my front porch. Across the street, on the opposite balcony, lived a video tape librarian named, Veronica. She gave me a tentative wave one morning. I waved back. She smiled. I smiled back. A couple of days later, I took my guitar across the street and played her, "Baby let me follow you down," by Eric Von Schmidt. Before long she was waking me up with nectarines and bringing me snacks at the zoo. One afternoon, we did LSD together and wandered around Stanley Park all night. If you want to find out how compatible you are with someone, try tripping together. Acid is the ultimate arbiter of compatibility. We aced the test.

In the morning, I moved in to her apartment across the street. We've been married now for forty-three years. At the time—and if I believed in fate—I might have given credit to the gentle, fortuitous caress of kismet.

Here's how we ended up married: after overstaying my twelve-day visa by two years, I was a veteran illegal immigrant. I wanted to stay in Canada so I decided to try and rectify the situation. Veronica and I went to see an immigration lawyer who advised us to get married, then turn myself in to immigration authorities, and take my chances. We made an appointment to get married at City Hall on Valentine's Day. It was 1979, the same year Eric Clapton married Patti Boyd and Isabella Rossellini married Martin Scorsese.

Two days before our appointment, I was busy giving a guitar lesson in our apartment when two immigration officers appeared at the door. They were looking for an illegal Chinese immigrant and asked if I had seen him. I had not. They got curious about my English accent and asked where I was from. I made up an elaborate story about being born in Sudbury, moving to England as a boy with my father who was a fuel technician etc. etc., blah, blah, blah. What was my name? Michael Sydney Willan. And to prove it, I produced my false ID. They had a good look, made some notes and left. Distracted, I went back to the guitar lesson. I had trouble concentrating because I could hear them in the hallway talking on a two-way radio. Minutes later, they were back at the door, wanting to know who I really was? The game was up. I handed them my British passport and was immediately handcuffed and thrown into jail.

Vancouver City Jail was a madhouse. I watched in horror as the police beat up a transvestite in the elevator. My cellmate was an enterprising Neanderthal who offered to sell me a discounted case of M-16 rifles. Despite the excellent price, I declined the offer. During the night, the guy in the next cell went kablooey. For hours he screamed obscenities at the guards while he trashed his cell.

The next day, I went to court and begged for bail. The judge read the pure terror in my eyes and granted it. Luckily, a friend of Veronica's had recently sold her car and put up a thousand dollars cash for my bail. The next morning, I was released from jail and ran to make our previously booked appointment at City Hall. Ever the romantic, I ducked into a florist on the way and hastily bought a bunch of flowers.

Veronica was waiting with a folk-singer friend of ours who, with nothing better to do that day, agreed to act as a witness. At the last minute, we found out we would require a second witness so we asked a girl from the office, who generously indulged us. We were not dressed for a wedding and were woefully unprepared. We giggled and joked around, finding the situation amusing and surreal. The Justice of the Peace became visibly frustrated and admonished us for not taking things seriously enough. At one point, he halted the proceedings to lecture us on the gravity of the situation. We immediately straightened up and the ceremony continued. When he asked for a ring, we had none. Veronica quickly removed her Turkish puzzle ring from her right hand and relocated it to her left hand. After the ceremony, we went back to our rented room and celebrated with a half-bottle of Asti Spumante and a tin of canned peaches.

It was essentially a passport marriage because, like Joni Mitchel, we were both of the opinion that we didn't need a piece of paper from the City Hall to keep us tight and true. In the end, regardless of legal documentation, a relationship either works or it doesn't. Contrary to popular notions, you should not have to constantly work at it.

A week later, I went to court and was deported back to England. It would be another five years before I was finally deemed worthy of being a Canadian citizen.

17

Deported, dejected, but not yet defeated, I took a flight back to London while Veronica remained in Vancouver to file a sponsorship application. She was told this could take six months or more so, a few weeks later, she joined me in England. Having an indeterminate amount of time to kill, we headed back to Europe for another busking tour along the familiar northern shores of the Mediterranean Sea. This would be my fourth tour of duty.

We moved from café to café, singing two songs per stop with Veronica following behind me, collecting the money in a hat. We were a money-making train strumming our way through San Tropez, Cannes, Nice, Monte Carlo, Monaco, and across the Italian border through San Remo, Imperia, Diano Marina, Andorra, Alassio, and on to Savona. Wealthy tourists frequented the many four-star luxury hotels. We slept happily on the beach in a tent, under the stars, or beneath upturned boats. At the end of the tourist season, we decided to travel overland to India. To make some extra money, we picked wine grapes in the south of France and then again in Switzerland.

At the Swiss vineyard, we were assigned a grubby apartment and set about cleaning it. As we were scrubbing and dusting, I accidentally put my hand through a plate glass window, severing the tendon in my right hand. With my exposed tendon twitching in the breeze, we jumped in a taxi and rushed to the nearest hospital in Lausanne where a very pleasant Afghani hand-surgeon with a crack team of assistants operated on me for over four hours.

Time is of the essence with tendon reattachment. A couple more hours and I might have been permanently handicapped. My guitar-picking days would have been over. Luckily, the operation was successful and I eventually regained full use of my hand.

Unable to work or earn wages, I kept house and cooked for the entire grape-picking crew. My right hand was covered in a bandage the size of a rugby ball. I chopped vegetables while holding them between my toes and learned to tie my shoelaces with a single left hand.

Terrified we would incur a massive medical bill and be crushed under the weight of the mighty Swiss franc, we plotted a midnight flit at the end of the harvest. As it turned out, the farmer had an excellent insurance policy which covered his workers. I made a claim and ended up with more money than Veronica did working in the fields every day from dawn till dusk. I've claimed many times that I've led a charmed life. Even my disasters turn out to be advantageous. If I believed in astrology, I might have thanked my lucky stars.

Now armed with a healthy wad of stashed cash, we hitchhiked through Yugoslavia and Greece and ended up, once again, in Istanbul, the gateway to Asia.

I showed Veronica around The Pudding Shop and we took in the Blue Mosque and other sites. In the center of Sultanahmet there was a large parking lot where travellers going east parked their vehicles and advertised for passengers. For a hundred US dollars you could get all the way to Delhi.

We shopped around and found a German fellow and his girlfriend driving a classic red, double-decker bus they had recently bought in London. The bottom deck had been converted into a kitchen and lounge. The top deck was a fourteen-person bedroom. Our driver, Helmut, was tall and sinewy with a mountain of black hair which hung down past his waist giving him the silhouette of a volcano. His girlfriend was a manic-depressive Visigoth witch we nick-named Broom-Hilda. She had a permanent scowl and an intemperate disposition. We paid up and jumped aboard. Resembling a ragtag delegation from the United Nations, our international crew of fourteen represented eight differ-ent countries. The bus had a maximum speed of forty miles an hour so we embarked on a slow-motion, one-month road trip to Delhi.

Travelling through Turkey was like a dream. The land-scape was barren but beautiful and we spent many hours lying around on the top deck, smoking chillums, watching the parched orange landscape drift by. Our frequent stops in small villages along the way were met with great interest. Crowds of locals marvelled at the red double-decker and, in the spirit of hospitality common to many countries of the region, we were welcomed, fed and entertained.

There were numerous stops along the way for Helmut and Broom-Hilda to work out their relationship problems. At least a couple of times a day we'd have to wait patiently while Broom-Hilda screamed and ranted in German at Hel-mut who stood, dejected, like a whipped dog waiting for the storm to blow over. Days turned into weeks as the bus ambled through mile after mile of desolate, rocky terrain. In eastern Turkey, we drove through a thousand miles of desert littered with wrecked vehicles and the petrified carcasses of dead camels.

The north eastern corner of Turkey shares a border with Iran and Russia, now Armenia. This area is disputed by nomadic Kurds who consider it a part of their homeland. The Kurds have been roaming freely across these three countries for centuries. At the time we were passing through, they had decided to make a statement about their claim to the land by attacking vehicles that passed through the disputed territories.

The Magic Bus was a legendary transit service in the sixties and seventies which had been immortalised in a peppy and poppy song by The Who. The bus ferried westerners on the 'hippie trail' through Turkey, Iran, Afghanistan, Pakistan and India. Several miles before the Turkish-Iranian border, we were stopped by police and told the area was too dangerous to pass. Two weeks earlier, The Magic Bus had been attacked by Kurdish rebels. The bus was torched and several bewildered hippies were dragged out and shot dead on the side of the road. It was to be the last voyage of The Magic Bus. The magic had finally run out.

Approaching the Iranian border, we were stopped by the Turkish police and taken to the local headquarters to await an escort through the troubled area. The police station was a non-descript, breeze-block building in the middle of a gravel parking lot. We parked the bus and were introduced to the youngest police chief in Turkey, an amiable man who seemed thrilled with our exotic company. With a flourish, he ordered food and drinks and invited a group of his friends over.

The guests arrived soon after, some carrying musical instruments. They began to play lively Turkish folk music on a long-necked plucked lute called a *tambour*, some sort of bowed fiddle, and various hand drums. Pretty soon we had a full-blown party going on. The youngest police chief in Turkey had his shirt off and was dancing with all the girls. Broom-Hilda was dancing like a possessed whirling dervish, attracting far too much attention with her lascivious gyrations. She was completely unaware of the cultural sensitivities at play. Helmut looked defeated as she sidled up to the police chief and bumped him with her booty. You could almost see the smoke coming out of his ears. Now thoroughly aroused, the youngest police chief in Turkey invited the men to watch some porn on a 16mm film projector in the back room.

Slightly nervous that we were partying in a police station, but careful not to offend, we tentatively played along. The girls were exempted from the invite and relegated back to the bus while the men filed into the dingy room. It was a creepy scene. The room was bleak with a faint whiff of urine. We stood around nervously while an old projector was threaded with a tiny roll of film. When the youngest police chief in Turkey produced a chunk of hashish and invited us to share a pipe, we politely declined and retreated back to the bus. Here's a tip: as a general rule, it's probably not a good idea to smoke hashish with Turkish police.

The next day, we were escorted to the Iranian border and made it across without incident. Our next stop was Tehran, which was in the throes of the hostage crisis.

Fifty-two American diplomats had been taken hostage at the US embassy in Tehran to protest American interference in Iranian affairs. The western-backed Shah of Iran was being ousted in favour of an Islamic regime. Anti-western sentiment was at an all-time high. The hostage crisis was in its third week when we arrived. It would captivate the world and last for another fourteen months.

Our double-decker bus stuck out like a western imperialistic sore thumb as we drove through Tehran and past the US embassy. Crowds of angry revolutionaries surrounded the bus, demanding to fight the men, fuck the women, and buy our blue jeans. We respectfully declined all offers. Rocks were thrown at the bus and cracked one of the back windows. Someone else struck a blow against infidel interference by stuffing a comic book into our gas tank. We retreated to a nearby suburb where the clogged gas lines finally choked the engine and the bus spluttered to a dead stop.

We held an emergency meeting to discuss our next plan of action. Helmut was determined to continue on to Kabul in Afghanistan. He had his heart set on buying some hand-made leather boots. Broom-Hilda was now redlining the needle on the crazy meter. She did not handle stress well. This was the early days of the Soviet-Afghan war. We had heard that Russian helicopter gunships were strafing Kabul and the surrounding areas and voted against the plan to travel through Afghanistan. It would be safer to head for the Pakistan border. To placate the irate Islamic insurgents we placed a large poster of the Ayatollah Khomeini on the back of the bus to feign our allegiance to the oppressive, theo-cratic Islamic revolution. This strategy seemed to work and the hostilities directed at us died down somewhat. We found a friendly garage that flushed the fuel system and got the bus running again, but the Germans were determined to buy footwear in Kabul.

Veronica and I parted company with the group and we boarded a local bus to Lahore in Pakistan. Things were still pretty tense so we huddled down in the back seat of the bus and sped through the night to the Pakistan border.

In Lahore, we checked in at a reasonably-priced hotel and I immediately became deathly ill. Some sort of alien amoeba had infiltrated my microbiome and was wreaking havoc. Weak with a high fever, chills and sweats, I was unable to stand or walk. The next day I was no better. While we were busy planning a medical intervention, we heard a disturbance down in the lobby. Several people were yelling in Urdu. This went on for some time until the hotel man-ager, Mohamed, burst into our room in a state of extreme agitation. He explained that a group of militant Islamic fundamentalists had come to the hotel looking for westerners to take as hostages. That would be us. He had appeased them temporarily but feared their return. Mohamed suggested we leave immediately for the bus station. We thanked him for his protection but explained that I was too weak to walk. After assessing the situation, he produced a matchbox from his pocket and took out a good-sized chunk of black opium. I swallowed the lump and hoped for the best. After an hour or so, I felt slightly better. An hour after that, my fever had subsided and I was able to dress and pack. On the way to the bus station, I was actually feeling pretty good, and by the time we got to the bus station I was feeling peachy. With one arm around Veronica and my guitar slung over my shoulder, I felt calm and serene, and unreasonably optimistic about the future.

At the bus station, we bought tickets to Amritsar in India, and once again slumped down in the back seat of a dilapidated bus and fled through the dark, black Pakistani night.

18

A mritsar is home to the Harmandir Sahib, also known as the Golden Temple. It is the spiritual center of Sikhism, a religion that cannot decide if it's monotheistic, monistic or pantheistic. Situated in the middle of a man-made lake, the Golden Temple resembles Disney's Magic Kingdom covered in gold foil. We passed through the temple with thousands of pilgrims marvelling at the lavish architecture. It was a surreal scene but it felt good to be in a safe place at last.

If Disneyland is the happiest place on earth, India might be the wackiest. A potpourri of colourful cultures, bizarre customs and mysterious rituals, its 1.4 billion people live in a delicate balance of chaotic harmony.

India's bureaucracy, adopted from the British, is pushed to the brink of obsession and absurdity. India is crowded and messy and hectic and dirty. Cow dung dapples the streets, sweetening the aroma of open sewers and piles of rotting garbage. The poverty is shocking but the people are surprisingly cheerful. Even lepers begging in the street manage to crack a joke and raise a smile.

In the West, many aspects of our lives remain private and hidden. We play our cards close to our chests. Indians live their lives out in the open, exposed and unguarded. They have no shame and nothing to hide.

There are naked sadhus wandering about the streets covered in ash with skewers through their cheeks or tongues, their only material possession, a brass pot. Cows and goats and chickens and dogs fill the streets. Apparently ownerless, they wander around aimlessly from place to place, begging at restaurants. Where crowds gather, they are massive and tightly-packed. The concept of personal space has long been abandoned. On overcrowded buses and trains people literally sit on top of each other.

In India, you can sit on any corner, on any street, in any town, and be endlessly entertained and amazed by a constant procession of absurd, implausible, and fascinating events that unfold before your eyes. It looks like the whole society might collapse into total anarchy at any moment but, surprisingly, it doesn't.

Hinduism is truly bizarre. The religion has no ecclesiastical order, no unquestionable religious authorities, no governing body and no founding prophets. Hindus can be polytheistic, pantheistic, monotheistic, monistic, agnostic or atheistic. It is a religion without any central doctrine, subject only to the whims and imagination of its whimsical and imaginative followers.

We visited temples that worshiped frogs, and monkeys, and rats, and even smallpox. It takes an extraordinary lack of rationality to worship an infectious disease.

Hindus practice animal sacrifice and self-mutilation. They make the outrageous claim to have millions of gods who come in a variety of implausible and colourful forms; a fanciful collection of super-heroes and mythical creatures. Hinduism makes the most convincing case that religion is solely manufactured in the imagination of human beings. And no one has a more active imagination than Hindus. They make talking snakes and virgin births look like peer-reviewed science.

After exploring the north for a month or so, we decide to visit Goa, a mecca for iconoclastic, non-conformist, transient, maverick culture. From Delhi, it was a fifteen-hour train ride to Bombay. To stretch our budget, we travelled third-class. Travelling third-class in India is an experience you will not easily forget.

Invariably, the carriages were filled with crowds of people, farm animals, piles of colourful plastic buckets, bales of various mysterious commodities, building materials, housewares, and a kitchen sink or two. Locals slept on the luggage racks and in the corridors. Indians have the enviable ability to sleep in any place, at any time, and in any position, including standing up. Hordes of excess, ticketless passengers hung on to the side of the train or rode on the roof.

To guarantee a seat on the train, we devised a strategy and carried it out with military precision. Veronica took our baggage and positioned herself at the far end of the platform. I walked back to the other end of the platform and waited for the train to pull in. As it arrived and began to slow down, I ran alongside, picked an open window and dove through it while the train was still in motion. Securing two seats, I then waited until the train came to a stop and Veronica passed the bags through the open window and jumped aboard. This would get us a seat but was no guarantee against someone sitting on our lap. From Bombay, we took a twenty-four-hour boat ride to Panjim in Goa.

On the boat, we met a Goan fellow named Krishna. After chatting with him for an hour or so, he offered us a job running his clothes store on Baga Beach. We gladly accepted.

Goa later become famous for its Goa Trance parties, named after its distinctive genre of frenetic, electronic dance music. It would be another five years before house music was invented but the stage was already being set for the rave phenomenon.

A series of beaches stretched up the coast north of Panjim and were filled with international travellers and hippies.

All-night parties, or proto-raves, were already in full effect but the music played was psychedelic rock and the drugs of choice were LSD and magic mushrooms. On full moon nights in particular, the beaches overflowed with revellers dancing with abandon, some naked, some covered in body paint, everyone high on something.

Krishna dropped us off at his store on Baga Beach. It was a small, simple cement structure built right on the expansive sandy beach. He gave us a range of prices for each item. The first was a high starting price and the second was the lowest we were allowed to go. The idea was to start high and haggle. Since our clientele was exclusively fellow travellers, Veronica and I felt it was unfair to overinflate the prices so elected to offer the lowest price only. Customers could take it or leave it. This cut into our meagre profits but our altruistic values were maintained and we enjoyed the benefits of free accommodation.

Old Indian ladies baked fresh coconut hash cakes and sold them to tourists on the beach. Hashish, or charas, was freely available and smoked in chillums, a conical, wooden or clay pipe. Like most things in India, rituals were invented around the smoking of chillums.

First, a mixture of tobacco and hash was worked and rubbed into the palm of the hand then lovingly packed in the bowl. Not too tight. Not too loose. A damp rag was wrapped ceremoniously around the mouth piece as a filter. The chillum was then held up to the forehead and various incantations employed. Some favourites were, 'Boom Shankar,' or 'Boom Shiva Shankar,' evoking the Hindu God, Shiva who was apparently a big fan of hashish. The idea was to take in as much as possible and then blow out a great cloud of smoke, the bigger the better. Smoking chillums was practically a competitive sport. The Germans usually came in with a silver or bronze but were no match for Team Sadhu.

Sadhus are Hindu mendicants who have renounced earthly life. Typically, they wear very little clothing and sometimes cover their entire bodies in ash or dust. They have also renounced the use of hair care products, brushes and combs, preferring a more naturalistic approach. This results in some truly outlandish hairdos which include knotted nests, tangled messes of matted locks, braided topknots and dreadful dreads that would cause a western hairstylist to recoil in horror. Sadhus also smoke a lot of dope, believing it connects them to the spirit world.

Tell that to a judge.

The best place to do LSD is in nature. You cannot go wrong on a beach, in a forest or jungle, or hiking in the woods. On acid we imprint on our environment like baby ducks. We soak up and synchronize with our surroundings. Nature appears harmonious, beautiful, and awe-inspiring. The visuals of wind, water and trees take on a super-natural splendour and can be truly transcendental. Lower doses are recommended for parties or social gatherings but the more expansive, amplifying effects of LSD are best suited to the great outdoors. Goa, with its golden beaches, swaying palm trees, and lush jungle is the perfect setting for a psychedelic experience.

One day, while tripping on acid, Veronica and I saw a familiar red double-decker bus parked on the beach. At first, I thought it was a flashback. On closer inspection, we recognised Helmut and old crazy-knickers Broom-Hilda arguing as usual about nothing. They had survived their detour through war-torn Afghanistan and to prove it, Helmut showed off his new pair of hand-made leather boots.

We had planned on a week in Goa but ended up staying over a month. This is a common experience. Some people who arrived as tourists never left. Some are still there today. But, in the wise words of the quiet Beatle, "All things must pass," and we eventually bade a fond Namaste to this tropical paradise and like migrating birds, headed south.

On the way to Sri Lanka, our interest in meditation drew us to a Buddhist monastery. The monastery provided free accommodation and the opportunity to meditate with a bone-fide Bhikkhu, an ordained Buddhist monk. He was a good-humoured fellow with the typical bald head, black robes and the prerequisite fat belly. The Buddhist monk curriculum is all meditation and no exercise. The night after we arrived, he beckoned us over and invited us into his private chambers.

That afternoon, he'd been showing a group of Japanese tourists around the monastery. As a parting gift, they had given him a large bottle of sake. He proceeded to pour us all a glass, then another, and another. After a while, we were all feeling the warm glow of enlightenment. He regaled us with stories about life in the monastery and then produced some hashish and a small, clay pipe from a wooden box. We were surprised but pleased. As we smoked together, he told us he was going on a trip to Europe and was planning to take some hash to raise money for the monastery. He asked us for some smuggling tips. We suggested he tape the hash to his body under his robes. Who would pat down a monk? He seemed pleased with the advice and we continued well into the night, getting stoned and drunk.

I have to say that in all my dealings with self-proclaimed gurus, sadhus and spiritual masters, I never met one who was not flawed, like any other human being. I have since come to reject the whole concept of enlightenment.

There is no doubt that meditation can be a valuable tool to quiet and strengthen the mind and free ourselves from distracting thoughts. I recommend everyone learn how to do it. Most of us are lost in a maelstrom of egotistical self-absorption that inevitably leads to conflict and confusion. Learning to detach from our ego can bring peace of mind and clarity of thought. It takes some time to learn but is well worth the effort. However, the idea that we can achieve a permanent state of perfect peace, free of duality and conflict, I now believe is a misguided notion.

Our human brains are thinking machines. This is one of our greatest strengths and the reason for our incredible success as a species. It's attachment to certain rigid ideas and beliefs that creates a multitude of problems. The only way to be completely free of thought is to surgically remove the brain. Even the brain that thinks it's not thinking is a thinking brain. Something to think about.

Moreover, the supernatural claims made by gurus and spiritual leaders are not only misleading but obviously fraudulent. Paramahansa Yogananda, for example, claimed to be able to dematerialise and levitate. Sai Baba claimed to be a saint and have the ability to remove and reattach his limbs. The list of ridiculous claims goes on and on. But none of these fantastical claims have ever held up to even the most cursory investigation. However self-deluded, they are clearly the products of deception and deceit, not qualities we usually associate with spiritual enlightenment. Whether it's Bhagwan Rajneesh surrounded by heavily-armed guards or Guru Maharaj Ji shagging his female devotees, these fakers demonstrate an obvious corruption of power that negates any spiritual teaching. The road to a fulfilling, moral, and virtuous life is paved with reason, logic, and critical thinking. Just ask the Stoics.

The ultimate goal is to learn how to be who you are. You will waste a lifetime trying to be someone you think you should be, or someone you would like to be. As the witty and flamboyant Irish poet and playwright, Oscar Wilde once said, "Be yourself; everyone else is already taken."

If you can allow yourself to be who you are, you will find peace of mind. You will be unique, incomparable, and extraordinary. You will be an individual.

After many years of experimentation with various meditation techniques and so-called spiritual practices, I can honestly say the most powerful and valuable states of meditation I ever achieved were dancing at raves on MDMA.

More about this later.

19

In Sri Lanka, we attended a festival in Kandy with a million people and hundreds of decorated and illuminated elephants. It was called the Festival of the Tooth. The local Buddhist temple claimed to possess one of the Buddha's back molars. They keep it locked away in a wooden box and take it out for a tour around town once a year. A likely story.

There are thousands of Christian churches around the world that claim to have a fragment of the cross on which Jesus was crucified. If you gathered all the pieces together, you'd have enough wood to build Noah's Ark.

Being in a crowd of that size was terrifying. When it came time to leave, we were crushed into the middle of a vast moving mass of humanity, unable to adjust speed or direction. For safety, Veronica was sandwiched between me and our travelling companion, a Frenchman named Pierre.

When tightly packed in a crowd, Indians have a curious habit of covertly pinching both men and women on the buttocks. These are not affectionate, gentle or playful pinches. They are aggressive, antagonistic, and decidedly unfriendly. By the time we had extricated ourselves from the crowd, both Pierre and I had bruised buttocks that looked like they'd been worked over with a baseball bat.

In a beach town called Hikkaduwa, we tried surfing for the first time. This did not go well. If you're thinking of taking up the sport, I can save you some time. In an effort vs. benefit analysis, it fairs very poorly. As a novice, you spend ninety-seven percent of the time paddling like a lunatic until your arms fall off for the momentary thrill of falling off your board. While there may be some value in communing with nature and experiencing the power of the ocean, this can more easily be achieved by body-surfing, swimming, or simply frolicking about in the waves. Save yourself the frustration and exhaustion and take up an easier sport. I recommend snooker.

I had written to a friend in England asking him to mail me some guitar strings. We spent the next three weeks waiting in the capitol city of Colombo for them to arrive. The postal service in Sri Lanka, like most institutions in that country and in India, is anarchic, unreliable, and often stymied by a tyrannical bureaucracy. For westerners used to a certain standard of organised efficiency, this can be a difficult adjustment. It is not an uncommon sight to see foreigners cracking up under the pressure.

Here's a typical example of bureaucracy gone mad: Jaipur is the capitol of Rajasthan, located in the center of the Great Indian Desert. Also known as the Pink City, Jaipur gets its name from the terracotta pink-coloured paint which covers most of the buildings in the walled historic center. It looks like an ancient colony on Mars. Jaipur's streets are filled with a menagerie of animals including camels, packs of rabid dogs, cows, Brahman bulls, and donkeys. Transiting troops of giant baboons rattle the rooftops and elephants cause traffic jams.

We arrived in Jaipur in forty-five degree heat which, even after several months of traveling in India and Sri Lanka, took us by surprise. It was like walking around inside a blast furnace, making even the most mundane tasks challenging. We learned to move about in slow-motion with wet scarves wrapped around our heads. We checked into a budget hotel misnamed The Evergreen. By necessity, we discovered a

unique cooling technique which involved throwing a bucket
of water at our bedroom wall. This caused a rapid evapo-
ration effect that lowered the temperature in the room for a
few glorious moments.

The hotel featured a rock pool which consisted of a
crudely-dug hole in the ground, lined with rough-hewn flat
rocks. It was just big enough for the two of us to squeeze
in. We spent hours submerged up to our noses sipping cold
drinks as a respite from the extreme heat.

Veronica is a black belt in the art of inferred suggestion.
If you ask her if she's enjoying her curry, you will not get a
yes or no. She's likely to mention a past curry she enjoyed
more, but avoid any direct criticism of the curry in question.
A comment like, "There's a fair bit of bite to this curry,"
translates as, "This curry is way too hot. It totally sucks and
I'd rather die than eat another bite." But you will never get
an answer that direct. Over the years I have developed the
capacity to interpret these circuitous suggestions and react
appropriately. So, when Veronica casually mused, "I wonder if the weather might be cooler in the north?" I immediately headed off to the train station to buy tickets to Delhi.

Arriving at the station, I was confronted by multiple line-
ups at multiple ticket windows. I picked the shortest line
and took my place behind a hundred or so Indian com-
muters. The temperature in the station was unbearable.
The line moved slowly as every ticket had to be hand-writ-
ten, signed, double-checked, filed and subjected to multiple stamps. Rubber stamps are a national obsession in India
and an essential part of any transaction. Officials take great
pride in stamping documents and do so with great relish
and zeal. One stamp is never enough. Numerous stamps
are required to imbue the document with sufficient legal
weight and authority. After a sweltering two-hour wait in the

oppressive heat, I finally reached the ticket window, "Two third-class, one-way tickets to Delhi, please."

The clerk looked confused and went to consult with an associate. They mulled over a schedule for a few minutes and the clerk returned with some bad news. "Next wicket," he said, pointing to the adjacent line-up. I pleaded my case but apparently didn't have one worth pleading. There would be no further discussion. I reluctantly took my place behind another hundred people in the next line over, which moved even more slowly than the first. It is said that patience is not the ability to wait, but the ability to keep a good attitude while waiting. I kept these wise words in mind as I endured another grueling two-hour wait. Moments away from a full-blown case of heat prostration, I confronted the next dedicated clerk and once again made my request, "Two third-class, one-way tickets to Delhi, please."

This time things looked more promising. He filled out the ticket and reached for one of his five rubber stamps. Following a double-fisted stamping frenzy, he asked for my passport. I didn't have it with me. When I enquired as to the necessity of a passport, I was told that tourists had to buy tourist-class tickets. The passport was needed to prove that I was not an Indian. As a six-foot four, pasty-faced westerner, I stood head and shoulders above a sea of five-foot Indians. I proceeded to make an airtight case as to my obvious status as a foreigner. The clerk insisted that without a passport this fact could not be legally verified. A lively debate ensued. I demanded to see the station master. The clerk reluctantly made a call. After an additional twenty-minute wait, another railway employee appeared and escorted me to the station master's office at the end of the platform. I was told to wait on a wooden bench outside the office. The station master would be along shortly. An hour later, I began to have my doubts and peeked into the office. It was empty. I asked a passing conductor if he knew the whereabouts of the elusive station master. I was told he'd gone on vacation. He'd be back in two weeks. My ability to maintain a good attitude evaporated like a bucket of water on a bedroom wall. Thoroughly defeated, I made my way back to The Evergreen. Veronica was sympathetic and offered to go back to the station with the passports and buy the tickets. I got back in the rock pool where I belonged.

Delhi is an impossible glut of humanity. It shouldn't work. It cannot work. But, inexplicably and against all odds, it does. We rested for a week in a modestly-priced hotel and then made the long journey to Nepal to trek in the Himalayas.

We learned the safest way to travel on buses and trucks was on the roof. Every day in the newspapers there were reports of overloaded and poorly maintained buses and trucks veering off the perilous mountain roads. Inside a bus, you didn't stand a chance, but on the roof you were able to sit on your backpack, enjoy the scenery, and leap off at the first sign of trouble.

The ambient noise level in India is a constant roar. Cocks start crowing at dawn. Dogs bark all day long. Radios are cranked up and set permanently to maximum loudness. Engines rev up and hawkers yell at full volume selling their wares. Every morning, the air is filled with the all too familiar sound of people clearing their noses and throats of phlegm. The hills were alive with the sound of mucus.

After the deafening din of India, Nepal was a breath of Himalayan fresh air. As soon as we crossed the border the noise level dropped. The air was cleaner, the people calmer. In Kathmandu, we rented a cheap room and set off to explore the ancient city.

Kathmandu was famous for its hash shops. Signs advertised an impressive list of choices. In front of the many temples, sadhus spent their days lounging around smoking chillums and, for a few rupees, they were only too happy to share. It's another place you could get stuck for longer than planned. And we did.

From Kathmandu we took a five hour bus ride to Pokhara, a beautiful town on a beautiful lake. Only a few weeks earlier, a prominent Hare Krishna guru had been drowned in Pokhara Lake. It was a murderous power play by a group of his demented devotees in another tangled web of delusional belief. In some sort of spiritual dispute, they had thrown him out of the boat and bashed his head in with an oar.

It brings to mind the old adage credited to Baron Acton, about how power corrupts absolutely. Religion and its attendant assemblage of irrational beliefs take this maxim to a whole other level. It appears that those who claim the highest degree of non-attachment from worldly control and power have the hardest time relinquishing it.

Trekking in the Himalayas is as exhilarating as it is exhausting. With only three main roads in the whole country, if you want to get somewhere, you walk. We made a two-week trek up the Jomsom Trail to Tatopani which translates as 'hot water,' named after the hot springs there. The trail follows the Kali Gandaki River which snakes through lunar landscapes covered in silver mica and punctuated by rhododendron forests filled with monkeys. Miles of ancient stone steps rise and fall with the topography and perilous rope bridges span rushing rivers fed by the snow-capped mountains of Annapurna and Dhaulagiri.

Several times a day we were passed by five-foot Sherpas who strode by carrying impossible loads on their backs. Their stubby, muscular legs looked better suited to supporting a grand piano. For one US dollar, they walked all day long carrying everything from tourist's backpacks to building materials, stopping only briefly to swig some barley beer or smoke a chillum. They were always happy to have us join them on their breaks.

Another mainstay in the many Tibetan villages along the trail is Tibetan tea. It is very strong, salted, black tea served with a lump of thick, oily Yak butter floating on the surface. In the rarefied, oxygen-poor environs of the Himalayas it can be quite invigorating. If you served it in a Devon tea shop, you would likely be garrotted.

After almost six months wandering about in the Indian subcontinent, we made our way back to Delhi and then flew to France. During our travels in India, we had periodically purchased goods and mailed the parcels back to Avignon in the South of France. Almost anything you buy in India is worth ten times more in Europe. We bought bags, sandalwood pens, jackets, pants, shirts, and so on. On arrival, we picked up the goods and sold them at the street markets in Avignon during a month-long film and theatre festival.

One auspicious day, a letter arrived from the Canadian Immigration Department summoning us to an interview in London. This was the news we had been waiting for. We hitchhiked back to England to pick up my Canadian passport.

20

B ack in jolly old England, we bought an old post office van and drove up to the Canadian Embassy in Trafalgar Square.

A Dickensian character with a lumpy face and a swollen, red nose pulled out a massive dossier from an old filing cabinet. This was my immigration file. It looked like the New York telephone directory. He thumped it down on his desk and began to paw through it while mumbling underneath his breath.

"Mmmmm, overstayed visa by two years."

"Ahh, working without a permit."

"Oooh, producing false ID to an immigration officer."

And then the kicker, "Ah ha! Narcotics arrest."

Things were not going as smoothly as we had anticipated. I tried to explain that the narcotics involved were no more than a microscopic trace of cannabis on a few strands of Drum tobacco. It was hardly worth a mention. But to the Canadian government, dope was dope and I would have to serve a five-year rehabilitation period from the time of the crime. I would have to wait another year to be eligible. I was also surprised to find out that I was subject to a lifetime ban from Canada.

Disappointed but never deterred, we returned to Brighton. There, we teamed up with a couple of old friends and hatched a mad-cap plan to form a theatre company. We wrote some short plays and skits and I honed my juggling skills. For the next few weeks, The Eyebrow Theatre Company toured the south of England playing pubs, theatres and country fairs. The tour was a grand adventure but a financial disappointment.

Upon our not-so-triumphant return we had an opportunity to house-sit a three-hundred-year-old thatched cottage near Braintree in Essex. The cottage was called, Sleepy Hollow, and more than lived up to its name. The heavy thatching, dark beams and low ceilings, created a soporific effect and we set new world records in the sleep marathon category. Being mid-winter, it was pitch dark by four o'clock in the afternoon and a mile trudge across muddy fields to the nearest pub. As we were already planning our next move, we received an unexpected visitor.

Jack Grimshaw had been an apprentice waiter at the Sackville Hotel at the same time I had served my chef apprenticeship. We had travelled in Europe together years earlier and crossed paths in Brighton many times on my frequent visits. Jack was a miscreant and a malefactor. His moral compass obeyed an alternative set of magnetic laws. He also had a volatile temper, which had gotten him into some trouble over the years. I once saw him stuff a busboy into a dumb waiter. Not an easy feat, and not entirely successful. But despite ne'er doing well and his penchant for flaunting the law and irascible disposition, he was likeable enough and a loyal friend.

I don't recall the exact charges, but he informed us that he was on the lam and was looking for a place to hide out, preferably out of the country. We suggested Amsterdam. While extolling its many virtues and advantages, we managed to talk ourselves into joining him. We locked up the sleepy cottage and all set off to the 'Venice of the North.'

It was December the 8th, 1980. I remember the exact date we left because, while packing, we were listening to a

Dutch radio station. We didn't speak a word of Dutch but all of our ears pricked up as the announcer ended his report with an emphatic, "John Lennon es dood."

Amsterdam is the equivalent of a gateway drug to the rest of Europe and perhaps the most cosmopolitan city in the world. It is said that over a hundred and twenty nationalities live there. There are also one hundred and eighty-five coffee shops. Coffee shop is a euphemism for pot store where cannabis of all sorts can be legally sold and consumed. Amsterdam was the undisputed pot capitol of the western world.

Our first address in Amsterdam was a canal barge which we shared with some artists who were refugees from Uruguay. The weather in December was unseasonably cold and the barge was frozen in place by thick ice that had formed on the canal. Through our kitchen porthole we could see ducks skating around like drunken penguins. The heating on the barge was woefully inadequate and our living quarters cramped so after a short time, we rented an apartment off Leidseplein Square.

Two blocks from our apartment on Lijnbaansgracht was the Melkweg or Milky Way, a three-storey alternative entertainment complex named after the abandoned dairy it had once been. It was home to a concert hall, three fringe theatres, a movie house, a coffee bar, a restaurant, and a market place. The Milky Way fulfilled all of our entertainment needs so we went there every Friday, Saturday, and Sunday night for months.

The market place on the second floor featured a hashish emporium. On the other side of the canal was a police station. You could smoke your brains out while watching uniformed police officers doing their daily paperwork. Occasionally they would glace over and give you a friendly wave.

Veronica got a job as a house-keeper for a Dutch psychiatrist named Dr. Louis Tas. I busked on the subway trains.

I'd board a train, play a song, collect the money, disembark, get on the next train and then repeat the process. Later, Jack Grimshaw and I were also employed by Dr. Tas as handymen, painting his office and sanding his floors. There was something poetic about standing on top of a step-ladder, watching a Freudian psychoanalyst wander around his office, deep in thought, while eating a whole cucumber. When clearing out his bookshelves one day, preparing to paint, we discovered numerous tiny packets of cocaine stashed behind the books; the mark of a true Freudian.

After a while, word got out that we had an apartment in the cannabis capitol of the world. Friends from England and other parts of Europe began to arrive. At one point we had eight people staying in our one-bedroom apartment.

One morning, we received another missive from the almighty and exalted Canadian High Commission in London. We were ordered back for another interview. Leaving the apartment to our house guests, we headed back to London, excited to pick up my newly minted Canadian passport. Our enthusiasm was duly crushed as it became clear that the Canadian government was hell-bent on doing everything in its power to ruin our lives.

In order to qualify as my sponsor, they now demanded that Veronica return to Canada to 'establish residency'. Having no legal status in Canada, I had to stay in England and wait. We bid a reluctant farewell and Veronica returned to Ontario to open a bank account and register a Canadian address. Meanwhile, I moved in with my old alumni from The Eyebrow Theatre Company in a squat in Brixton and waited for news.

The year was 1981, Prince Charles foolishly married Lady Diana, the Pope got shot, and the Brixton Riots were about to explode.

Brixton was predominantly an Afro-Caribbean neighbourhood. The police had been heavy-handed with the residents for some time and the proverbial pot finally boiled over. Disgruntled residents took to the streets, looting stores, burning police cars and buildings. Things came to their inevitable conclusion on what was dubbed, 'Bloody Saturday,' when five-thousand people rioted in the streets. Over a hundred vehicles were burned, including fifty-six police cars. At one point the police retreated to defend the police station which was under siege.

I spent that day wandering around the streets, ducking in and out of alleyways, watching from the periphery. Despite the unbridled protestations of discontent and outbreaks of violence, there was an underlying spirit of celebration.

This was a revolution with a reggae sound track.

A couple of months later, Veronica and I were informed that this stage of our immigration process might take another six to eight months, give or take a year. I was still under a life ban from Canada, and Europe was a bit pricey for our budget. So, desperate to be together, we hatched a plan to meet up in Merida on the Yucatan peninsula of Mexico.

21

Stepping off the plane in Merida to a tropical blast of heat, Veronica and I were reunited in a scene out of a Hollywood movie. The music swelled as she ran to my arms in slow motion. The swaying palms and exotic vegetation were a welcome counterpoint to the Brixton Riots. We had at least several months to wait so we travelled south to San Cristobal de las Casas near the Guatemalan border.

San Cristobal is a town in the mountains of Chiapas and is home to a community of gringo artists and musicians. We quickly made friends and established residency at Los Baños, a public bathhouse and motel in the center of town. The courtyard of our humble lodgings was also home to a large gaggle of turkeys who at the slightest provocation, would engage in a deafening group gobble. This cacophony became the soundtrack to our lives.

Every Saturday, San Cristobal hosted a large public market where indigenous people from all over the region gathered to buy and sell wares. It was an astonishing and colourful sight to see groups of different Mayan tribes wandering about in traditional dress and feathered head gear. My favorites were the petite Lacandon Indians with their jet-black bangs, white belted tunics and bare feet. They had a regal confidence about them. And they carried bows and arrows.

Originally planning to stay a month or so and then move on to Guatemala, our plans were thwarted by an international dispute. The UK government had awarded Belize its independence. Guatemala disputed the move, claiming that Belize had always been one of their provinces, and always would be. In protest, they decided to ban British passport holders from entering the country. That would be me.

With the border closed, we made the best of it and ended up staying in San Cristobal for the next three months. Veronica, a talented artist, got the use of an art studio and painted while I jammed with the local musicians. We also got pregnant.

Eventually, we heard the border with Guatemala had temporarily opened to British passport holders. We made a beeline down to Guatemala City and on to Panajachel on Lake Atitlan. The lake is surrounded by three volcanoes and we ensconced ourselves in the picturesque village inhabited by locals, American ex-pats, and international travellers. Back then, Panajachel was a sleepy, laid-back, one-horse, one-street town. It has since become a major tourist hub. Don't go there. Go to San Pedro on the other side of the lake instead.

It quickly became apparent that the region was the epi-center of a civil war. With echoes of the Brixton Riots, ethnic Mayan indigenous groups and Ladino peasants were tired of being pushed around and had taken up arms against the Guatemalan government. At night, while smoking dope on our veranda we often heard the gentle pops of gunfire in the hills around the town. Occasionally, the boom of a hand grenade rattled the silence. And sometimes the rebels came into the town on hit-and-run expeditions.

I was playing guitar in a local bar one night when gunfire erupted in the street outside. We quickly turned out the lights and everyone hid in the shadows. Moments later, government forces burst into the bar demanding to know in which direction the rebels had gone. We pointed in the opposite direction and they set off in pointless pursuit.

In another incident, that same week, a band of heavily-armed rebels drove into town in a pick-up truck and shot the chief of police and the mayor. Their bodies were dumped in the lake. A couple of days later, an American tourist got shot in the bum on her way to a bar. It was an unfortunate accident; a stray bullet had ricocheted off a wall and embedded into her left buttock. But regardless of the war raging around us, we felt relatively and strangely safe. Everyone had a vested interest in not shooting gringos. The government forces had a policy of not bothering tourists for fear of losing their western funding, and the rebels were afraid of increased government funding which would be stepped up if they killed any Westerners. So in the middle of a civil war, we carried on with our lives and ran a small movie theatre aptly named, The Poco Loco, where we screened VHS movies bootlegged from American TV stations.

After a couple of months in Guatemala, Veronica's belly was starting to resemble one of the volcanoes around Lake Atitlan. We began a letter-writing campaign to the Canadian government pleading for clemency due to our extenuating circumstances and Veronica's extended midriff. Our friends and family wrote letters directly to the Minister of Immigration and vouched for our integrity and honesty. My mother, in a ten-page petition, begged for mercy for her unborn grandchild. Our impassioned pleas finally pierced the armour-plated heart of the Canadian Immigration Department, but there would be one more hoop to jump through. Now that my probation period was over, I would have to prove that I was rehabilitated from marijuana. So, I rolled up a big spliff and formulated a plan of action.

I needed testimonials from professionals who would vouch for my commitment to sobriety. I first called upon my old Freudian employer, Dr. Louis Tas who, in between snorting lines of coke, wrote an eloquent letter extolling my virtues as an exemplary, sober human being. An old school friend and fellow psychonaut, Dr. Bob Bagshot— now a senior surgeon at a London hospital—wrote another, asserting my complete and unequivocal rejection of the devil's weed. The third reference came from a therapist friend who had a well-earned reputation for smoking heroic amounts of pot.

The accumulated effect of this mail blitz finally yielded results. My lifetime ban was rescinded and I was granted a temporary visa to Canada. It would be another two years before I was granted a passport and full citizenship.

With nesting on our minds, we moved back to Guelph, Ontario to start a family. With my long-awaited Canadian status in hand, I vowed never again to return to England. I kept that promise for the next twenty-five years.

22

Guelph is a university town in Southern Ontario also known as the Royal City. It gets its curious name from the British Royal Family's German heritage. Apparently, they were forced to import some German genes to avoid embarrassing genetic traits resulting from inbreeding. You only have to look at Prince Charles' ears to see that they were not entirely successful. The name also brings to mind the sound of someone swallowing a small vole and is therefore the brunt of many cruel jokes and inept choking impersonations.

Veronica is an alumnus of the University of Guelph where she received an honours degree in fine art. While art was her major, dealing LSD became her minor. During her final year, her extra-curricular activities were cut short by a tip off. One of her professors informed her she had become a person of interest with the police. She ceased operations immediately and avoided a potentially embarrassing situation. It was one of the many things we had in common.

Veronica still had many friends in Guelph and we were welcomed into a vibrant community of artists, musicians and hopeless optimists. We rented a cheery two bedroom apartment on the wrong side of the tracks and I set about revving up my music career while dealing pot on the side.

I played around town as a solo folk-singer for a while and then as a duo with a saxophone player. I went on to form a band with keyboards, cornet, sax, bass and drums. We were called The High Hats and specialised in performing novelty jazz tunes from the thirties and forties while singing four-part harmonies.

Veronica had an old friend with a farm a couple of hundred miles north of Guelph. As a failing farmer, he grew pot in between his corn rows to help pay off his massive debt load. The farm was called Stoney Acres. Periodically, we'd visit him and load up with garbage bags full of marijuana. I sold it in ounces and made a reasonable profit.

Veronica was now the size of a beautiful, bulging Beluga whale. We planned a home birth, secured a midwife, and signed up for birth classes. I had previously been the birth coach for some close friends in Brighton and had been through prenatal training classes with them. There was only one doctor in Guelph willing to attend a home birth and he agreed to come as well. We were ready for anything.

On the 27th of August, 1982, Veronica's waters broke like a ruptured water main and she went into labour. The doctor and midwife arrived and we all galvanized into action, prepping the room, checking the fetal heart rate and monitoring dilation. I grabbed a pair of white shoelaces and put them on the stove to boil.

Hours went by.

We tried walking up and down the stairs to increase the contractions. At one point, we went for a walk to a local park and tried some African dancing.

More hours went by.

We tried the single-assisted squat and then the double-assisted squat. My fingers and thumbs went numb from intensive lower back massage. We tried jumping up and down on the spot. After about twelve hours, the doctor diagnosed a prominent lip on the cervix and suggested we go to the hospital, induce the birth with oxytocin, and use forceps to get the baby out. This was not what we had in mind.

I consulted with our midwife who assured me that this was not unusual for a first baby. They were often long and slow affairs. Veronica's heart rate was normal and so was the baby's.

After twenty hours, the doctor again suggested the hospital. He also said that his wife might divorce him if he missed their planned camping trip. We refused again and decided to give it some more time. Clearly frustrated, the doctor packed his black bag and left us to it.

Veronica was exhausted but remained determined. The contractions picked up, and then slowed down, and then picked up again.

More hours went by.

Finally, after thirty-three hours of labour, Donovan Fritz exploded from the birth canal like a bloody torpedo. I caught him, laid him on Veronica's breast, grabbed the boiled shoelaces, tied and cut the umbilical cord, took a deep breath, and stared into the face of my first-born son. It was like looking into a mirror.

Over our bed, I had built the frame-work of a pyramid with the exact dimensions of Cheops' Great Pyramid at Giza. Donovan's wicker baby basket hung at the exact height of the King's Chamber. Pyramid power was all the rage at the time. This was back when I believed in such baloney. I understand the new-age magical mind because I used to have one. But despite the erroneous invocation of Egyptian magic, Donovan grew into a happy, healthy baby, and we settled into family life.

Veronica had long been fascinated by magic mushrooms so we tried our hands at growing some. This proved a lot more difficult than we imagined. First, we built a controlled environment in the basement. It was a large, purpose built, insulated box, lined with tin foil, where temperature and humidity could be precisely controlled.

We obtained some spore prints from the Amazonian Psilocybe Cubensis mushroom. The spores were cultivated in a petri-dish lined with agar, a gelatinous, nutrient rich, growing medium. The spores grew into mycelium, a white, fibrous material which is the fruiting body of the mushroom. After the mycelium was fully developed, it got chopped up and deposited into mason jars full of sterilized rye grain.

Everything had to be meticulously sterilized. Transferring the mycelium from the petri dish to the mason jars was done with an autoclave, a machine used to sterilize surgical equipment. The grain and jars had to be sterilized in an oven. We swabbed every surface with alcohol and disinfectant. One speck of mould could ruin the whole batch. Despite our best efforts, microscopic airborne particles of bacteria and mould infiltrated our systems and proved more tenacious than our delicate mushroom spores. We grew black mould, red mould, brown mould, bread mould, yellow slime mould, acremonium, aspergillus, chaetomium, fusarium, and a fascinating variety of other unidentifiable microscopic interlopers, all of which out-competed our wimpy mushrooms.

With further refinements to our techniques, we did eventually produce some viable magic mushrooms and enjoyed the fruits of our labour. But the amounts produced were insufficient to be commercially viable. There was more money to be made in buying mushrooms from accomplished growers and reselling them at a profit. So we did that instead.

And then, as if someone, somewhere, had rubbed a magic lamp, Jack Grimshaw appeared out of nowhere with his eighteen-year-old girlfriend. Since we had last seen him, Jack had become a Maître d'. His girlfriend, Dolly, was a budding waitress. They suggested that with my chef credentials, we should join forces and open a restaurant. Apart from the fact that we had no access to credit, and a complete lack of start-up money, it sounded like a good idea. Sometimes it's best to move ahead with an idea, regardless of how unlikely the outcome. It's forward motion that creates momentum. Jack and I immediately began scouting around town for a suitable location.

Due to its proximity to New York State, Guelph had a reputation as a safe haven for the mafia to house their families. True or not, there was indeed a healthy population of shady-looking Italians about town. Often they had businesses that seemed questionable in their financial viability. One such character, Tony, owned a pool hall above a failed Italian restaurant. The empty restaurant was perfect for our needs, having a fully-equipped kitchen and dining room. Jack and I went upstairs to the pool hall to sweet talk Tony.

The place was a dead ringer for the pool hall in *The Hustler*. Tony was Jackie Gleeson as Minnesota Fats. Jack Grimshaw was George C. Scott as the unscrupulous and villainous manager, Bert Gordon. And I was Paul Newman as Fast Eddie Felson. I couldn't miss.

Using my rudimentary Italian, we introduced ourselves. Italians love it when you make the effort to speak their language. After I'd exhausted my preliminary repertoire, we lapsed back into English and explained that, with our credentials and enthusiasm, we could make a go of the unused opportunity downstairs. It had already failed several times so Tony was open to suggestions. We made him an offer he could well have refused, but didn't.

We asked for a free month's rent, then half-price for the next two months and then full rent for the rest of our tenure. To our surprise, Tony agreed and we began preparing for the opening of The Bo Tree, named after the tree under which the Buddha sat for seven years and attained enlightenment. Another likely story.

The restaurant already had everything we needed. It looked as though the previous owners had just walked out the door and left everything as it was. We had only to hang Veronica's paintings and put our sign in the window. Five-hundred dollars bought enough food and booze to last for a week. We printed menus and opened the doors.

The Bo Tree was a vegetarian restaurant and wine bar with live entertainment six nights a week. We hired a slight-of-hand conjurer to work the tables and had a tarot card reader in the back corner, or what I more commonly refer to today as a card shark. This was back when I believed in that sort of malarkey.

Entertainment at The Bo Tree featured various local musical acts, poetry readings and we also hosted numerous community benefit nights. Donovan was one year-old and both Veronica and Dolly served tables with him perched on their hips. We kept our deal with Tony and three months later made enough money to pay full rent. The place quickly became a thriving hub for the local arts community. Regulars arrived at 11 a.m. and were still there at one the next morning. Creatively and socially, it was a roaring success but financially, despite our sixteen-hour days, we barely managed to make ends meet.

Then, like a rerun of an old B movie I really didn't want to see again, my old nemesis, the Canadian Immigration Department, reared its capricious and bureaucratic head. Six months after opening, Veronica and I took our first night off. Jack was working in the kitchen. Dolly was serving in the restaurant. Apparently, immigration officers had been staking out the restaurant for over a month. They were spying on Jack and Dolly who were illegal immigrants.

That night, two immigration officers came into the restaurant, ordered a meal, had a drink, paid the bill and tipped Dolly who had just served them. They then arrested and handcuffed both Jack and Dolly and hauled them off to the slammer. Regardless of the fact that we were all equal partners in the business, Veronica and I were charged with employing illegal immigrants. In the following days, it was all over the local newspapers which ruined our reputation. Taking full responsibility, I accepted a plea deal and offered to take the rap if they dropped the charges against Veronica. In the end, I was fined a thousand dollars and we closed up shop.

During the final throes of The Bo Tree, Veronica became pregnant with our second child. I was still playing music with The High Hats and Veronica was painting portrait commissions and selling her original oil paintings. It was at a local High Hat's gig one night that I met Donny Winslow from North Carolina.

Donny was a barefooted, red-necked hippy with long blond hair. He also made money roofing and doing tree work. Both figuratively and literally he offered to show me the ropes. When I had gotten up to speed, we started our own company called Residential Roofing. Our by-line was, "For a hole in your roof or a whole new roof." Catchy stuff.

With Donovan approaching two-years old, Veronica was once again the size of an African elephant. We planned another home birth and arranged for a midwife. One night, she woke up and was crowning, already in advanced labour. I immediately rushed to the stove and put the white shoelaces on to boil. Things were progressing very quickly as I called the midwife. Over the phone, she asked me to describe exactly what was happening. I put down the phone, returned to the bed, caught the baby, put him on Veronica's breast, picked up the phone, and reported, "It's a boy."

Nolan Fritz was born in forty-five minutes on the 4th of July, 1984. A Yankee-Doodle baby.

Finally, a long awaited letter arrived announcing that I

had become eligible for Canadian citizenship. After a written test to assess my knowledge of Canadian history, I attended a ceremony at a Government building in Guelph. There were twenty-seven other immigrants present, from eighteen different countries. Some of them shed tears of joy. I felt only relief after what had been a long and frustrating, seven-year journey. I was more than delighted to finally see the back of the Canadian Immigration Department.

Good riddance to bad rubbish.

At the citizenship ceremony, there were speeches and declarations and pomp and circumstance. After much blathering and babbling, I stepped up to the podium where a Royal Canadian Mounted Police Officer, in full ceremonial dress, pinned a miniature, enamelled Canadian flag on my lapel.

It was 1984, Ronald Reagan won the popular vote, Marvin Gaye was gunned down in the street, and I was finally declared a genuine, certified, grade A, five-star, Canadian citizen.

23

Donny Winslow was from Ashville, North Carolina, and spoke with a soft, southern drawl. Apart from his roofing prowess and arborist skills, he was also an accomplished guerrilla pot farmer. He was planning to return to North Carolina for another growing season and suggested we all move down to Ashville, grow mass quantities of marijuana, and make a fortune.

It sounded like a cracker of an idea so, like the Beverly Hillbillies, we scooped up the kids, now one and three, loaded up our yellow Dodge window van, stacked all our worldly possessions on the overloaded roof-rack and drove south. Up until now, I had been inadmissible to the USA. I was excited to flash my brand new Canadian citizenship card. I had it clutched in my sweaty hand as I approached the border checkpoint. They didn't even ask to see it.

Ashville is located in North Carolina's Blue Ridge Mountains. It is the birthplace of the Enfield rifle, home of the moog synthesizer, and the resting place of authors Thomas Wolfe and O. Henry. In national polls, it is consistently voted one of the best places to live in the USA. But for all its glowing accolades, don't even try to order a cup of tea there, or for that matter, anywhere else in the United States of America. You are likely to get a lukewarm cup of swill with a stale lemon rind floating in it.

In Ashville, we rented a big house with Donny, his girlfriend, Bernice, and their two young children. Donny and

I did some roofing and tree work in between tending to six plots of marijuana plants in the hills around the city. We named one, the Billy Graham patch because of its location near the Billy Graham Evangelistic Training Center. It was the largest of the patches and contained about thirty plants. The dense woods surrounding the center provided perfect cover. The weather and the altitude in Ashville are well suited to growing pot. Each plant can reach over ten-feet tall and yield up to a pound and a half of dried marijuana.

Most of the work is in the preparation of the soil. Heavy bags of prepared soil had to be hauled into the deep woods under the cover of night. We dug holes in the ground and loaded them with soil mix and nutrients. Water barrels and irrigation systems were installed. Donny climbed up trees with a one-handed chain-saw and cut holes in the canopy to let in the light. At one patch, we installed grow bags in the crooks of branches in the tops of trees. At another, we hollowed out bushes and concealed the plants inside.

The biggest drawback with outdoor growing is theft. Despite our efforts at concealment, by the end of the season we had lost three out of six patches to bandits. Ashville was well known as a center for cannabis cultivation and towards the end of the season, local pot-pirates often scoured the landscape with the intention of stealing whatever they could find. One day, while tending a patch, we heard a buzzing overhead and saw a power-assisted hang-glider flying just above the tree tops. We ducked into the undergrowth while it passed. These intrepid, opportunistic thieves followed the rivers upstream looking for easy money.

There should be a law against it.

We harvested the remaining three patches and started the trimming and curing process. For the next few weeks we all worked tirelessly, manicuring the leafy flowers into perfect nuggets worthy of a High Times center-fold.

The strain we grew was called Skunk #1, first developed by The Farm in Tennessee, a hippie commune led by Stephen Gaskin, which was devoted to spiritual pursuits, and the cultivation and breeding of high potency marijuana.

As they say in Goa, "Boom Shiva Shankar."

When the trimming and curing was completed, we were left with several large garbage bags full of stalks, stems and leaves. A lot of the smaller, undeveloped buds were also in the debris. Although not worth selling, there was still a lot of good smoking to be had. Donny suggested we dump the leftovers in Brown Town, a not-so-affectionate term for the area in Asheville populated exclusively by Afro-Americans, essentially a black ghetto. At 3 a.m. one morning, we filled several large garbage bags with the trimmings, threw them into the back of the yellow Dodge window van and drove to Brown Town. After checking that no one was around, we emptied the bags onto the side-walk and sped off into the night.

With money from the harvest, we all took a well-earned vacation in sunny Myrtle Beach, South Carolina. We found a house to rent on the beach and spent the next month playing in the sand and surf with the kids. We also smoked a lot of Skunk #1.

We returned to Ashville to find our house had become infested with rats. At first we tried a catch and release program to no avail. On closer inspection of the basement, we found dozens of rat holes in the mud floor. There were hundreds of rats, far too many to catch or kill.

Our relationship with the Winslows had become strained. The rat problem didn't help. Notwithstanding Donny's long hair and bare feet, I began to detect more than a tinge of racism in his off-handed remarks and comments. During our last meal together in a pizza restaurant, his neck turned a deeper shade of crimson as he joked about the stringy mozzarella cheese having the consistency of "nigger snot." The black family at the next table overheard the remark but said nothing. They'd heard it all before. I was appalled. With that comment, our relationship was instantly and permanently terminated. Despite being hailed as one of the most desirable destinations in the US, Ashville had a racist streak that ran as deep and wide as the Mississippi River. It had only been three and a half decades since racial segregation had been lifted. They still had a very long way to go.

Racism is a big, frustrating subject rife with willful ignorance. I'll leave it for others to talk about endlessly. But I will make a couple of relevant points.

Race is a social construct. There is only one race of Homo sapiens. Skin colour is the result of melanin which has modified over time to protect us from the sun in warmer climes. Darker skin is nothing more than a genetically-acquired suntan. Also, every human being is a direct descendant of a tribe originating in Ethiopia. We are all Africans. In any discussion about so-called black, white or brown people, try substituting the word hair for skin and see how ridiculous it sounds. If we ever want to arrive at anything close to a post-racial society, we simply have to stop colour-coding people.

One of the great benefits of world travel and exposure to different cultures is that no matter how conspicuous our superficial differences may appear, it quickly becomes apparent that we all have the same basic fundamental goals and ambitions, the same hopes and dreams. No matter where you go, everyone has the same basic human needs. We all want to love and be loved. Show me a racist and I'll show you someone who doesn't get around very much.

Veronica and I decided to leave Ashville but needed some extra cash to make the long trek back to Vancouver,

Canada. Donny had kept the bulk of the money from the pot harvest and left us, like the pot, high and dry. We never spoke again. The Winslows moved out and left us with a house full of rats.

Veronica advertised her portrait skills in the local newspaper and was contacted by the CEO of a large corporation. In the basement of his mansion, he had a secret, luxury man-cave behind a hidden door and wanted several large oil paintings to fill the walls. For a hobby, he took photographs of his secretaries with their panties down around their ankles, or with their skirts pulled up to their waists revealing hairy bushes. These were not sophisticated shots but crude Polaroids. He requested four portraits painted from the photos and was willing to pay eight-hundred dollars for each one. After some discussion, our high-minded, moral objections slowly melted away under the incandescent heat of financial gain. We reluctantly accepted the commissions and Veronica brought the photos home and went to work. A few weeks later, we delivered the dubious works and picked up a great, sweaty wad of US greenbacks.

Once again, we overloaded our yellow Dodge window van and drove across the Southern States to California, and then headed north to Vancouver.

Let me take a few moments to extol the virtues of the yellow Dodge window van. I bought the van in Guelph for six-hundred dollars. It was well used, full of rust and belched blue smoke. I was informed by a mechanic that the engine was shot and in desperate need of a thousand-dollar ring job. I ignored the recommendation and continued to use it to haul roofing materials and heavy loads for the next six months. In Guelph, another mechanic told me it would never make it to North Carolina. Not only did I drive the yellow Dodge window van to North Carolina, I worked it hard with tree work and roofing for another six months and then drove it thousands of miles across the US to California, and then up to Vancouver where it served another year as a work truck. I eventually sold it and recouped my original six-hundred dollars.

There is surely some wisdom to wring from this parable? I will leave that for you to discover.

24

It is said that travel is the ultimate test of any relationship. It subjects both parties to unique and unexpected pressures. The stress can produce fractures which in turn can lead to cracks. Plans can change in an instant, requiring flexibility and adaptability. A failure to adapt can vent minority impulses best left under wraps. Let the record show that after our seven-year honeymoon, Veronica and I had passed every test with a perfect score. In all our travels, we never had a single fight, quarrel, or cross word.

Donovan was now four-years old and Nolan was two as we drove the miraculous yellow Dodge window van into Vancouver, BC. It was 1985, CDs and the Sony Discman had just arrived on the market and The Rainbow Warrior was bombed and sunk—spoiler alert: the French did it.

For the first two weeks we were back in Vancouver, we lived in the van in Stanley Park. Seven years earlier we had been wandering around the same park high on LSD. The park itself looked much the same but the zoo had closed and the flamingos had flown.

I attempted some busking around town but the results were disappointing. Playing on the street in Europe reliably yielded up to a hundred dollars an hour. Europeans embraced the long tradition of street performing and were happy to support it. To West Coast Canadians, it was tantamount to begging. In Vancouver you were lucky to make twenty dollars an hour.

In an effort to increase income, I upped my game and built a one-man-band with a bass drum mounted on my back. My right foot operated a high hat on top of the drum and my left foot activated the bass drum. While simultaneously stamping out the rhythm with my feet, I played guitar while hyperventilating into a harmonica and a kazoo. Veronica painted a beautiful coiled dragon on the bass drum. But the rig was heavy and exhausting to play for any more than an hour. It did attract a little more attention than playing solo guitar, but still only made about thirty dollars an hour. After a couple of weeks, I retired from busking and never played on the street again.

To rise to the financial challenges of the day, I resurrected Residential Roofing and worked on my own or with a helper. Roofing gave me the freedom to work when I wanted, make decent money, and spend lots of time with Veronica and the kids. Veronica pursued her painting career and began to produce and exhibit regularly. Selling oil paintings for a thousand dollars apiece augmented our income nicely.

We rented a large house and sublet the extra rooms to further supplement our income. This worked for a while but roommates proved to be problematic. They were unreliable, unpredictable, and sometimes turned out to be certifiable nutters. It quickly became apparent to us that we needed our own house. We scraped together a small down-payment and I went to the bank for a mortgage.

For over two hours I engaged in a battle of wits with a humourless woman at the Royal Bank of Canada. In the West End, we had found an old heritage house at the bottom of the market. I had to convince this buttoned-down banker we had the resources to cover a mortgage.

She requested tax returns. I had none. I lied about being in the process of making a multi-year filing. I had never filed a tax return or paid income tax in my entire life. The questions came fast and thick as I struggled to make up believable answers. I fabricated non-existent savings. I made up a phony full-time job and forged a letter to prove it. I gave her the phone number of my employer and had an unemployed friend waiting by a phone, ready to verify the story. After much deliberation and a heroic effort on my part, I was finally and flatly refused. My application was denied and I was told not to bother applying again.

For my part, we were already paying six-hundred dollars a month for rent and since the loan payment would be about the same, I felt confident we could take on the responsibility of the mortgage. We called our real estate agent and told him we would be unable to borrow the money or buy the house. Unfazed, he suggested that we go and present our case to his mortgage broker. A few days later, I presented the exact same pack of lies to him. He said he'd get back to us.

On Christmas Eve, 1988, while decorating the tree with the kids, we received a call from the broker. He had placed the mortgage with the Bank of Nova Scotia and we had our own house.

For the next year, we knocked out walls, refinished floors and painted every square inch. The property also featured a full-sized basement. I promptly built a hidden grow room with a concealed entrance and began to grow pot.

The room was twelve feet by twelve. I installed two, one-thousand watt halide lamps, an air circulation system, and plumbing. With another hidden room in the attic for cloning, I could grow in a continuous cycle, producing three pounds of high-grade marijuana every ten weeks. This provided an income of approximately forty-thousand dollars a year. I did this for the next fifteen years.

Growing pot is not as easy as you might think. The plants

are a product of intense inter-breeding over many generations. Each iteration gives higher yields, increased potency,
shorter flowering cycles etc., but these improvements come
at a cost. The plants become hyper-sensitive, more finicky,
and require extra attention and closer monitoring.

Over the years, I never stopped fine-tuning the operation. I experimented with many different plant foods. I tried
blood meal, bone meal, enzymes, various micro-nutrients,
worm-castings and bat guano. I tried CO_2 enrichment, negative ion generators, magnets, and electrical stimulation. I
fiddled with the temperature, humidity, and the light cycle.
I tried bending, topping, stressing, training, pruning, pinching, lollipopping, flushing, mainlining, and monster cropping.

Producing a harvest every three months requires a lot of
trimming. At the end of every harvest, Veronica and I spent
many hours sitting around a table trimming plants into perfectly manicured buds. This became a family affair. We were
what people refer to as a mom and pop operation. Only ours
was an operation that included mom, pop, two kids, and
both grandparents.

At the time, my parents, Hazel and Bert, were in their
seventies. They had recently immigrated to Canada and
were getting a thorough education in the world of cannabis
cultivation and consumption. Hazel had had some success
using pot as pain control for shingles. She had a particularly
nasty case and was bedridden for months. When every conventional pain killer had been exhausted, she tried cannabis
and found it to be surprisingly effective. She later smoked
the occasional joint to elevate her mood.

Bert, on the other hand, couldn't understand why anyone
would take a drug without a medical condition. There were
a lot of things Bert didn't understand. But he did try smoking
pot a couple of times, both with disastrous results.

The first time was at a party at our house in Guelph. A beautiful young woman, half his age, approached and offered to give him a shotgun. Not the firearm but a smoking technique which involves blowing pot smoke backwards through a joint into someone else's open mouth. This involved the participant's lips coming into very close proximity. Bert accepted the offer without hesitation. After a couple of hoots, he began to cough uncontrollably. His face turned a deep shade of purple and the veins in his neck bulged and looked fit to burst. The coughing turned to heaving as he ran into the bathroom to throw up. Just in time, he puked into the toilet with such force it blew out his dentures. They shot out of his mouth like a grinning bullet into the porcelain bowl and disappeared around the u-bend. It was left to me to fish them out.

Bert's second, and last attempt to consume cannabis, also occurred at a social gathering at our house. This time it was a simple misunderstanding. Again, a beautiful young woman half his age was passing around a tray of cookies. As he went to take one, he asked what kind of cookies they were. She smiled and told him they were laced with marijuana. Thinking she was joking, he laughed and scarfed one down in two bites. A short time later, his heart started racing. Then he experienced shortness of breath and was showing all the symptoms of a major heart attack. Unsurprisingly, he was never tempted to try pot again.

25

While banging away on the roof one day with a wide view of the horizon, I began to muse about what I might do in terms of broadening my own. It was time for a new challenge. What did I want to do that I hadn't already done? The answer I came up with was filmmaking. I decided to become a film director.

Since childhood, I'd been fascinated by the process that produced hypnotic, flickering images on a screen. The idea that I could create those images filled me with excitement. But I would first have to learn every aspect of the process. To this end, I enrolled in film school.

I hadn't stepped inside a school since leaving Hazelwick as a disgruntled fourteen-year old. As a child, I remembered the sick feeling in my stomach every morning walking to school. The feeling of impending dread as the summer holidays came to an end, marking the return to that house of horrors. And the feeling of exhilaration when I finally left for the last time, ripping my school uniform to shreds and festooning it in a tree in front of the school in a final act of defiance.

Film school was a horse of a very different colour. I was actually learning something of value and soaked up every second. Upon completion, I had all the skills necessary to produce, direct, and edit my own films. I teamed up with another film school graduate and we approached the local cable TV station. We proposed a series called 'Alternating

Currents,' a monthly, half-hour show that would explore the soft, eccentric underbelly of the local arts scene. It proved to be a great success and an excellent training ground where we could hone our skills. We had free reign, access to equipment, complete editorial control, and ended up winning several awards.

As a community station, we were unpaid volunteers, so my income from pot-growing and Veronica's painting sales financed the project. After producing eighteen shows, I left the cable channel and formed a production company called Scarlet Sky Productions producing educational, promotional videos, and documentaries. Our films covered global warming, teenage pregnancy, juvenile prostitution, false memory syndrome, and a theatre company operating in a federal prison. But the ultimate goal was to write and direct a feature film and, to this end, I made a 16mm short film entitled, *House of Cards*.

In the film business, this is known as a spec project, a self-financed, resume piece. I submitted the film to various festivals and received an invitation to screen the film at Local Heroes International Screen Festival in Edmonton. The festival offered to pay my return airfare and four days accommodation.

As an independent filmmaker with 'several projects in development,' rejection was a way of life. Most projects die on the vine and you get used to being ignored and refused. Idealistic enthusiasm is constantly met with indifference and apathy. These small victories are to be relished.

The day before leaving to attend the festival I was faxed a list of the delegates. To my surprise and delight, Werner Herzog's name appeared on the list. He was presenting a new film and would be the keynote speaker. I had been a fan of his films for many years and was thrilled at the prospect of meeting him in person.

Before leaving for the festival, I had decided I would meet this man by any means necessary. Herzog himself is legendary for his persistence and determination. To achieve his goals he has walked hundreds of miles, forged government documents, stolen cameras, picked locks, thrown himself into a cactus patch, and once dragged a 340-ton steamship over a mountain in the Amazon jungle. On one occasion, to prove a point, he even ate his own shoe.

I would follow his tenacious example. If necessary, I would knock on every door of the four-hundred-room hotel. I was prepared to camp out in the lobby, eat amphetamines to stay alert and ambush him at the check-out desk. If necessary, I would question each and every guest at gun-point as to his whereabouts and, yes, if needs be, I would even eat one of my Birkenstocks.

Luckily, I ran into him at the hospitality suite ten minutes after I arrived.

It took me a moment to recognize him, but as soon as we made eye contact there was no mistaking that intense and enigmatic Bavarian stare. I told him I was showing a film at the festival and would like to interview him for a local film magazine. He agreed to meet me in the lobby of the hotel that evening. Armed with a tape recorder and a camera, I arrived fifteen minutes early.

Through his films, Herzog looks at the world with an uncompromising, penetrating gaze which elevates his subject matter from mere cinematic storytelling to a unique form of subconscious film poetry. The end result achieves a hypnotic effect which seems to transcend the medium of film altogether. He transports us to an unknown world of mad beauty where we are no longer just looking *at* things, but into the very heart of things. Few filmmakers have achieved this elusive quality and for this reason, Werner Herzog is one of the greatest visionary film artists of our time.

In a world of compromises, Herzog asks us to believe that anything is possible, that no matter how big we dream, if we have the courage and passion of our convictions and can inspire enough people around us, we can create a climate where the impossible becomes possible, where thought forms and dreams are made manifest, and where 340-ton steamships can be dragged over mountains by manpower alone. The sad fact is, in a world influenced only by commercial concerns, and dominated with blockbusters and superhero movies, the true film artist is a dying breed. If the current trends continue, we may never see another Orson Welles, or Fellini, or Godard, or Herzog.

Movies, like literature, became an integral part of my continuing education. Here, once more, there is a clear distinction between conventional entertainment and film art. Like the dichotomy between pulp fiction and literature, auteur filmmakers offer a unique perspective, a window into the psyche of the filmmaker, the vicarious experience of another human mind.

I consider my short time with Herzog the zenith of my film career. I went on to write two feature-length screenplays, one of which almost got made.

The Love Encyclopedia was a riveting, hilarious, comedic romp about a fellow named Jimi Fritz who was busy compiling an encyclopedia on all aspects of love. His girlfriend leaves him in the first scene and he spends the rest of the movie trying to win her back, employing every trick in the book.

The project was moving along nicely. We had a shooting script, a budget, and Veronica had illustrated a complete storyboard. We'd done some of the casting, secured a completion guarantor, and had a couple of interested distributors, including Miramax. The only major stumbling block was the lack of a lead actor. The distributors were demanding a name or a face.

In my cover letter to agents, I described the lead as a young Elliott Gould. Soon after, I received a call from Sam Gould, Elliott's son. He was interested in the part so I flew to Los Angeles to meet him. We arranged a meeting in a hotel room in Anaheim, California. Veronica and I took the kids with us and bought tickets to nearby Disneyland.

The day before our meeting, there was a great flurry of activity in the lobby and we went down to investigate. A crowd of people were gathered around, watching the news, transfixed to a report about O.J. Simpson in a slow-speed car chase. While we were watching, we realized the car was coming our way and rushed to the window just in time to see O.J's white Ford Bronco cruising by followed by twenty-two police cars. One of his old football buddies drove the car, while O.J. sat in the back seat holding a gun to his head with one hand, and a written confession in the other. In a just world, he would have pulled the trigger and saved everybody a lot of time and money.

After a long day at The Magic Kingdom, Sam Gould arrived and we talked about the movie. He was also a fan of Disneyland and told us they had closed the entire park one time to give him and his mother, Barbara Streisand, a private tour.

Sam liked the script and agreed to do the film. He also agreed to ask his dad to play a small part. This led to a very frustrating and confused telephone conversation a couple of weeks later.

I had sent Elliott Gould a rewrite of his part as the wacky psychiatrist. He seemed satisfied with the changes and agreed to do the cameo for five grand. I was in the middle of making dinner for the kids one evening and was having trouble hearing him over the noise. He was getting more and more agitated as we spoke. I asked him for his contact information and he gave me his address at Pacific Palisades.

This was apparently one of the most famous addresses in the world. I had never heard of it. "Pali what?" I said.

"Palisades," he repeated.

"Can you spell that?" I pleaded.

"It's Pacific Palisades," he said more emphatically. "You've never heard of Pacific Palisades?" He was incredulous.

"The *what* Palisades?'

"Pacific Palisades!" he barked.

"Is that one L or two?" I said, struggling with my pen and paper.

"Oh, for God's sake, look it up."

And with that, he hung up the phone.

Elliot was clearly used to a higher level of geographical literacy and shortly after that disastrous phone call, withdrew from the project. This was the first of a series of unfortunate events that led to the film going into 'turnaround.' This is filmmaking jargon for cast into the pit of hell, never to return.

Despite my failure to ultimately write and direct a feature film, my eight years as a filmmaker were some of the most satisfying experiences I've ever had. As the great Soviet director and film theorist, Sergei Eisenstein once said, "There is nothing more fun than making movies.

26

Shortly after my film career went into turnaround, something happened that would inexorably change my life.

Jack Grimshaw had followed me to Vancouver and set up shop as the biggest pimp in town. Ever the innovative entrepreneur, he established several brothels and ran a stable of a dozen girls. His latest girlfriend, Delores, assumed the role of Madame. But this was not my catalyst for change.

It came in the form of Jack's twenty-one-year-old son, Dwayne, who had come to Vancouver to visit his wayward father. I had babysat Dwayne as a one-year-old back in Brighton. He was a cheerful lad, full of misguided and naive optimism. He had been involved in the rave scene back in England and regaled me with stories of clandestine, hedonistic love-fests held in abandoned buildings, fuelled by electronic dance music and the drug MDMA, also known as ecstasy, molly, X, or E.

Dwayne invited me to an event in an abandoned Salvation Army building downtown. I had never tried MDMA and had never heard any electronic dance music. My curiosity was peaked and I agreed to go. Dwayne said he knew where to get some high quality ecstasy.

Dwayne came by the day before the rave to prep me on the scene. He told me everyone was extremely friendly at raves and the music was truly new and exciting. He told me that a nice big hit of MDMA would open up my heart chakra and enable me to dance all night long. I was somewhat sceptical, especially about the chakra reference. I no longer believed in that sort of irrational balderdash.

Also, I never particularly liked electronic music. As a musician, I was faithfully devoted to the acoustic, organic qualities of the guitar, piano, and ukulele. My experiences with electronic keyboards had always been disappointing. No matter what instrument they attempted to reproduce, they invariably sounded like the disturbing whine of a low-tech kitchen appliance. An annoying electronic buzz is not improved by varying its pitch or frequency. This merely turns a high-pitched annoying buzz into a low-pitched annoying buzz. The sounds produced by synthesizers in the seventies seemed to lack an important human quality that I believed essential to good music. When mixed with 'real' instruments synthesizers could produce some interesting effects, but on their own, they were somehow cold, sterile and lifeless.

Another thing: I had not found any music worth dancing to in almost twenty-five years. The last time I had danced with total unbridled enthusiasm was at a rock concert in 1973. The Who were in their heyday and twenty-thousand hippies and leftover mods went berserk in a soccer stadium in London, England. That night I also learned a valuable lesson about thermodynamics: you cannot use the plastic packaging from a refrigerator box as a sleeping bag, especially if you are sharing it with a close friend.

It was not that I disliked dancing. I found it quite entertaining to watch other people dance, but I had rarely come across any music that inspired me enough to express myself on a dance floor. Consequently, I had become certified as a chronic, non-dancing individual. I had certainly never danced all night.

I patiently explained my position on electronic music and my limited dancing experience to Dwayne who remained undaunted. I detected a mischievous twinkle in his knowing eye but he was steadfastly convinced that I would benefit from the experience. I countered with a host of good reasons as to why my worldly wisdom would render me impervious to this fleeting teenage fad. Dwayne listened patiently. He had heard this story before. A wry smile crept playfully across his youthful face. Or was it an impish grin?

Armed with a capsule of ecstasy, I marched downtown to a building that until recently had been home to The Salvation Army. At around 10:30 p.m., a crowd of partygoers began filing into the building that was slated for demolition in a few weeks. From outside, the music sounded like a muffled and messy explosion of bass drums. I popped my pill and went in.

Inside, the music was very loud but crystal clear. At first, I thought it sounded a little stuck in a groove, but I had never heard anything quite like it. These were not the depersonalized electronic sounds of the seventies. They were rich, textured sounds, fat and juicy and warm and friendly.

The once sedate chapel, with its high ceilings and vaulted roof, was transformed into a psychedelic grotto. Large screens suspended from the rafters displayed footage of outer-space inter-cut with tribal imagery, while on another screen, a newborn baby was spinning in space, superimposed on a computer-generated, futuristic landscape. Japanese animation, pirated from local video stores transformed the entire back wall into a moving panorama of colour and forms.

The DJ was set up at the head of the room on a raised platform that had once served as a pulpit. Crinkled aluminum foil lined the walls surrounding the stage, causing light from the lasers to zigzag back and forth as if struggling to escape from the inside of an astronaut's underwear.

For a while I sat behind the DJ and watched him spinning records on two turntables while fiddling with a mixer in between. Although I had some experience with sound systems and recording studios, I couldn't quite figure out how the sounds were being created but was fascinated by this mysterious process. I finally gave up trying to demystify the mechanics and began to listen to the music more closely. I checked the time. It was almost midnight. Dwayne was right; everyone seemed very happy and friendly. And the music was definitely growing on me.

The one hundred and forty milligrams of methylenedioxymethamphetamine I had ingested were now barrelling down the highways and byways of my blood vessels, looking for an off-ramp to my cerebral cortex. Inside my brain, billions of cells were bucking and jockeying for position in my jumbo can of neurochemical soup. Some were now quivering with anticipation, as if telepathically sensing the arrival of a surprise package from a wealthy but distant relative.

Deep within each cell body, the ancient council of DNA were casually discussing the pros and cons of cytokinesis verses binary fission, unaware of the impending alkali onslaught. From each neuron, dozens of dendrites were waving like branches of seaweed in a tide pool, organic aerials monitoring all frequencies for incoming instructions. Something was coming down the pike. Something that smacked of smoke and mirrors and fire and magic.

Protruding like pointing fingers from swollen cell bodies, erect axons were pulsing electrical signals out to twitching terminals. Sacks of serotonin at the end of each terminal were stuffed and ready to be delivered to any address with the correct postal code. Axons deep within the gray, purple folds of my cerebellum were now creeping closer to the dangling dendrites of other nearby neurons. Like drunken nymphets swaying in a water ballet, their spindly arms reached out in anticipation of a friendly handshake.

The small vesicles in my cranium containing serotonin molecules quivered in anticipation of their impending liberation. The hug drug, the X, the bean, the Adam, the roll, the E, was penetrating the deepest recesses of my brain. Electrical charges went off like firecrackers, triggering a massive release of serotonin into the synapses. In other parts of my cerebellum, other neurotransmitters in the form of dopamine and norepinephrine flowed into the mix. The hairs on the back of my neck began to bristle. A warm, healthy glow spread through my torso. The slight fatigue I had felt earlier now melted away, giving way to a lighter, more relaxed mood.

As the MDMA began to really kick in, I started to hear complexities in the music that had previously gone unnoticed. I felt myself beginning to move to the music, so I headed back to the dance floor.

The mood on the dance floor was electric. I had never seen so many people dancing so enthusiastically and with such fervour. The energy level in the room could have easily powered a small town. People were smiling from ear to ear, as if amazed at the ability of the music to affect them so completely.

Heavy tribal beats continued to build in intensity. Just when any further increase in power seemed impossible, a plateau of swirling sounds suggested an ultimate zenith. Then, suddenly, the music exploded into another rhythm even more penetrating and profound than before. This upward spiraling cycle of pulsating sound continued to build relentlessly, hour after hour, throughout the night. Like a musical river, it swept everyone along with its irresistible momentum. A wave of positivity swept through the crowd as we surrendered to this new musical form.

I was completely astonished at the intensity of this new experience and, by the look on everyone's faces, I was not alone. The atmosphere in the room was one of turbo-charged celebration. At forty, I was one of the oldest people present, but age, like so many other social conventions, melted away and meant nothing. Complete strangers came up and introduced themselves to me with a warm hug. They told me they were glad to see me and hoped I was hav-ing a good time. From time to time, experienced ravers approached me with a reminder to drink water or to offer me candy. I felt protected and safe, as if surrounded by close friends and family.

The music was getting louder and clearer. Either some-one was gradually turning up and tweaking the sound sys-tem, or my ears had developed new and improved powers of hearing. My whole body vibrated as the sound waves pene-trated every bone and sinew. When I closed my eyes, incred-ibly intricate geometric patterns danced behind my eyelids, each pattern more detailed than the last, pulsing and mor-phing in perfect time to the music.

Like members of an alien tribe adorned in candy-coloured garb, glow beads and furry animal backpacks, ravers greeted each other with hugs and childlike whoops of excitement. I had never before seen a group of people so connected, integrated, and familiar. It was the kind of close-ness usually associated with small groups, close family, or friends.

The normal formalities and protocols of everyday social activities, the polite smile, the civil but rehearsed greeting, were replaced with spontaneous displays of genuine affec-tion and camaraderie. It was a world where the social rules had changed. A society where people had transcended their petty, superficial differences and embraced a reality in which everyone was accepted for who and what they were, without judgment or fear.

As the night drew on, I found myself reflecting back on

past events in my life. People, places, incidents, flashes of conversations ran through my mind like a street parade, each more detailed than the last. But, rather than analyzing the information, I found myself calmly surveying this procession of memories as a passive observer, without judgment or criticism. I experienced a kind of omnipotent benevolence. I realized that no matter how foolish or misguided or selfish an action may appear, it is ultimately driven by some underlying, virtuous urge. People are not innately bad or evil. People are merely inept or foolish or misguided. My newly developed, high-powered, non-critical perception peeled away the layers of judgment, revealing intrinsic truths about human nature. It was a form of super-charged, accelerated, enhanced meditation.

A combination of the music, the MDMA, and the environment conspired to create a unifying, transcendental, group-mind experience. At some point, the personal experience of the individual became a collective one. No longer a group of separate people dancing in a room, we had become an integrated single entity connected by the music and feelings of empathy produced by the MDMA. Like a shoal of fish or a murmuration of starlings, the participants moved as a synchronized whole, becoming greater than the sum of its parts. This unifying connective experience is at the very heart of rave culture and by far the most interesting and compelling aspect.

Throughout the night, ravers approached me with friendly greetings, or to inquire about my physical or mental health. They sensed I was a novice and wanted to make me welcome. I could barely hear a word above the music, but I smiled and nodded and gave the occasional thumbs-up. I was offered Vicks Vapour Rub to inhale. The menthol fumes clear the head and refresh the mental palette. Someone else casually handed me a bottle of water as they passed by. I was given gifts of stickers and incense and pieces of fresh fruit.

The next time I checked the time, I was amazed to find another hour had passed in what had seemed like minutes. I felt like I was speeding through a wind tunnel, barely able to register the events as they rushed past. At the same time, I felt frozen in time and was able to concentrate on each and every individual change in the music. I felt stronger, lighter and healthier than ever before. An incredible sense of optimism and enthusiasm filled my entire being. I was simultaneously calm and energized. A feeling of tranquility emanated from somewhere deep in my stomach and spread slowly throughout my body, encompassing the totality of my being.

I then found myself jigging about, hopping from foot to foot. The hopping and skipping developed into bouncing and jumping. I leapt into the air, both feet leaving the ground at the same time with all the grace of a Thomson's gazelle.

I was dancing about like a mad fool.

That night, I danced for seven hours straight with barely a break. As the dawn light flooded in through the stained-glass windows, the party was still in full swing and the music was still climbing to impossible heights.

It was quite a shock when the music suddenly ground to a halt just after 7 a.m. and the lights came up revealing hundreds of exhausted, sweaty, and exhilarated ravers. The carefully combed, coifed, and gelled hairstyles from the night before now hung limp, tousled, and damp with sweat. Wide-eyed, dilated pupils blinked defensively under the harsh fluorescent lights flooding the former chapel. Most people, including myself, stood in stunned amazement, unable to believe the night had ended. The bubble had burst, the dream was over. I wandered outside into a crisp new morning.

Dawn was breaking over the rooftops casting a warm pink glow reminiscent of a Maxwell Parish print. The world looked new and different, as if polished and buffed to an improbable shine. Even the air felt different. With each breath, I imagined I was filling my lungs with rarefied oxygen imported from the summit of Everest. I couldn't remember ever feeling so alive and satisfied, so inspired and fulfilled.

One of the people Dwayne introduced to me that night was Mr. X. He was a likeable, easy-going chap dressed as the Easter Bunny. I later found out he'd been the source of my high quality MDMA. This would mark the beginning of a very long, and very fruitful relationship.

27

I was still growing pot in the basement but my modest room could no longer keep up with the increasing demand. I had developed a solid and enthusiastic customer base which wanted a greater variety of choices but I was only able to grow two or three strains at a time. Buying from other growers gave me the ability to offer many more varieties. Consequently, I started buying pounds from other growers to expand the business. This meant more money. For the first time in my life, at the age of forty, I was financially independent. I could now direct my energies to more serious pursuits—like raving. The rave scene in Vancouver was just kicking into high gear and I couldn't wait for the next event.

Raves were underground affairs advertised with flyers. They provided information about the event, which DJs were playing, and a phone number to call on the day of the event. A recorded message revealed the location or a pick-up point. The pick-up point was usually a parking lot or industrial area where the attendees gathered to get final directions. This cat-and-mouse game was in an effort to throw off the authorities as the events were usually unlicensed, uninsured, and therefore illegal. The subterfuge added to the general sense of excitement.

Veronica and I started to go to raves every weekend and became deeply involved in the local scene. Early on, I knew I would need a steady and safe supply of MDMA for me and my friends. So I went to see Mr. X., the Easter Bunny, and my soon-to-be Fairy Godfather.

Mr. X. was one of those rare human beings who was well-liked by everyone who knew him, an exemplary human being you could trust without question. He was also chummy with a couple of clandestine labs which made the finest quality MDMA and LSD.

I began buying twenty or thirty pills at a time. This was enough for my personal supply and I sold any excess to cover my costs. At that time, most of the E came in the form of pressed pills. Sometimes they were clean but more often than not, they were cut with various fillers and additives. This is one of the direct and dangerous consequences of prohibition. Quality control is out of control.

There are many people who produce MDMA for purely financial reasons. Hells Angeles and Vietnamese gangs dominate the Vancouver market but also dealt in coke, speed and heroin. Theirs was a dirty business. But there's another category of intrepid, underground chemists and psychonauts who believe in the transformative effects of psychedelics. They strive to make the highest-quality products with integrity and a sense of purpose. These are the labs I was able to access through my Fairy Godfather.

For some historical perspective, MDMA was first patented in 1913 by Merck, a German pharmaceutical company. Its early use is not well documented and it didn't surface again until 1953, when it was supposedly tested by the US army. Perhaps they theorized that spraying it onto an opposing army might diminish their will to fight, while increasing their desire to dance to house music, thus making them easy targets. It's a controversial theory at best. The British army conducted similar tests with LSD. The results were hilarious.

In the early eighties, a Ph.D. biochemist from the University of California at Berkeley named Alexander Shulgin developed a pesticide for Dow Chemicals that made them a lot of money. Consequently, they gave him an independent research grant and free reign to explore any biochemical avenue he saw fit. Shulgin, like Huxley before him, was fascinated by the mescaline molecule and began to tinker with its benzene rings and molecular structure. This led him to rediscover the old Merck patent for MDMA. He was intrigued and cooked up a batch.

Shulgin and his wife Ann were self-experimenters, following a long tradition in science. They were impressed with the effects of MDMA and suspected it might have therapeutic applications. They began to distribute it amongst their psychiatrist and psychologist friends who reported miraculous results in their therapy practices.

At this point, MDMA was still legal. Shulgin went on to monkey around with psychedelic substances in his private lab, making analogues, stressing benzene rings, switching out nitrogen molecules and this amine for that.

Alexander Shulgin is credited with creating over three-hundred unique psychedelic compounds including ALEPH 1, DIPT, 5-MEO-DIPT, DOM, MMDA, 2C-E, 2C-T-2, 2C-T-7, 2C-B and on, and on. These compounds were summarily scheduled by the DEA as fast as Shulgin could file the patents. To this day, they remain illegal and for that reason have yet to be clinically tested.

In 1984, MDMA leaked into dance clubs in Dallas, Texas and could be purchased legally at the bar with a credit card. The authorities quickly figured out that people were having far too much fun and swooped in, declaring a public emergency. Originally meant to be a temporary measure, MDMA was banned and has remained a Schedule 1 drug to this day. Schedule 1 drugs are classified as addictive and having no therapeutic value. They were dead wrong on both counts.

Despite its illegal status, MDMA migrated across the Atlantic and took up residence in Ibiza, a Spanish island in the Mediterranean off the coast of Spain. There it melded with a burgeoning house music scene and soon after migrated north to the UK. By 1987, rave parties were springing up all over England. This became known as the Summer of Love, a name recycled from 1967's Summer of Love which marked the peak of hippy culture twenty years before. What goes around comes around.

Thanks to Mr. X, I quickly shared his reputation for having the best quality MDMA and my customer base continued to grow. I progressively bought larger amounts and found I could make several hundred dollars per night dealing on the dance floor at parties and clubs. I was careful to only deal with people I knew, or friends of friends. Often, I'd be approached by strangers on the dance floor enquiring as to where they could find some good E. I ended up turning away more people than I sold to.

Because I was only selling to people I knew and liked and cared about, I felt a responsibility to test every batch of MDMA. First, I used a marquis reagent testing kit. This is a method used by law enforcement to test substances on location. It's a crude test but can give you some useful information. A few grains of the powder are placed on to a plate and a couple of drops of the reagent liquid mixed in, turning the sample different colours. If it turns yellow, amphetamines are present. Purple/black is confirmation that it's an MDMA-type substance. It's not an exact science because an MDMA-type substance can be MDA, MDE or MDAI. So, after first getting a strong purple/black reaction, I employed a thorough field test.

For years, Veronica and I attended a rave club on most

Wednesday and Saturday nights. As the conditions at the club were always the same, it became a controlled environment in which to test drive new batches of E. We'd take 125mg at precisely 10 p.m. and monitor the results. If it checked out, I sold it. On the extremely rare occasion it didn't cut the mustard, I returned it. And this is one of the reasons my Fairy Godfather became paramount to my success. He offered a full, money-back guarantee and I was then able to pass along this assurance to my customers. If, for any reason, a customer was dissatisfied, I offered an exchange or full refund. This policy extended to all the psychedelics I sold. Satisfaction was always guaranteed.

With the complicit permission of the club owner, I became the house dealer. Sometimes on a Saturday night, after the club closed at 2 a.m., the regulars waited in the back while most of the customers left the building. We then locked the doors and carried on until six or seven in the morning.

I have since calculated that in ten years of parties and club nights, I consumed over four-thousand doses of MDMA and never experienced any negative consequences.

28

A reasonable assumption could be made that after an all-night party, at which you'd been dancing for eight hours or more, you might be ready for bed. But you will have underestimated the euphoric, after-glow of MDMA.

Fact is, by the end of a long, sweaty night with the sun coming up, the feelings of exhilaration and overwhelming buoyancy override any mundane considerations for sleep. This leads to the inevitability of the after-party.

In rave culture, there exists a dedicated band of insomniacs and die-hards who, by virtue of being too high, too charged up, too easily influenced, or just too dumb, refuse to give in to the normal biological imperative for sleep.

Bodies may ache for rest, eyes may droop and involuntarily close, large areas of the brain may shut down or malfunction, but no matter, going home to bed is not an option. The raver is driven by an unconscious desire to push a little further, delve a little deeper, and wander a little further away from the beaten track of conventional reality.

After-parties exist as a phenomenon unto themselves. They dwell in a twilight zone, a liminal layer between waking life and a semi-conscious dream state where the sharp, well-defined edges of the 'real world' blur and bend into something less familiar. This is a place where the ordinary checks and balances of everyday social life are broken down and a new order takes over. Social barriers are breached and discarded, exposing the spongy underside of raw and unguarded psyches.

At any given after-party, the first order of business is music. Without the constant barrage of beats serving as a metronomic massager, kneading the last drops of energy from mind and body, the after-party can very quickly degenerate into a slumber party. Music that is subdued or moody will not do. The energy will be lost, the balloon popped. At the after-party, the music must be hard and fast and loud.

If decks and a mixer are not already set up—an operation requiring forethought and planning, and therefore unlikely to succeed—a posse will immediately be delegated and dispatched to collect the components necessary to continue the seamless soundtrack from the previous evening. This can take time and can involve a number of phone calls. If the after-party looks like it's going to flourish—some fizzle out due to apathy, ineptitude and incompetence—then more people are invited. Small groups drive off into the early morning light, in cars driven by drivers who should not be operating machinery of any weight.

The second most important order of business is more drugs. Whatever it takes to kick the brain into another cycle of distended perception and warn off, for as long as possible, the mundane curse of ordinary reality.

For me, sixty micrograms of LSD usually did the trick. Not enough to elicit hallucinations but enough to wake up the brain and cast a new neural net. This was typically followed by an MDMA chaser to sweeten the mood. With the warmth produced by the shared camaraderie of the previous evening, social connections are heightened and unguarded. A communal, unspoken bond connects the participants in a web of intimacy. This can be a powerful experience for those who are normally locked into a stifling life of guarded conformity.

MDMA in particular can act in a similar fashion to sodium pentothal, the truth serum used by CIA operatives. This is why it is so effective in therapeutic settings. It has the ability to bypass and suppress anxiety levels while allowing the user to access inner feelings and to express them without fear or self-judgment. For many, this is the closest they will ever come to tasting true freedom.

During the next decade of raving, I was witness to countless examples of lives transformed for the better. People were routinely being saved by the Church of Rave.

29

My parents, Hazel and Bert, were thrilled with their move from England to Vancouver. They'd spent their whole lives in a dingy council house and were grateful to find a better life in Canada. Hazel once described the rows of houses that lined her street in Crawley as tombstones. She saw them as portents of an ignominious end, monuments to a wasted life. She found the prospect of dying on that street without ever having left, a bleak one.

They loved the relaxed, West Coast life-style, adapted quickly and spent their last decade enjoying life while spending as much time as possible with their grandchildren.

Hazel started smoking as a teenager and never stopped once to catch her breath. It came as no surprise when, at the age of 73, she finally succumbed to lung cancer. It was diagnosed as stage 4. There is no stage 5.

I would love to report that medical marijuana came to the rescue and cured her cancer. There are many people who will tell you this is possible but there is no credible evidence to support this view. Perhaps with future research, cannabis may yield treatments for cancer but, for now, it can be a grave mistake to think that smoking dope or eating hash oil will cure your cancer. Numerous friends of mine have chosen to reject conventional treatments, proven to extend life expectancy or even affect cures, in favour of medical marijuana. In every case, they have died at the same rate predicted for a patient with no treatment at all.

Terrified of dying in a hospital, Hazel asked me to facilitate a home death. I agreed, and when the time came, moved into her apartment for the last month of her life. I installed an extra bed in her bedroom and we spent every one of her last moments together.

Hazel was what is politely termed as high-strung or, less politely, a nervous wreck. Given her neurotic disposition, I fully expected her to crack up towards the end but was pleasantly surprised to witness her rising to the occasion and dying with dignity and grace.

A doctor dropped in once a week with a steady supply of syringes containing atropine and morphine. Every four hours, I injected a dose of each drug into shunts permanently installed in both of her thighs. I read to her and sang her favorite songs. We talked and talked. She confided in me that her only regret was not leaving my father when I had left home at fifteen.

With one of her precious last breaths, she warned me about the dangers of ecstasy use. I smiled and nodded at a woman who was literally dying from her drug addiction.

Near the end, she was barely able to lift her head off the pillow for a smoke. After only a couple of puffs, she puked green bile into a bowel and flopped back on the pillow. After a short pause, she went back for another puff.

Hazel loved a good smoke.

In the last few days, she stopped eating, and then drinking. She dipped in and out of consciousness, speaking in whispers, her body shrunken, her face collapsed, her skin transparent. We joked about our role reversal. She was a helpless baby and I was the vigilant parent. She was toothless, wore diapers, and was frozen in the fetal position. Death is birth in reverse, a completed circle.

A parent accepts the responsibility of caring for their child unconditionally. Similarly, a fundamental contract exists between an adult child and an aging or dying parent. Check it out. It's in the fine print.

Death remains our biggest and baddest wolf. When I shared with friends I was helping my mother die, they clammed up, froze, or ran screaming into the hills. I could read the fear in their faces. I was given plenty of space. My phone stopped ringing.

A lot of people are ambivalent towards death and reluctant to get involved. It's other people's business, too personal, too serious, and too scary. One day they will have to face the beast, but they will put it off for as long as possible.

Death is always a surprise. Even when you have watched each and every last second tick away, the actual moment of death is strangely unexpected. And, no matter how prepared philosophically and intellectually you may be, it is not enough to protect you from the tidal wave of emotion that comes from nowhere and hits you like a sucker punch. Death is easy, loss is more difficult.

Bert was not far behind and died a few years later. A blood clot in his leg shot up to his heart and attacked it. It didn't survive the ambush.

My mother had requested that her ashes not be put in the same place as my fathers'. She made it clear that she'd had enough of him in this life and didn't want any potential entanglement in the next. Despite the infinitesimal probability of an afterlife, I honoured her request. Hazel's ashes were sprinkled on the rose garden. Bert's were dumped on the compost heap. We also put a small amount of each in two small brass pots and placed them on either end of the mantelpiece—not too close so as to avoid any ectoplasmic transference.

On Christmas Eve, a year after Bert died, we hosted a party. The stockings were hung on the mantelpiece, the tree ablaze with Christmas cheer, and sugar plums danced in our heads to house music. A few days before, I'd read a news report about Keith Richards in which he claimed to have snorted a line of his father's ashes. I had once dripped liquid LSD into my eye-balls at an after-party, but this was next-level stuff and read like a challenge.

Call me sentimental, but I decided to include my deceased parents in the family celebrations. Veronica and the kids agreed it would be an appropriate demonstration of respect at this special time of the year.

I made two thin lines of MDMA on the mantelpiece and sprinkled my father's ashes onto one line and my mother's on to the other. Careful to avoid any commingling, I snorted one line up my left nostril and the other up my right.

30

For the next few years, Veronica and I regularly attended raves and club nights. The clandestine events were advertised by flyers left at local music stores. Some flyers came in elaborate shapes or high-tech plastic finishes and could range from business-card-size to two-foot-square posters. Generally speaking, if the flyer had high production values there was a good chance the party itself would be of a higher quality. Of course, this was not always true, but the promoter who promised the earth and did not deliver very quickly lost the support of the notoriously ethical-minded raver.

A promoter's reputation was often the deciding factor in the decision to attend an event. Rave promoters survived or perished on their reputations. If the location was too small or overcrowded, if a DJ didn't show up, if the sound or lighting was inadequate, or even if the party got shut down, the promoter was held responsible and ravers would be reluctant to buy tickets to their next event.

The appropriation and re-working of corporate logos was a common pastime with flyer designers. This is another example of rave culture's attitude towards a corporate mentality that puts profits before people.

Like music, logos were sampled and endlessly recycled into something new, a practice known as slamming or byteing. The notion of ownership was challenged in a whimsical way. But although light-hearted, there was a larger political statement being made. These symbols represent the amount of corporate control or influence that a company commanded in the marketplace. The more familiar the logo, the more powerful an influence the company had with its customers. By stealing and reusing these potent symbols, ravers were doing more than merely thumbing their noses at big corporations. They were challenging the power and authority of these mega businesses by showing that they may have less power than they would have us believe. By blatantly flaunting their illegal handiwork in the faces of corporations they perceived to be the antithesis of rave philosophy, ravers were demonstrating that these companies were powerless to stop obvious copyright infringement, influencing a new generation to re-think the concept of absolute corporate control.

And so the flyers led us, beckoned, and bade us to abandoned buildings, industrial areas, blacked-out stores and restaurants, country houses, and embark on wild goose chases up logging roads, deep into the woods. We gathered at pick-up points in parking lots and boarded busses on magical mystery tours to remote locations. These operations were carried out with military precision by an anonymous army of dedicated volunteers.

Essential supplies for a rave included a towel, a change of clothes, chewing gum, a fan (manual or electric) a water bottle, electrolytes, snacks, and blinky lights. The first order of business was to locate the washroom and stash the backpack. Next, ascertain the sweet spot for maximum sound quality. This entailed walking up to the DJ booth and then backing up until a perfectly balanced stereophonic image filled each ear, usually one third of the way to the back of the room. Then it was time to pop an E and let nature take its course. With Veronica by my side, we would remain glued to that spot for the next eight hours, leaving only briefly to take bathroom breaks or replenish water supplies.

These were powerful transpersonal journeys and some of the most meaningful meditation experiences I ever had. Nothing else existed apart from the music and the moment. The fat, velvet, hammered beats vibrated through our bodies like an inner massage while our minds became intensely focussed. We fell in love over and over again.

Synaesthesia is a common phenomenon where the sound of the music translates itself into light and colour. Impossibly complex patterns dance behind your closed eyes. MDMA produces intense feelings of empathy which focus not only on the people around you but on yourself. You feel a sense of deep peace, are energised, buoyant and calm. For some, this is the first time in a long time that they will have felt so positive and connected.

At first, one 125mg capsule was sufficient to see me through the night. But as time went on, I found that by two or three in the morning, the effects wore off. My next strategy was dosing at 10 p.m., then again at 2 a.m. This worked for a while until a third hit was added at 4 a.m. Other experiments included taking threshold doses. This is where a half dose is taken in between full doses to increase the effects, a method employed by doctors with pain medication. There were also trials with double doses and triple doses—not recommended. On a couple of occasions, I did as many as ten hits in a single evening—also not recommended. We live, we learn.

Bottom line is, at some point you have used all of your available serotonin resources. The sacks that contain and secrete this nifty neurotransmitter have been thoroughly wrung out and it takes time to make more, or for the reuptake function to kick in.

One thing that helps guard against serotonin depletion is 5HTP. This supplement is an amino acid and a precursor that your brain converts into serotonin. Our standard practice was to take 100mg of 5HTP the night before an event to bolster serotonin levels and 200mg the following night to replenish depleted stocks. Some people are known to suffer serotonin depletion after MDMA use which can include depression and anxiety. With this method, I never experienced any of these symptoms. In fact, I usually felt fabulous for days after a good rave.

Over the years, Veronica and I also travelled to raves outside the country. For our twentieth anniversary on Valentine's Day, we flew to San Francisco to a party called Love Affair. San Francisco had long been the epicenter of the rave scene in California. The event was held at a warehouse complex in Oakland. It featured world-class DJs, several massive rooms, and fourteen thousand candy ravers.

San Francisco ravers had a particular flair and sartorial style. They were known for wearing 'candy.' These are Technicolor plastic beads strung on elastic and worn as necklaces and bracelets. There appeared to be an implicit competition as to who could wear the most trinkets. Hundreds of candy bracelets were worn, covering the wrist to the shoulder, and a similar number of necklaces hung around necks, like great multi-coloured yokes. Other fashion accoutrement ensembles included giant, oversized bell-bottom pants, enormous mad hatter top hats, animal backpacks and baby pacifiers.

Raves in general are an invitation to dress up. Every event is a theme-less costume party where everyone is encouraged to freely express themselves. At any event you might encounter robots, fairies, steampunks, cartoon characters, tuxedos, Ghostbusters, or even the Easter Bunny.

Another memorable anniversary took us to Montreal for the Bal en Blanc, or White Party, an annual event held at the Montreal Olympic Stadium. Thousands of people dressed in white are illuminated by a barrage of black-light cannons and dance for twelve hours straight to the sounds of the world's best DJs. By 4 a.m. most of the fifteen thousand participants have stripped down to their white underwear and lingerie. It's quite a sight to see a vast sea of undulating undies bobbing about, bombarded by a glowing cloud of ultraviolet light.

As the decade progressed, the events became bigger and bigger. The intimate and spontaneous vibe of underground events was being supplanted by corporate takeovers. Sponsorships by breweries, energy drinks, and even cigarette companies muscled in for a piece of the action. Some of the original promoters burned out and retired. DJs achieved the status of demi-gods and started to charge exorbitant fees. Calvin Harris, a Scottish DJ, made sixty-six million dollars one year. Some DJs were tempted to play with offers of new cars. And as raves gained a higher profile, the police began to take a greater interest. During the early years, the smaller, more discrete events were easier to conceal. The advent of mega raves gave way to a more diverse, inexperienced crowd which led to a lot more irresponsible drug use. GHB or Gamma Hydroxybutyrate began to infiltrate the party and club scene in the mid-nineties and wreaked no small amount of havoc.

In the seventies, GHB was sold as a work-out supplement purporting to build muscle and burn fat. It was popular with body builders who took small amounts at the gym. Some of them soon discovered that taking larger amounts induced a euphoric feeling similar to having a few drinks.

The problem with GHB is that it's extremely dose-specific. Four milliliters can produce a pleasant high; six to eight can cause convulsions and vomiting. The difference of one or two milliliters can be the difference between a good time and a disastrous one. Mixed with alcohol, GHB can cause forced sleep. While not technically a coma, when someone collapses on the dance floor and becomes unresponsive, it amounts to the same thing. You have to be very smart to use a drug as dumb as GHB.

Normally measured carefully in milliliters, it wasn't uncommon to see people on the dance floor swigging GHB out of water bottles. After knocking back a few drinks they were dropping like flies. As GHB is a clear liquid, these water bottles became a minefield of accidental dosing. Most of the ambulances called to events and clubs during the nineties were due to rampant and irresponsible GHB use. Unfortunately, because most folks also had MDMA in their system, many of these incidents were unfairly chalked up to MDMA overdoses. The truth is, there have been remarkably few problems with the use of MDMA.

A survey in 1995 found that, in England, it was estimated that one million doses of MDMA were being consumed every week. This is an extremely large sample group. But even from a group this large, there were only a handful of verifiably negative reports. Most of the problems that have been attributed to MDMA use are due to other causes such as overheating from insufficient ventilation, dehydration due to the unavailability of water, or overdoses of other, more harmful drugs. And while on the subject of harmful drugs, let's not forget society's most available and frequently used drugs, tobacco and alcohol. These two legal drugs are responsible for more deaths than all other illegal drugs combined. Similar figures around the world have confirmed time and again that alcohol is without doubt one of the most dangerous and destructive drugs on the planet. But when was the last time you heard anyone calling for a total ban of alcohol?

The statistics on tobacco are even worse. The World Health Organization now estimates that up to four million people a year die from tobacco-related diseases. Comparing

MDMA to alcohol or tobacco is like throwing Mike Tyson in the ring with Minnie Mouse.

By the beginning of the twenty-first century, our favorite rave promoters were coming to the end of their tenures and began to retire. The events were getting too big, too commercial, and too crazy. They were rife with tom-foolery, skullduggery, and jiggery-pokery.

The best parties had a specific formula which I had been carefully studying during my years of extensive field research. I now decided to apply this formula to promoting my own parties. To that end, I founded an underground rave cult.

31

I named my underground rave cult SPEC and began a four-year adventure in rave promoting.

I'd coined the phrase from my filmmaking days. A spec project was a labour of love with complete editorial control. The idea was to produce small, intimate, non-alcoholic, invite-only events for up to two or three hundred hand-picked participants. The requirement for membership was an unconditional love of progressive house and trance music and a penchant for ecstasy. Members were also required to be certified—by me—as 100 percent cool and groovy. Membership cards were issued and everyone was placed on a group email list which announced the events and gave instructions about location, where to park and who was playing. This forum was also used to educate, inform and indoctrinate. Group emails informed members about responsible drug use, appropriate behavior, and other relevant issues. The net effect was a tight-knit, family group of responsible partiers dedicated to the fine art of raving.

The mandate of the society was to construct and detonate love bombs.

I reached out to the membership for a suitable acronym for SPEC and received an avalanche of exotic appellations, a veritable festival of frivolous nomenclature. Here are a few of the suggestions: The Secret Peoples Ecstasy Club, Soul-Powered Ecstatic Children, The Society for Psyche-delic Exploration and Celebration, Sexy People Experiencing Creativity, The Simply Perfect Energy Club, Secret People Enjoying Confidentiality, Smart People Enjoying Connections, The Self Perpetuating Endorphin Cartel, The Smile Powered Euphonic Cabal, The Sacrilegious Pranksters Eschewing Conformity, Strategic Pantheists of Enduring Charisma, Special Projects Encompassing Coolness, Savvy Proletariats Eating Cake, The Seriously Pushed-Envelope Committee, The Self-Proclaimed Entertainment Czars, The Sudden Pleasure Elevation Contingent, The Superlative Penultimate Epiphany Cavaliers and, one of my personal favorites, The Selective Protective Enchanted Collective.

After careful consideration and much deliberation, I finally settled on: The Society for the Perpetuation of Empathogenic Celebrations. Veronica, my dedicated and perpetual art department, painted a large psychedelic, fluorescent banner to hang behind the DJ booth.

The SPEC Projects were an extraordinary and beautiful experiment. It didn't take long before over two hundred members were signed up and certified - by me - as 100 percent cool and groovy.

Members were allowed two guests for whom they would be wholly responsible. This avoided having to hire security. Every member was responsible for their own security and safety. In over thirty-five events we never had a problem that wasn't dealt with quickly and efficiently by the members themselves.

Members were instructed to park several blocks away and walk to the venue in small groups. A truck was often parked in front of the entrance to obscure any activity from the street. Arrival time was 10 p.m. till midnight, after which the doors were closed and no one else allowed in. This avoided the bar crowd who roamed the city after 1 a.m. like packs of unhinged, drunken hyenas searching for easy prey.

The music we played was exclusively progressive house and trance. This was key to creating a unified musical journey. Although other techno and break beat genres were played at raves, they were generally relegated to secondary or tertiary rooms. For over a decade, the main room at raves was the exclusive domain of progressive house and trance music. Its unique characteristics were perfectly suited to the empathetic effects of MDMA and provided a seamless vehicle for transcendental, transpersonal journeys.

This kind of music was not about entertainment or information. It harboured no ambition to top the pop charts, win prizes, or go platinum. It was not about musicians becoming stars or influencing a mass audience with a particular philosophy, opinion or viewpoint. It did not compete or strive for money or power or status, or any of the other goals and ambitions of most contemporary popular music. It was about spontaneity and change, emancipation and revolution, personal exploration and freedom.

Unlike the egocentric, pain-filled, opinionated voices of pop culture, rave music did not seek to influence or manipulate. It simply created a musical environment designed to free the mind, open the heart and inspire the imagination. More a transportation system than a final destination, the music served solely to provide an environment of irresistible momentum, a musical heart beat that unified and connected the participants. And my Fairy Godfather provided as much high quality ecstasy as needed.

In December 2000, as Bill Gates and Charlie Brown both quit their jobs, The Inaugural Solstice SPEC Project was launched.

It was held in a downtown Mexican restaurant run by a Guatemalan wise-guy named Manuel. The restaurant had been failing for some time and was grinding to a halt. For five-hundred dollars, we were given free rein to run amok.

The front windows were blacked out, lighting and sound installed, and the SPEC banner was ceremoniously hoisted and bombed with black light.

The event was a great success, until the police barged in at 3 a.m. The party was raging as I dealt with three uniformed officers at the door. They asked for my event license. I didn't have one. Insurance? Nope. My pleas for leniency fell on deaf ears. The party was shut down and I was written a violation ticket. They also confiscated my money box from the table at the front door. This was a bridge too far.

The officer placed the stolen box, stuffed with my cash, behind him on a shelf while he proceeded to fill out the ticket. I sidled up beside him pretending to study the content. With my right arm, I reached around his back, retrieved the box from the shelf and wedged it into the back of my pants. I politely accepted the ticket and slowly backed away, fading into a crowd of people who were now leaving the building.

This was the only time a SPEC Project was ever shut down by the police and, although disappointing, I had learned a few valuable lessons. Commercial events required licences and insurance. Private parties with no ticket sales were another matter. The police did show up at other SPEC Projects from time to time but I was always able to placate them and avoid a shut-down. I retired the money box at the door and instead collected cash which I promptly stuffed into my cargo pants. Visiting authorities were told that we were a private, ad hoc group of filmmakers and artists, (partially true) I assured them the events were alcohol free, (mostly true) I told them we had the full permission of the landlords, (sometimes true) I told them the event was over and we were just about to shut it down and go home to bed, (never true) And I explained that the events were strictly drug-free, (a blatant and bold-faced lie.)

In all fairness, the police were generally amicable and reasonable. Usually, by the time they got around to noise complaints, it was after 3 a.m. and they had just finished dealing with the bars and clubs emptying out downtown. After battling hoards of belligerent and drunken louts trying to kill each other in the streets, it was a breath of fresh air to arrive at a rave where everyone was polite and respectful. The police were routinely greeted with beaming smiles and friendly handshakes.

The Valentine's Day SPEC Project in 2001 was held in an industrial building, legally zoned for eight people. There was only one washroom so we set up five-gallon plastic buckets behind screens in a back corridor. The fire exit was covered with a large mattress to muffle the sound. At 4 a.m., five uniformed police officers marched in and pushed their way through a crowd of two-hundred ecstatic ravers. Four of them wandered off to inspect the premises while I stood at the back of the room chatting with a sergeant who introduced himself as Colin.

The party carried on around us as I gave him the usual spiel. No alcohol, no underage kids, private party, responsible adults etc. I told him that we didn't want to party with the drunks downtown. He could relate and nodded sympathetically. He asked me if anyone was on ecstasy. I told him that we had a zero-drugs policy but there were likely a couple of people breaking the rule. Luckily, he failed to notice my pupils, which after three hits of E, were the size of saucers.

He then said something surprising for a police sergeant. He said that everyone seemed well-behaved, there was no alcohol, and that if people wanted to do E, it was their business and no concern of his. I shook his hand and said, "Colin. You're a cool guy."

Just then, the other officers gathered around and began

debating whether or not to shut down the party. They took a vote. It was two for and two against. Colin cast the deciding vote and we danced till dawn.

The SPEC Projects were unique in that they were not purely commercial ventures. Although I did make a little money on the events, and even more on sales of MDMA, we were united in a common purpose. As the events continued on a monthly basis, the group became more and more unified. Everyone became close friends. We became one big, wonderful, outrageous family.

Our door policies were also a little different to most events. If someone arrived unable to pay the twenty-dollar entrance fee, I asked for ten. If they didn't have any money, I'd ask if they could borrow some. If that wasn't possible, I'd let them in for free and give them a free hit of E.

We instituted a program called The Broke Ass Ravers Fund, or B.A.R.F. Members could apply, plead poverty, and get a free pass. There was also a policy of free tickets and E for single mothers or fathers, or anyone else with even a half-assed story.

Occasionally I was criticized for being an elitist due to our members-only policy, but this was the secret of our success. Generally our screening process worked well, but we did get the occasional gate crasher.

During one SPEC project, after the doors had been sealed, someone climbed over a barbed-wire fence and gained access. I was called to the door and confronted by a dishevelled drunk with a bottle of whiskey in one hand and a nasty wound on the other. He had cut his hand on the barbed-wire and was dripping blood all over the floor. We cleaned up his wound and told him he could come in if he surrendered his whiskey and traded his tipple for a free hit of MDMA. He agreed and joined the party.

His shock of red hair and love of rugby earned him the

name of Red Rugger. Obviously a novice to the rave scene, he looked on in amazement at the spectacle unfolding before him. At first a little reticent, he soon warmed up and began to gently sway to the music. An hour later, as the E kicked in, he was smiling and dancing and making a lot of new friends.

As the love bomb fully detonated, he was swept away on a wave of euphoria. For the first time in a long time, his defenses melted away. Afterwards, he told me this had been the first time in his life he had felt a sense of belonging to a family. The transformation was remarkable and one that I witnessed repeatedly over the SPEC years.

From then on, Red Rugger was the first to arrive for set-up and the last person to leave in the morning after clean-up.

32

I had an opportunity to study DJ culture during the SPEC years. They are a curious and enigmatic breed. They share an obsessive compulsion to play records anywhere, at any time, and at any cost. They are driven to do this for reasons known only to themselves. It's probably something to do with dopamine receptors. Given half a chance, they would stand behind the decks for four or six or twelve hours straight, refusing to budge. Even when driven to exhaustion, they would beg to spin one more track. With only one DJ in the house, their obsessive compulsion was an asset, but when several DJs were hovering around the decks eager to spin, things got tense.

At all my events, I had a large clock in the DJ booth with written instructions on what time to start and finish each set. This avoided a lot of unpleasantries. Without clear instructions, a DJ would assume they could play indefinitely. I also made a point of telling them what to play. My aim was to create a seamless musical journey throughout the night, building in intensity, reaching a final climax. I had a specific goal for each set with exact requirements for beats-per-minute and genre.

For a party with four, two-hour sets, it went something like this: begin the first set with tribal or deep house at about 124bpms, progress through the set to harder house finishing up at 128bpms. Start the second set a tad louder with progressive house and ease up to 130bpms. For the third set, the volume increases, we move to progressive trance, and creep up the beats per minute to 134. The last set depended on the mood of the crowd. If they were pumped and jumping, we proceeded to some hard trance or psy-trance and finished up at 138bpms. If the troops were flagging, we finished with some deeper melodic tracks and brought it back down to 128bpms. This was a formula that worked consistently. But it only took one DJ going rogue to upset the plan.

Most of the time DJs were compliant, but occasionally they would nod and smile, agree to the plan, assure you they understood and were in full compliance, and then go ahead and play whatever they wanted. There is nothing more disruptive to a musical flow than a DJ with a mind of their own.

And there seems to be some confusion as to exactly what a DJ does. There are many misguided fans who believe DJs are creating music as they go, adding every sound and effect. They describe their favorite DJs as musical geniuses. I'll let you in on a little secret: most DJs play tracks and beat-match. This means synchronising the speed of the tracks, fading one track out, and another in. It's a skill that can be learned after a few hours of practice. Anyone can do it. These days, more often than not, it's an automatic function on a laptop. All that knob twiddling is mostly just for show.

Adjusting the EQ is unnecessary as the track has already been mixed and mastered, at great expence, in a professional studio. Of course, the best DJs are also musicians who write their own tracks. But being a musician is not a prerequisite for being a DJ. A musician is someone who composes music, or is proficient on a musical instrument. MP3s, turntables and CDJs are not musical instruments, and playing a Beatles record does not make you a Beatle. DJs are more akin to a master of ceremonies with musical taste.

DJs know two things: louder and faster. This is why strict limits had to be imposed on speed and volume. At most of my events, I was forced to adjust both at least a couple of times per set. Left unchecked, the music became progressively louder and faster until it was either impossible to dance to, or damaged everyone's ear drums.

The DJs greatest skill is track selection. Here's the thing: if a DJ plays music you like, he's a good DJ. If he plays music you don't like, he's a bad DJ.

33

By the end of the nineties, it seemed to me that rave culture was an important cultural movement with a lot to offer. Although it drew much of its allure from its underground status, I became frustrated that the only reporting on the subject was negative. Reports of drug-crazed reprobates, overdoses, madness, and mischief filled the news. MDMA was demonised and blamed unfairly for deaths from other causes. It was widely touted as a dangerous and toxic drug. This was far removed from my own experience, which had been entirely positive. I felt compelled to set the record straight.

I teamed up with my associates at Scarlet Sky Productions and we put together a pitch for a documentary about rave culture. We approached the CBC, the National Film Board, BC Film, Telefilm Canada, and a number of distributors. They all said no thanks, and don't bother applying again.

Undeterred, I decided to write a book instead. It took a year to write and another year to publish. I called it, *Rave Culture; an Insider's Overview; a primer for the global rave phenomenon*. Veronica provided the many illustrations, collages and paintings. On the front cover, she created an irreverent but beautiful collage depicting the Dalai Lama as a DJ.

I did a number of radio and print interviews to promote the book and was labeled a rave guru on more than one occasion. I quite liked the sound of that.

Most rave promoters at the time towed a strict party-line which avoided any recognition of drug use. They maintained that the use of drugs at raves had been overstated and their events were strictly drug free. They claimed that people were getting high on music alone. My book was unapologetic on the subject. Rave culture could not have happened without MDMA. It was essential to the rave experience. I made more than one interviewer nervous with my full-throated endorsement of psychedelics.

In one on-camera interview with a local TV station, I wore a ball cap pulled down over my ears and a pair of oversized yellow sun-glasses as a disguise. At one point, I stated that no one had ever died from taking one hit of ecstasy. Months later, a venue which had hosted many raves in the past received some complaints and was under review. The local promoters involved were required to attend an information meeting by the Royal Canadian Mounted Police, and I was invited to attend. The RCMP arrived on foot and opened the meeting by screening an educational video on the dangers of ecstasy use. The first thing to appear on the screen was a clip from my previous TV interview. It was a shot of me, pointing directly into the camera saying emphatically, "No one ever died from taking one hit of ecstasy." Luckily, my disguise held up. Not one of the four police officers present recognised me.

Due to the success of my book, I became known as a local expert on the subject of raves. There was a local, city bylaw stating that no public event could go past 2 a.m. It was being employed by the police to shut down numerous events. I decided to take our case to City Hall.

I scheduled a presentation to the mayor and city council and assembled a crew of experts and concerned citizens. We made three requests: rescind the 2 a.m. bylaw, create a permit for all-night dance parties, and issue a new class of business license to cover all-night, non-alcoholic dance clubs.

Municipal politics are the epicenter of grass-roots democracy, the point of contact for the general public to lobby local government, a bastion of the supreme and sacred power vested in the individual to be represented by their elected officials. As we waited for our curtain call, I found myself humming a few bars of John Lennon's *Power to the People*. After a short time, we were ushered into the main council chamber to exercise our democratic rights and issue our demands.

The mayor and city councilors lined up behind their benches like jurors at the Last Supper. They were sincere, earnest, community-minded folks, but what could loosely, but not inaccurately, be referred to as straight, as in, straight and narrow, straight-laced, straight lined, straight up, straight jacketed and straight down the middle of the road. They were well-intentioned folks who lived behind a public persona, rarely giving free rein to their authentic selves. They looked tired, bound by duty and procedure, bogged down by bureaucracy, compromised and compartmentalized, filed and rubberstamped.

The mayor, a tough-minded businessman, sat in the middle of a large semi-circular table flanked by three councilors on either side. These were people you don't want to be around on acid.

The conference room was lined with highly polished wood paneling which shone like dark mirrors and smelled like lemony-fresh turpentine. The windows were hermetically sealed to prevent contamination from the unfiltered air outside.

The meeting began and we made our case. We had a promoter make the argument that events could be both safe and responsible. An owner of an equipment rental business pleaded that raves were a necessary and significant percentage of his business. A member of a local DanceSafe group outlined the implications of harm reduction versus prohibition. A university professor, and the oldest member of SPEC at 73, made the argument that rave culture had legitimate ancient roots in neo-paganistic, tribal rituals. And I provided an impassioned, expert testimonial as to the historical and social importance of the movement.

A number of supporters from the rave community had also turned out to show solidarity, adding more than a splash of colour to the monochromatic proceedings. The last two rows of wooden benches at the back of the room were lined with ravers sporting a variety of multi-coloured clothing, frenetic hairdos, and a veritable rainbow of beads, bangles and piercings. The group resembled an alien delegation from planet Psychedelia.

To their credit, the mayor and city councilors were receptive and listened attentively to our concerns. Several weeks later, we were informed that all three of our requests had been approved. Democracy and reason had won the day.

The Ancient Greeks would have been delighted.

34

Veronica and I smoked dope openly around the house. We hid nothing from our kids. If we thought what we were doing was wrong, we wouldn't have done it.

When they were old enough to ask questions, we gave them direct and honest answers. Nolan was thirteen and Donovan fifteen when they became curious as to what we were smoking. We offered a frank explanation. We told them we smoked pot to relax, to heighten our senses, to change our minds, to make ordinary experiences less ordinary, and to make other people more interesting. We explained the long history and social context of cannabis use and the complex web of intrigue surrounding its illegality. At school they were getting a different story.

They were told to "just say no." They were told that marijuana made people fat and lazy. We were neither. They were told that pot would turn them into hopeless heroin addicts. It didn't. Our arguments were so convincing, they decided they'd like to try some, so we rolled up a joint and smoked it together. It was a positive experience for all of us. We laughed and joked and all had a jolly good time. We came to the decision that, like most teenagers, they would be experimenting with booze and drugs anyway and we'd prefer they did it with us rather than sneak around in back-alleys buying who knows what from who knows who. Not long after, we took them to their first rave.

Donovan and Nolan are only twenty-two months apart

in age and this led to some sibling rivalry. As teenagers, they squabbled and argued constantly, both claiming superiority in the pecking order. The conflict subsided somewhat after we smoked dope together. But when we did E together as a family, it transformed their relationship in a single night. They instantly became best friends. This is why MDMA has been so successfully used in relationship counseling. It amplifies feelings of empathy and connection. It was a wonderful experience to be in the middle of the dance floor in a family group-hug with our kids openly professing their love for us, and each other. In terms of family values, it doesn't get any better than that. We raved as a family regularly for the next few years and Donovan and Nolan ended up running the juice and snack bar at most of the SPEC Projects. One morning, while tending my grow room, there was a knock at the front door. A uniformed police officer informed us that Donovan had been caught selling mushrooms at his high school. I acted shocked. How could this have happened? The officer explained the seriousness of the offence. I agreed wholeheartedly. Something had to be done. We needed to nip this in the bud. We both decided it would be better handled outside the judicial system and I assured the officer I did not take the matter lightly. I was horrified that any son of mine would engage in such a heinous act. What next? Heroin? Crack? I promised to give him a good talking to and was confident I could deter him from a life of addiction and crime. The officer seemed impressed that the matter was well in hand and buzzed off. That night I smoked a joint with Donovan and told him to be more careful in the future.

During Nolan's and Donovan's teen years, our house became a social hub for our kids and all their friends, and their friends and girlfriends, and the girlfriend's girlfriends, and the boyfriends of girlfriends, and their friends, etc. For many years we fostered a thriving subculture of raging teenage brains trying to figure out who they were. Many of them grew up at our house. They saw it as a safe harbour, a place where they could be themselves. We made great vats of food and most evenings, entertained a multitude of extra dinner guests. We talked about love and death, politics and sex, and the meaning of life. Today, we babysit their kids.

Many of them had tenuous or strained relationships with their parents. Some were branded as problem kids, rebellious and non-conforming. I could relate. Truth is, most of them were smart, creative, intelligent people trying to make sense of this topsy-turvy, cockamamie world. Something else I could relate too.

At heart, they were good kids with a lot to offer but tragically, their parents had become estranged. The more they tried to express and explore their independence, the more control their parents applied, which resulted in total rejection. It's a mistake a lot of parents make. With the best intentions, a parent's impulse is to lay down the law and maintain control at all cost, believing it best for the child. It's an appropriate strategy up until twelve or thirteen. After that, it creates a war that can never be won.

In those critical teen years, rather than exercising more control and judgement, energies are better directed into creating trust and a sense of worth. At some point, you have to redefine your role. You have to stop being a parent. You can be a confidant, a mentor, an advisor, or a trusted friend, but you cannot maintain or exercise the authority you once had as a parent. You've had your chance. It's now time to step back and see what kind of parent you've been.

To gain trust and respect, you first have to give it. Responsibility cannot be dictated. It must be given unconditionally. It's a sad fact that, even as adults, most parents have no idea who their kids are.

From very early, I hammered home to our kids that we are all autonomous human beings with the power to make decisions about our own lives, that we always have the power to change our minds and therefore change our behaviour. Too often, we think of addiction and destructive behaviour as being out of our control. We are hopeless victims of forces beyond our sovereignty. But to change the world you must first change your mind. If we teach kids from grade one that they always have the power to change their minds, we might find ourselves living in a different world.

Donovan and Nolan are now pushing forty. Donovan became a Vipassana meditation teacher and a world class athlete. During his party years, he dabbled in just about everything but never had any issues. For the past fifteen years, he has chosen to lead a 100 percent sober life. Nolan remains a bon-vivant and still enjoys a good party, but is productive, hard-working and well-liked. He has yet to end up a hopeless addict up an alley.

Instead of teaching kids that drugs are radioactive and to be avoided at all costs, we should be giving them good information about how to use them safely and responsibly. We should teach them how to differentiate between use and abuse, how to be smart people doing smart drugs.

The 'scared straight' school of drug education is ineffectual and out-dated. It's astounding that after a half century of psychedelic investigation, the average cop on the street still doesn't know the difference between a magic mushroom and a flap of crack.

35

Despite the fact I have never sold cocaine, I am all too aware of its prevalence.

Cocaine falls squarely into the dumb drug category. That's not to say that everyone who dabbles in it is dumb, although with prolonged use, they come perilously closer to falling into that category. Apart from being highly addictive, the business of coke is rotten to its core.

Coca farms in South America are run by subsistence farmers who are exploited by cartels made up of heartless criminals. The farmers live in abject poverty, unable to feed their families, while producing one of the most profitable commodities in the world. The middle men who buy the raw cocaine from the farmers are bullied and threatened by distributors above them. The business is powered by fear and intimidation. The whole chain of command is a tangled, malignant web of violent hoodlums and malfeasance. With each step on the road to the final user, the product is diluted and adulterated to increase profits. It's a rip-off from start to finish.

Year after year, Mexican cartels battle for supremacy of the market, causing an all-out war on the US border. According to the Mexican government, between 2007 and 2014, more than 164,000 people were murdered by warring cartels—more than the wars in Afghanistan and Iraq combined during the same period. You might wonder how many people died for that ounce of coke you just purchased.

Coke's forte is lighting up the reward pathways of the brain. For those with the right brain chemistry, it gives a short-lived, euphoric lift and an increased sense of confidence. But the effect is fleeting and requires constant top-ups to maintain a buzz. And the inflated confidence is wholly subjective. If you've ever been cornered by a coke-head at a party, you'll know what I mean.

With increased consumption, the user becomes more edgy and aggressive. This happens at the same rate they lose the ability to perceive themselves objectively. Subjectively, they are intellectual giants, thrilling the crowd with their witty repartee and rapier wit. Objectively, they are boorish nitwits, repeating themselves endlessly, hammering home the same inane point. Coke is a real vibe killer at a rave and stands in stark contrast to a room full of people on MDMA.

I'm probably fortunate that I don't have compatible brain chemistry for cocaine. If it made me feel fabulous, I'd probably have done a lot more of it. As it is, the very few times I have indulged were less than enjoyable. It makes me instantly tired and gives me a headache.

Not so with lab rats. Given the opportunity, rats will press the cocaine button until it kills them. With LSD, they press it once and never again.

36

After fifteen years of growing pot in the basement, I retired my grow room.

Maintaining a grow room became a chore needing constant attention, plus I discovered I could make more money buying pounds from other growers and then selling ounces. I also expanded my product line to include LSD, mushrooms, DMT and, of course, MDMA. This meant more money, a lot more money.

Financial freedom is a beautiful thing. Don't listen to that old adage about money being the root of all evil. Don't believe that money is dirty or filthy. Believe this instead: money buys you freedom, freedom from debt, freedom to travel, freedom to eat out in restaurants, freedom to take your friends on vacation, freedom from reading price tags in grocery stores, freedom to set your own schedule and chart your own course.

Money also buys you time, the most precious of all commodities. Time to pursue creative projects, time to learn new skills, time to parent your kids, time to think, and time to dream. It buys you access to nutritious foods, and a gym membership, and a healthy lifestyle. It creates opportunities and possibilities and, most importantly, peace of mind. It may not buy you love, but it can go a long way to increase your desirability, creating more favourable conditions for a successful relationship. As someone's Jewish grandmother once said, "It's as easy to fall in love with a rich one."

Veronica and I also had the financial freedom and time to pursue our artistic interests. Veronica continued to paint, exhibit and sell her work. She also continued to expand her box of therapeutic tools by studying new counseling techniques and methods. Friends could drop by for an ounce of pot and a hypnotherapy session.

In the constant enterprise of keeping myself amused, I combined my filmmaking and song-writing skills and made twenty-eight music videos of my original compositions. You can find them on my YouTube channel. Just dial up Jimi Fritz.

As the money continued to pile up, it created a storage problem. I spent the twenties and stored fifties and hundreds in bundles of a thousand. You can fit about thirty grand in a gallon paint can.

On one occasion, to accommodate the surplus cash, I turned to bird houses. I installed four wooden bird boxes around the back garden and stuffed them with cash wrapped in freezer bags. You can get about twenty-five grand in a bird house.

This created two problems. One: no matter how well-sealed, moisture eventually seeps in and can damage the bills. Half-way through the winter, I checked the boxes and found the plastic bags had begun to deteriorate. The corners had become damp and mouldy. I had to remove and renovate them one by one, bill by bill. And two: it confused the hell out of the birds, who relentlessly tried to set up home in the boxes. It was sad to watch them desperately trying to peck their way into a blocked hole.

Drug dealing is like any other retail business. There's a supply chain to maintain, quality to control, public relations, packaging, pricing, etc. And, as with all businesses, customer satisfaction is paramount. This last point is why I retained such a loyal and enthusiastic following for so long.

I always strived to have the highest quality product and my customers came to rely on, and trust my judgment. My no-questions-asked, full money-back guarantee went a long way towards earning their confidence. Superior quality and competitive pricing also helped. But my forte was creating a climate of normality.

Buying drugs can be a nerve-racking affair. Is the price fair? Is it cut? Is it the correct weight? Am I about to get busted? To me, selling these substances was no more controversial than selling condiments. I facilitated and maintained a casual atmosphere, putting my clients at ease. I rarely ever counted the money they gave me. Trust is reciprocal: if you give it, you get it. Also, I thought it likely that the money they handed me had already been double checked. We are far more concerned about the money we spend, than the money we receive.

There was another little trick I played on my customers to elicit trust. I slightly over-weighed everything I sold. My expectation was that my clients accepted the stated weight, but if they did check later, they were pleasantly surprised.

The ethical dealer is in a very different situation to those who deal dumb drugs. If your customers are meth-heads, speed-freaks, coke-fiends or junkies, your life will be a series of bitter disappointments. Turmoil and trouble will be lurking around every corner. This is what's known as the sketch factor. Sketchy people do sketchy drugs and lead sketchy lives. It was a world with which I had no contact and was blissfully unaware. With psychedelics, you get a different class of clientele. They are independent, free-thinking adults who use drugs responsibly and safely, people who enjoy a better life through chemistry, and people you don't see getting taken away in ambulances on the evening news.

Consequently, I never sold dumb drugs or had to deal with sketchy people. If I suspected anyone was abusing a substance—and this is extremely rare with psychedelics—I recommended counseling, wished them well, and promptly dropped them from the roster. The same was true of anyone with mental issues.

Strangely, people who are bi-polar and/or have psychotic tendencies are often hopelessly attracted to LSD and amphetamines. I've seen this repeatedly over the years and often questioned them about it. They claim their anti-psychotic medications turn them into zombies and the only time they feel truly alive is when they're in, or near psychosis. Like moths to a flame, they are drawn to psychoactives which put them into a kind of controlled psychosis. I'll leave it to psychiatrists to figure that one out. In my opinion, anyone with psychotic tendencies should stay well away from psychedelics.

My clientele included doctors, military personnel, teachers, therapists, lawyers, government workers, and professionals of all stripes. People who are held up as respected pillars of the community and considered to be the bedrock of a civilised society.

Consider this: your doctor may be toking on a big fat doobie at the weekends while your MP is hiking in the woods on magic mushrooms. Your trusted therapist might be a closet raver who dances the night away on ecstasy. And that dedicated and beloved primary school teacher with the cheerful disposition, may well be micro-dosing acid.

37

No matter how many photos or videos or documentaries you may have seen about Burning Man, nothing will prepare you for the onslaught of the actual event. It is incomparable to any other festival on the planet.

Its uniqueness comes from the fact that it's entirely created by the participants and is located in the vast and inhospitable Black Rock Desert in Nevada. The only respite from the unbearable heat is the frequent, blinding dust storms. It's like partying on the surface of Venus.

The Burning Man organization provides the basic infrastructure and the attendees bring themed camps and art projects. The scope and scale of the event is truly awe-inspiring. 'Burners' are a unique amalgamation of techno-hippy, steampunk, and thrill-seeking yahoo. They are wildly creative, self-directed, unconventional pranksters with a fierce sense of independence. And like me, they love a good party.

Veronica and I became ensconced in the Burning Man community and went to the event for the first time in 2005, the year Charles married Camilla, and another Pope kicked the holy bucket—strengthening the exceedingly unlikely possibility that a just god exists.

We were invited to join an established theme camp called Slacktoria. Their interactive offering was to invite people over to watch them eat. We rented an RV and packed it with costumes and food and too much stuff. From Vancouver to Nevada it's a three-day drive. Along the way, we picked up our good friend and SPEC aficionado, Rush-the-Fish-Stick.

Like a good boy scout, I wanted to be prepared, so I planned to smuggle in a stash of psychedelics to distribute at the event. With its many nooks and crannies, an RV is a perfect smuggling vehicle. The US Canadian border is so busy, it's impossible to search every vehicle. I decided to roll the dice.

I took a couple of hundred hits of MDMA, a hundred hits of acid, various other bits and bobs, and packed them all into tennis balls. These are a common item with burners who use metal rebar to peg down tents in the high winds. The exposed ends of rebar can be treacherous and placing tennis balls on the tips makes them visible and harmless. With a utility knife, I cut open the balls along the seams, stuffed them with the contraband and carefully glued them back together. These balls were placed at the bottom of a bag and covered with twenty more empty balls. The bag was then buried under half a ton of baggage in the luggage compartment. It would have taken several hours to sort through, and there are 30,000 cars a day to process. Unlike the casinos in Nevada, the odds were in my favour.

At the border, a customs officer who was a ringer for Burt Reynolds' younger brother, asked a few perfunctory questions. I smiled sweetly and told him we were going to Las Vegas to roll some dice. He waved us through and we headed for the Black Rock Desert.

We spent our first day setting up our camp and then ventured out on to the Playa for the first time. The Playa is an open area, one kilometer across, at the center of Burning Man. 'The Man' is a huge wooden structure that stands at the center of this circle and is surrounded by art projects. These can range from hundred-foot-tall sculptures to elaborate, interactive environments. Hundreds of art cars weave through the installations. Some are as big as two double decker buses. The vehicles are created to look like galleons and insects and space ships and prehistoric beasts. Many of these mutant vehicles contain dance floors and bars and huge sound systems.

At night, the Playa is a fantastical explosion of light and colour. Propane burners shoot flames into the sky and random explosions punctuate the night. Sixteen hundred theme camps surround the Playa in a maze of streets that cover seven square miles. The streets are organized into neighbourhoods. Some feature yoga camps and meditation centers. There are designated areas for sound camps and restaurants and bars. There are coffee camps and even tea camps. Don't get your hopes up, even camps that profess to specialise in tea-making lack the most rudimentary skills.

There's a Red Light district with orgy camps and cunnilingus competitions. At Camp Kwiki-Lube you can get a hand job from a San Francisco leather boy. Burning Man is famous for being a money-free, gifting society. Everything is free. Free food, free drinks, free shows, and free hand-jobs.

That first year was an eye opener and a mind blower. We spend the first couple of nights walking around with our chins on our chests. On the Thursday night we organized an art walk. Sixteen of us dropped acid and ventured out onto the Playa.

Rush-the-Fish-Stick was sporting a skin-tight, lime-green onesie. I wore my custom-made top hat festooned with a hundred flashing lights. Veronica was covered head to toe in gold lame. The Playa was a whirlwind wonderland of twinkling lights. Our senses were amplified and overloaded as we toured the art installations, each more awe-inspiring than the last.

As the sun came up, we found ourselves in a disco camp with a stripper pole. Rush-the-Fish-Stick took to the stage, wrapped himself around the pole and gave us a show. He invented half a dozen heretofore undiscovered dance moves that night and we watched in rapt attention as he gyrated his lithe, green body around the pole like a rubber lizard. Shafts of morning light streamed into the tent leaving lime-green trails in its wake.

It's hard to give justice to these kinds of experiences. They defy the limitations of our usually discursive minds. Our descriptive and analytical powers fail against the enormity of these psychedelic expeditions. Suffice to say, 'twas a night to remember.

Peak experiences are what define our lives. What we take to the grave. It's why we line up for a Ferris wheel or a roller coaster. It's why we travel, and why we do psychedelics. Looking back on your life, you will not remember all the days you went to work, or to the grocery store, or renovated your basement. You will remember the times you spent connecting with close friends and family. Your memory will favour extraordinary and novel experiences which inspired or motivated. Any psychologist will confirm that this kind of social interaction and connection is essential to human flourishing and critical for mental health. The notion that getting high and partying is somehow frivolous and superficial is a false one. On the contrary, it may be one of the most important and significant activities we engage in. It is turbo-charged social cohesion.

The sense of belonging to a community or family, to be accepted for who we are, and to feel solidarity within a group is the cornerstone of psychological health. Behind every trauma lies a fractured, dysfunctional family or broken social connections.

While making the documentary, *Theatre Behind Bars*, we followed the inmates in a federal prison for eight months while they staged a theatre production. During our many interviews with the prisoners, it became apparent they all had the same story. Without exception, they came from broken homes with addicted, alcoholic or absent parents. It's no wonder they lost their way. They never stood a chance.

So, in the pursuit of psychological health and mental stability, we went back to Burning Man the following year. This time we took our own theme camp.

After several years of lying dormant, The Society for the Perpetuation of Empathogenic Celebrations was resurrected. SPEC camp offered a gin and tonic chill-out lounge with free LSD. This proved to be quite popular. Rush-the-Fish-Stick and I had full-sized cardboard cut-outs made of ourselves and we served behind the bar dressed to match our flattened doppelgangers.

The most impressive of all the many soundstages at Burning Man is Opulent Temple. Run by a non-profit from San Francisco, it features a colossal sound system with DJ-controlled flame-thrower effects. A multi-level scaffolding structure at the back of the dance floor provides an excellent vantage point to dance and watch the show.

Rush-the-Fish-Stick and I climbed up the scaffolding one night and got a ring side seat for back-to-back sets from Christopher Lawrence and Infected Mushroom. I hadn't done any MDMA for about eighteen months. The energising rush of euphoria I had once reliably experienced had all but disappeared. My serotonin sacks had packed their bags and hit the road.

The reason MDMA is not often associated with addiction or abuse issues is that with increased use comes diminishing returns. Once your serotonin sacks have been thoroughly exhausted, the beneficial effects subside and the less desirable side-effects like overheating, eye-wiggle and jaw clenching increase. You can end up a sweaty mess with a twisted grimace and twitching eye balls.

Given the extraordinary location and circumstances, I decided it was time to try an MDMA refresher course. Rush-the-Fish-Stick and I double-dropped and waited for take-off.

About forty minutes into Christopher Lawrence's set, I began to feel the old magic coursing through my veins. An old friend had come back to visit. My serotonin sacks were back, unpacking their bags, and making themselves at home.

Periodically, the DJ pulled down on a lever above his head and shot giant flames over the dance floor. Like a bolt of lightning, the whole area was illuminated, revealing eight-hundred Burners in full regalia. Before Christopher Lawrence had finished his set, I had mastered the art of levitation. By the time Infected Mushroom started their set, I had ascended into something akin to a secular version of The Rapture. Just then, Rush-the-Fish-Stick tapped me on the shoulder and pointed across the Playa behind us. Like a scene from *Blade Runner*, the landscape was lit up with puffs of fire and smoke belching into the air. It was the Hajj on acid.

One of the art installations, a hundred and fifty-foot tall wooden tower in the shape of an oil derrick, stood on the far side of the Playa. We watched in disbelief as it blew up in a giant mushroom cloud. The explosion rose into the air, sucking up the smoke beneath it in what looked like stock footage from Hiroshima. Apparently, the world record for the biggest propane explosion had just been broken.

Talk about a peak experience.

The weather at Burning Man can be problematic. Violent dust storms can rear up at any time. The first year we went was relatively mild, with only three or four blow-ups lasting a couple of hours. This can be fun. You strap on your goggles, pull up a bandana, grit your teeth, and party on in defiant celebration. The second year was different. The windy conditions threw up one storm after another, some lasting eight or nine hours. Fine playa dust, the consistency of talcum powder, permeated every nook and cranny and was impossible to escape. The day we arrived, we spent all day building our camp into a thing of beauty. The second day, we spent watching every piece of it mashed and smashed and thrown into the air like crumpled paper.

As the Burners like to joke, "It was better next year."

Later in the week, Veronica and I heard that Alexander 'Sasha' Shulgin and his wife Ann were scheduled to give a talk. We arrived early to get good seats. Poised and dignified, the Shulgins held court like tribal elders and emphasised the importance and potential of psychedelic research. Like Leary and others before them, they truly believed in the power of psychedelics to alter human psychology and change behaviour. As Stanislav Grof, the eminent Czech psychiatrist and founder of transpersonal psychology put it, "Psychedelics are to psychiatry what the microscope is for biology or the telescope is for astronomy."

After the Shulgin's talk, I lined up with many others to meet the great man. I shook his hand, thanked him for his pioneering work, and gave him a copy of my book on rave culture. He smiled and thanked me but looked tired. He'd been harassed by the police who had recently raided his lab. The authorities continued to pester him for some time, eventually fining him twenty-five thousand dollars before closing down his lab. A few years later, at the age of eighty-nine, he died of liver cancer.

At the same event, I ran into Rick Doblin, executive director of The Multidisciplinary Association for Psychedelic Studies. He also got a copy of my book. More on Rick and MAPS later.

Following a three-year hiatus, which is how long it took to clean the dust out of our kit, we returned to Burning Man for the third time. Once again, we prepared our gin-and tonic LSD chill-out lounge, loaded up the RV, and headed back to Black Rock City for the last time. This time, we hid our illicit booty in the freezer, concealed in the center of a frozen vegetable curry.

2011 was the twenty-fifth anniversary of Burning Man. There were seventeen hundred theme camps, the most ever. And it was the first year it had ever sold out. There were more fire features and art installations than ever before, and the weather was perfect for the whole week, another first.

The Man is a beautifully constructed wooden effigy that stands at the geographical and psychological center of Burning Man. It burns on the Saturday night and is the highlight of the event. Sixty-five thousand people and hundreds of art cars gather around in a great circle. Hundreds of fire dancers perform around the base of the man which is then ignited with a propane fire bomb. The crowd goes wild as The Man burns and then collapses into a fiery heap. The proceedings culminate with hordes of naked bodies dancing wildly around the burning embers of The Man. As self-created pagan rituals go, this is a good one. The meaning is intentionally left open for everyone to interpret as they wish. For many, it's a statement about the impermanence of all material things.

Sunday night, on the last day of the week-long event, is reserved for the more sombre and serious Temple Burn. The Temple is a massive, elaborate structure that takes all year to design and build. During the week, obituaries and memorials are posted and painted on the walls commemorating fallen comrades and loved-ones. I posted a eulogy to a DJ friend of mine who had recently committed suicide. Rush-the-Fish-Stick printed a touching tribute to his recently-deceased and much-beloved 1984 Toyota Tercel.

On the afternoon before the final burn, Rush-the-Fish-

Stick and I took our cardboard cut-outs to the temple and installed them on a second-floor balcony. That night, as the temple and our cardboard clones burned in front of sixty-five thousand Burners, a reverent silence hushed the crowd. Smoke billowed into a vast, starlit desert sky, and Rush-the-Fish-Stick shed a tear for his dearly departed Tercedes.

38

N,N-Dimethyltryptamine, or DMT, is the most powerful psychedelic known to man. It has the ability to instantly catapult you at light speed into a geometric universe, producing visions that are truly breathtaking. DMT is not a party drug and should be treated with the utmost respect.

Until recently, DMT traditionally came in the form of an orange-coloured crystal which is smoked in a pipe. If you eat the powder, it does nothing. This is due to monoamine oxidase inhibitors, also called MAO inhibitors, or MAOIs, which block the actions of monoamine oxidase enzymes, rendering the DMT useless. To experience its psychotropic effects it must be burnt on a benign herbal mixture, usually garden herbs or pot leaves. This can be messy and problematic, making it difficult to regulate the dosage. It also tastes like burning plastic.

Smoking DMT is a fleeting experience. Onset is rapid and the whole trip is over in a few minutes. It happens so fast and is so disorienting that the benefits can be elusive. To slow down the effects and make it more ingestible, it is sometimes mixed with harmaline, which is a reversible inhibitor of monoamine oxidase.

Harmaline inhibits the enzyme breakdown and allows the drug to be absorbed into the blood stream and travel to the brain. Ayahuasca is a blend of two plants: one contains DMT and the other harmaline. In the right balance, it produces a long, slow DMT trip lasting several hours. Like any psychedelic, if used properly, this can be both rewarding and therapeutic.

Ayahuasca has been used by indigenous people of the Amazon basin for a thousand years in religious ceremonies. It is not surprising that the pre-scientific minds of South American shamans explained this powerful and mysterious experience in supernatural and mystical terms. All of our early attempts to understand the natural world involved supernatural explanations. It was the best we could do at the time. As human beings, we have a tendency to ascribe agency to natural phenomenon we don't fully understand. The sun comes up and goes down so there must be a sun god. The wind blows so there must be a wind god. Thunder? No problem. It's probably Thor with his red cape and mighty hammer.

In the absence of a reasonable explanation, we tend to make stuff up. This is the basis of all religious belief. There are good Darwinian reasons for this, but as our scientific knowledge has increased, better answers have emerged. Supernatural and paranormal explanations have become increasingly obsolete. Consider this: in two-hundred years of scientific exploration, nothing has ever turned out to be magic. This kind of superstitious or magical thinking is nowhere more apparent than in our understanding of the psychedelic experience.

The American ethno-botanist and author, Terence McKenna, believed that DMT is the gateway to a super-natural, parallel dimension inhabited by alien entities he named Ayahuasca Machine Elves. To anyone applying even the slightest smidge of critical thinking, the proposition is obviously highly improbable. McKenna's 'stoned ape' the-ory claimed that our evolution from Homo erectus to Homo sapiens, and our increased cranial capacity was due to eating magic mushrooms. There is no evidence for this. He was convinced that large amounts of DMT are released by the pineal gland at the point of death, hurtling us into an after-life. To date, there has been no DMT detected in the human brain. McKenna also predicted that the end of the world would coincide with the end of the Mayan calendar in 2012. I'll leave you to figure out the accuracy of that claim your-self.

See what I mean about making stuff up?

Not to pick on poor Terrence, who seems like a nice enough chap, but he's an excellent example of how an other-wise intelligent person can hold deeply irrational beliefs. It's an all too common problem. It's tempting to buy into these extravagant and fanciful explanations for the psychedelic experience. When you are in the throes of a psychedelic experience, it does feel like you are transported to another world. It can appear as if information is coming at you from an outside source, or that your consciousness is travelling through space or time. But our human perceptions are noto-riously unreliable. Our senses and intuitions cannot reliably be trusted.

Consciousness is a mysterious and hard problem, but like all scientific explorations, we must follow the evidence. As of yet, there is no credible evidence that consciousness can exist outside of the human brain. Every attempt to find it has failed. Everything we currently know about neuroscience, biology, and psychology points to the fact that consciousness is an emergent property of the brain and cannot exist with-out it. Which brings us to so-called shaman.

Ayahuasca has become increasingly popular over the past few years, with retreats popping up all over North and South America. These therapeutic sessions are run by facil-itators who call themselves shaman. They claim to act as intermediaries between the natural and supernatural worlds, using magic to cure illness, foretell the future, and control spiritual forces. Shamans believe in a spirit world inhabited by animal and plant guides. They'd have no problem with McKenna's Machine Elves, or ghosts or goblins, or fairies at the bottom of the garden.

While people can get therapeutic benefits from shamanic rituals, the same can also be said of faith-healers and witch doctors. Belief systems can yield both powerful and motivating results, but I would argue that truth always has a greater value than a consoling fantasy. The last thing I need, to get real benefits from a therapeutic psychedelic session, is someone pretending to be a wizard.

But let's not throw the baby out with the holy water. Under the right conditions, psychedelics can change your mind, change your behaviour, and change your life. We are only just beginning to realise their true potential. We are on the cusp of an exciting new era of psychedelic psychotherapy. The effects are real, but the supernatural trappings, imaginary and inadequate explanations, and magical thinking are, as they say in Crawley New Town, a load of old bollocks.

One of the finest technological advances of the twenty-first century is the DMT vape pen. A gram or half gram of DMT is suspended in a solution of vegetable glycerine and smoked with a vape pen. There are a number of advantages to this method. Unlike smoking, nothing is wasted. It's good till the last drop. All you have to do is put it in your mouth and suck. Dosage control is the biggest advantage. A small toke will give you a pleasant lift and put a smile on your face. A longer toke will put you on the launch pad ready for blast-off. And a couple of big hauls will sling-shot you into what might seem like an alternative universe but will, in fact, just be the wonderful machinations of your marvelous mind.

39

My clients had a few simple rules they had to follow. Come alone, text before you come, park a couple of blocks away, spend at least a hundred dollars and never mention my name.

Here's what a typical day used to look like back in the heady heights of my infamous heyday.

Get up and go out for a late, leisurely breakfast with Veronica (we are on an eternal quest for the perfect breakfast sandwich.)

Get text from A... Can I drop by today?... Yes... Be home in an hour... Finish breakfast... Walk home... Text from B... You home?... Yes... Come on down... Arrive home... A arrives... Tea?... Yes... Make some tea... A sits down at kitchen table and requests two ounces of pot and a half ounce of mushrooms... I stuff a wad of dough in my back pocket, serve tea and chat to A... B arrives... Tea?... No thanks, gotta run... What can I get you?... B buys two DMT vape pens, an eighth of E and twenty hits of acid... I stuff a tidy sum in my back pocket... B leaves and Veronica and I chat over tea with A... A is splitting up with their partner... Veronica and I both give A our best advice... She doles out sympathetic soft power... I offer the cold, hard steel of truth. Text from C... You around?... I'll be here... C arrives... Tea?... Sure... C buys a hundred lot of acid and an ounce of MDMA... I stuff a fair chunk of change in my back pocket... C chats over tea with A... They com-

pare relationship tactics… Get text from D… Can I drop
in?… Sure… Half hour later D arrives and buys an ounce of
pot, an ounce of mushrooms and six hits of MDA… I stuff
a great, sweaty wad of cash in my back pocket… A leaves
and D sits and chats to C and Veronica… D and C are both
therapists… They discuss with Veronica the thorny issue of
addiction and its potential solutions.

Text from E… Was thinking of dropping by?… Ok, see
you soon… I weigh up more pot… E arrives and wants
three ounces of pot and a DMT vape pen… I stuff another
fat wedge of cashola in my back pocket… Tea?… Sure…
Make more tea… E sits at the kitchen table with C and
D… D leaves… Text from F… You available?… Sure, I'm
here… F arrives and wants to sell me two pounds of pot…
I give it a quick sniff and a squeeze… It checks out and I
give him a pretty penny… He says hi and bye to E and C
and leaves… Text from G… Yes, I'm here… G stops by and
buys an ounce of MDMA and two ounces of mushrooms…
I stuff a chunky roll of moolah in my back pocket… E and C
leave together… Veronica shows G the garden… They talk
flowers and compost and relationships.

H drops in and is having a bad day… Veronica takes
him into her studio for an impromptu therapy session… She
talks him down from a ledge… G leaves… J texts and wants
to drop by… Ok… J is broke and wants to borrow money
to pay his car insurance… I give him a pile of shekels… K
shows up and buys a pound of mushrooms… I stuff a fat
stash of samolians in my back pocket… We invite J out for
dinner… He accepts… L arrives and picks up an eighth of
MDMA, an ounce of pot and a vial of liquid acid… I stuff
a crispy stack of sweet spondoolicks in my back pocket…
Veronica and I take L and J out to dinner at a nearby restaurant… I pick up the bill, pay in cash, and tip heavily.

Another day at the office comes to an end with a string of

happy, satisfied customers. The only danger is an overdose of tea.

My customers were trained to only come during the day. Not wanting to be on call at all hours, I shut up shop at 7 p.m. The last thing you want is someone knocking on your door at midnight for two hits of E. My texting protocol and hundred-dollar minimum nipped that one in the bud.

My business model was buying pounds and selling ounces so there was quite a bit of weighing involved. Pounds of MDMA had to be weighed into ounces, half ounces, eighths, and capped into gel caps for individual hits. Mushrooms and pot were weighed into ounces and half ounces. LSD came in sheets of one thousand and then chopped up into hundreds and fifties. DMT came in one-gram lots and in vape pens.

After a few decades of practice, I got very good at weighing. I could eyeball a half ounce of pot, throw it on the scales, and often get the exact weight. The same thing was true for MDMA or mushrooms.

I fantasized about competing in the drug dealers Olympics where the events would test skills inherent in the trade. There could be weighing events to test accuracy; the one-ounce powder event, the half-ounce pot challenge, speed trials on weighing a pound of mushrooms into one-ounce bags. A money-counting event could include sorting a pile of bills into their respective denominations, or guessing the value of a stack of bills. There might be races to roll joints or cap Es or bag up pot. This was surely my only chance to become an Olympic champion.

Although my chances of a world record in the drug dealer Olympics seemed like a long shot, I did get a fair bit of acclaim from my clients. Because of my unfailing commitment to quality, public education, and my superior tea-making skills, I received a lot of positive feedback.

I cannot count the number of people who have reported

life-changing experiences from psychedelics. Almost everyone who tries MDMA experiences some benefit. Even if they only try it a couple of times, they invariably report positive effects.

Nowadays, there's been an explosion of micro-dosing. A tiny amount of LSD or Psilocybin or even DMT is taken on a daily basis. It's not enough to get you high but will improve your mood and elevate your thinking. The result is similar to an antidepressant but much more effective, and with none of the nasty side effects.

Having supplied hundreds of people over the years with micro-doses of psychedelics, I can attest to their success with anxiety, depression, addiction, migraines, and relationship issues, and so on. New research and numerous studies are now validating many of these claims.

40

With the money continuing to pile up, we doubled our mortgage payments and paid off our first house in eight years. Then we borrowed a down payment from the equity in our first house and bought a rental property containing several apartments. The rental income covered all the expenses, so the house effectively paid for itself. We repeated the formula every few years and, at one point, ended up with seven houses.

Real estate and rental properties became another profitable business for us. Once you own a couple of houses, the equity builds up quickly and down payments can be borrowed against it. We could have kept going and ended up with dozens of houses, but we have always valued time and freedom above money. More houses meant more work. Dealing with tenants and repairs and maintenance can take up all of your time so, once we achieved financial security, we eventually retired with our family home and two rentals.

What did we do with all this money and free time? We became the social hub of our community. We hosted weekly gatherings at our house with free drinks and drugs. We took groups of friends on free vacations and getaways. We hosted large and lively dinner parties. We gave away tickets to concerts and theatre shows and movies. If tenants were struggling, we reduced their rent or gave them a free month or two. If friends were short of money, we gave them cash, or paid their phone bills, or had their cars repaired.

Veronica, as a trained counselor and therapist, used her skills to offer free counseling to anyone who needed it. I, too, had a lot of advice to give. We became very popular and maintained a large circle of friends.

It's worth repeating that it's these human connections and social transactions that give life its ultimate meaning. Not piles of money in off-shore accounts. Not another promotion at work. Not collecting cars or amassing accolades. Meaning is something that we create from human relations and interconnection.

Real wealth lies in the emotional capital we invest in family and friends.

41

New Year's Eve 2000 brought with it the hysteria known as Y2K.

It was widely believed that because computer programmers had assigned two digits to represent the date, instead of four, the world would come to a grinding halt. It was predicted that everything controlled by a computer would fail. The global economy was predicted to collapse, electrical devices would turn on their owners and planes would fall from the sky. We were all doomed.

So, in spite of this, or maybe because of it, Veronica and I decided to take the kids for a raving holiday to Thailand over Christmas and New Year.

Air travel used to be fun, something to look forward to. In the sixties and seventies, you dressed up to fly. It was a special occasion. The staff at the airport, and on the plane, would beam and grin from ear to ear. Nothing was too much trouble. Services were fast and efficient. Free gourmet meals were served on every flight. Drinks were free and unlimited. You could even enjoy a smoke on the plane. There was a tiny, flip-top, ashtray built into the arm rest of every seat.

These days, instead of being treated like royalty, passengers are herded about like farm animals and treated like common criminals. We wait patiently for hours for flights that are often cancelled or delayed. We are lulled into a false sense of security and hoodwinked by flight times. 11.06 or

4.49 appear so precise, so exact, we are fooled into thinking that schedules are meticulously planned. Fact is, you will likely wait several hours to appreciate that split-second timing.

We are poked and prodded and surveyed and interrogated. We are all suspects who cannot be trusted. It is the job of the customs officials to break us down, pierce our defences, catch us off-guard and reveal our true nefarious and evil intentions. Intensely aware of being watched and monitored at every moment, we overcompensate with clumsy efforts to act naturally. This invariably attracts more attention and perpetuates a vicious cycle of psychosomatic aberrations.

Air travel is now psychological warfare of the highest order.

Once aboard, passengers are strapped into seats designed for six-year-olds. These are seats formerly used to experiment on monkeys in a laboratory. The ones where the wretched animals are restrained while their skulls are surgically removed and their brains exposed.

During the flight, we continue to be eyed with suspicion by staff and passengers alike. There is no longer any such thing as a free lunch. Now we pay through the nose for a dried-up cheese sandwich in a plastic bag. The drinks are limited, expensive, and served in a disposable thimble. These refreshments are 'enjoyed' while virulent air is blown into our faces through a nozzle specifically designed to intensify harmful bacteria.

So, after a pleasant flight, we touched down in Singapore to make our connecting flight to Bangkok. In Singapore airport there are signs everywhere announcing that the penalty for international drug smuggling is death. Next to the word death is a crude illustration of a skull-and-crossbones. As our travel agent had failed to warn us of this draconian policy, I became a little apprehensive about the hundred hits of LSD in my shirt pocket. And this presents an opportunity to impart another useful smuggling tip.

With the advent of heightened security, X-ray machines, drug dogs, and modern scanning techniques, it is becoming increasingly difficult to smuggle drugs through airports. The exception is LSD. It is odourless, colourless, and cannot be detected by any human, dog, or machine. Liquid acid can be dripped onto the paper of any book, journal, notepad or business card.

One of my favorite methods is to use the loyalty cards issued by coffee shops and other businesses. These cards often feature a convenient numbering system entailing circles or squares which are punched with every sale. These spaces are a perfect repository for drops of liquid LSD. Just slip it into your wallet or purse for a bon voyage. On this particular trip, I was experimenting with a variation on the theme.

I bought a pocket-sized crossword-puzzle book, filled out the first few puzzles, then flipped to the center and doctored a few pages with liquid acid, carefully dripping one drop in each square. Then, I casually slipped the book, along with a pencil, into the breast pocket of my shirt and sailed through customs.

Back in the sixties, Singapore was famous for an entry stamp it used to identify undesirables. It consisted of a large, black stamp that took up half a page in your passport and read, S.H.I.T., an acronym for Suspected Hippy in Transit. Singapore has since dropped the stamp but retains its reputation as one of the most punitive and uptight places on earth.

From Singapore, we suffered a three hour flight to Bangkok. Like every westerner before us, after arriving at Bangkok airport, we proceeded directly to the Khaosan

Road. This is mandatory. There is no choice. Khaosan Road is the bustling hub of Bangkok and the center of everything. It's a crowded carnival jam-packed with raucous bars and restaurants, cheap hotels, junk stores and travel agents. This is where your Thai adventure begins, or ends.

There are many tales of rudderless travellers who got stuck in tawdry, fleabag hotels, got hooked on the white stuff and never left. Cheap heroin, opium, and an affordable lifestyle attract junkies from all over the world. You can see them staggering about in the streets like emaciated zombies, hungry ghosts searching for love in all the wrong places. This is where the guys from *The Deer Hunter* ended up. It was a teachable moment and we used it to tell our kids to lay off the smack.

Nothing broadens the mind like travel.

We rented modest rooms just off the Khaosan Road and hit the town running. Donovan and Nolan were in heaven. There was cheap food and drinks everywhere. No ID? No problem. They were like rats in a maze. We let them loose and did some sightseeing.

Later that night, we all met up in a street café. The boys had befriended a sixteen-year-old Australian girl named Alice. She was visiting Bangkok with her parents. We had planned to visit the notorious Patpong that evening and Donovan and Nolan had already invited Alice to join us.

Patpong is the Red Light district, renowned for its loose morals and lawlessness. Its seedy bars are full of girlie boys, rampant prostitution, and explicit sex shows. We were convinced our boys could handle it, but not so sure about the demure Alice. She'd have to get permission from her parents. She called them and said she'd be sightseeing with her new friends and their responsible parents. She handed the phone to us and we confirmed that we were indeed parents but strategically avoided any references to our level of responsibility. Alice's parents seemed satisfied and we all set off to the world's most famous sex circus.

In Bangkok, one goes everywhere in a tuk tuk, a three-wheeled auto rickshaw. Like swarms of angry bees, they buzz the streets, racing around wreaking havoc, leaving death and destruction in their wake. A tuk tuk has a back seat that can fit two or three people comfortably. But at a pinch, can accommodate up to a dozen adults, seven children, and a goat. They also have the unique ability to defy the laws of physics.

Normally, when a hundred and fifty vehicles enter a six-way intersection, Newton's three laws of motion are strictly observed. One: every object moves in a straight line unless acted upon by a force. Two: the acceleration of an object is directly proportional to the net force exerted and inversely proportional to the object's mass. And three: for every action, there is an equal and opposite reaction.

Tuk tuk drivers are blissfully unaware of Newton's laws and employ only one strategy: accelerate. They believe if they can go fast enough they will bypass the usual physical limitations of the universe and avoid any trouble. Miraculously this tactic serves them well, most of the time.

Veronica and I got our own tuk tuk while the lads and Alice took another. We goaded our respective drivers to race each other across town and they were more than happy to oblige. This made the trip a lot faster and a lot more exciting.

Bangkok's Patpong district is an endless marketplace of sexual desires and deviances. There are strip bars, pick-up bars, fetish bars, girlie-boy bars, live sex shows and the infamous ping pong bars. The name is deceptive and many a table tennis player has been disappointed by the lack of tables or paddles.

We ended up in a place called, The Pussy Ping Pong

Bar. What we saw there was about as erotic as a pap smear. Despondent young girls who looked about the same age as the horrified Alice lumbered onto the stage one after another and pulled various objects from their vaginas. Strings of flowers and ribbons were unceremoniously yanked out from that most sacred of caves and piled onto the stage. One wretched girl wheeled out a shabby looking, five-foot-tall cardboard effigy of a cake complete with lit candles. She spent the next twenty minutes contorting her body and cocking her leg in a grotesque effort to blow out the candles with puffs of air from her vagina. It was excruciating to watch. Alice was looking slightly peaky so we quickly paid up and left before the next act came on. We'd all had quite enough of Patpong.

Donovan, Nolan and Alice decided to go home so they flagged down a tuk tuk and zoomed off into the night. Veronica and I went in search of a rave club and found one called Euphoria which featured trance music and three levels of dance floors. The place was packed and jumping. Although I'd brought some acid with us, I hadn't brought any MDMA so we decided to try and find some.

Usually, I approached a promoter or a DJ and introduced myself as a world-famous rave promoter and author. I often carried copies of my book, *Rave Culture: An Insider's Overview*, to use as credentials. But on this night, I had spotted a likely looking character in the middle of the dance floor. He was completely lost in the music, covered in sweat, eyes closed, arms swaying in front of his face like water weeds. I wanted what he was on.

I danced up beside him and asked if he had any ecstasy for sale. He was a little defensive at first but I quickly assured him I was not a cop but a world-famous rave promoter and author. This worked. He took out several pills and handed them to me. It's always a bit of a gamble buying drugs

from complete strangers in underground clubs in the seedi-
est neighbourhood in Bangkok, but in this case, I could see
the effects with my own eyes, and they looked good.

Veronica and I both popped a pill and ventured onto the
dance floor. Soon we looked just like the guy who'd sold us
the E. It was some of the best we'd done in a long while.

At 3 a.m. the club wound down and we hit the street.
There was a merry band of Thai scallywags outside and
murmurs of an after-party. The guy we had bought the
E from was in the group and invited us to tag along. We
followed the group for many blocks, cutting through back
alleys and narrow streets until we were thoroughly lost.
Eventually we came to a place with a shiny red door which
opened up into a big, flashy gay night club. At the center
of the dance floor stood a large metal climbing frame, complete with swings and monkey bars. Veronica and I found
a spot on the second-floor balcony and watched as exuber-
ant, sweaty, shirtless gay guys performed for each other on
the jungle gym. This proved to be highly entertaining and
we marveled at their fitness levels, unbridled optimism, and
enthusiasm for life.

By 5 a.m. the MDMA was wearing off and our clocks
were winding down. We flagged down a tuk tuk and headed
back to the hotel. The rosy fingers of dawn were tickling
the morning sky as we sped through the mostly deserted
streets. Thai skies are famous for turning a particular shade
of peach. The cool morning air blew through our hair as
we relaxed in the back seat of the tuk tuk. As more of the
sun appeared on the horizon, its warmth began to fill the
cab. The honk of an Asian spot-billed duck greeted the day.
Some moments are made to savour.

Closer to the hotel, the traffic intensified. Heading for a
particularly busy intersection, our tuk tuk driver narrowed

his eyes and carefully planned his strategy. Approaching the grid-lock ahead at high speed, he stamped on the gas pedal.

The next morning, we discovered that Donovan, Nolan and Alice had also found some late-night fun. It was 4 a.m. by the time they dropped Alice off at her hotel. Her Dad was on the street to meet them and was hopping mad. No harm, no foul. I hoped her night was as memorable as ours.

Our final destination was Ko Pha Ngan, a small island off the south coast of Thailand. We had to take a twelve-hour train ride from Bangkok to Surat Thani in the South and then a ferry to the island. The four of us boarded the overnight sleeper train in Bangkok at 7 p.m. It was dusk as the train crept out of Bangkok at a snail's pace through the vast wilderness of the Khlong Toei Slum.

You won't see this advertised in your tourist brochure. Over a hundred thousand people are crammed into makeshift houses made of scrap building materials and cardboard boxes in what is Thailand's biggest shanty town. We pondered our good luck as mile after mile of desolation and misery rolled by. These people had lost the geographical lottery that we had won.

From Surat Thani, a ferry took us across the Gulf of Thailand to Ko Pha Ngan. On the southern peninsula of the island lies Haad Rin beach, a one-kilometer stretch of pure white sand lined with dance clubs, restaurants and bars. Haad Rin is most famous for its monthly full-moon parties but this year was Y2K. It was the end of the world. They would be pulling out all the stops for one last Christmas and New Year.

We checked into a guest house in a palm grove at the far end of the beach. Our polished, wooden cabins were elevated on stilts. A well-stocked bar and a full-sized snooker table kept the boys entertained for hours.

Mopeds, or motor scooters, are cheap and plentiful in

Thailand so we rented one each for the lads, and another one for me and Veronica. Our ad hoc scooter gang spent many days exploring the island, discovering remote beaches and waterfalls, while running into the occasional herd of elephants.

Christmas in Haad Rin was less than traditional. Some of the local bars and restaurants displayed the odd tree or Christmas decoration but the effect was somewhat lost on a white sand beach in thirty-degree heat. There were a few brave souls in Santa suits. One impressive group costume featured a dozen, drunken Australians all dressed up as that jolly elf.

One of the bars on the beach served magic mushroom milkshakes. The mushrooms were fresh and black and slimy. For two dollars, they'd throw a handful into a blender with a mango and some pineapple juice. On Christmas Eve we all toasted in the new millennium with a magic milkshake and hit the beach. Each establishment had different music and décor. Most of the clubs were simple wooden structures built with substandard materials, free from the pesky limitations of building codes.

In one such establishment, we were dancing on the second floor of what looked like a large bamboo barn. The place was really going off. About two-hundred people were jumping up and down in unison to hard house music. At one point, someone we assumed to be the owner, was also jumping up and down, but rather than enjoying the music, his pained and desperate expression told a different story. The frantic club owner was pleading with everyone to abandon the building. No one was listening. He eventually jumped up onto a pool table screaming at the top of his lungs. It was then we noticed the whole place listing dangerously to one side. We could hear the wood ripping and tearing. The building was about to collapse. We got out as fast as we could, as did everyone else. With disaster averted, we strolled down the beach and into the next club.

New Year's Eve was a truly epic bash, a hedonistic spectacle, a veritable bacchanalian cavalcade. Twenty thousand international partiers packed the beach. Every single bar and restaurant pumped out various genres of electronic dance music. We were given a few hits of MDMA from a local DJ who claimed to have read my rave culture book. He was excited to meet such an important and famous author and wanted to impress us with some superior ecstasy. His mission was accomplished and we were duly impressed. This was the night I discovered Sangsom rum.

There is much debate about this local spirit distilled from sugarcane. Some claim it contains a mild psychedelic, others say it has added amphetamines. The truth we may never know, but my curiosity was peaked. After the last E wore off, and in the spirit of scientific discovery, I drank a mickey of the fabled brew.

It was certainly no ordinary rum. At first, I felt like I was coming back up on the mushrooms and then had an enormous burst of energy. Time sped up and the rest of the night was a blur.

Long after Veronica and the lads had gone to bed, I found myself in a jungle clearing amongst a Japanese DJ collective, dancing like a lunatic in front of a giant stack of speakers blasting psy-trance at full volume.

Midnight had long since passed, but the world was far from over.

42

In Polynesian mythology, Maui is a trickster god best known for creating the Pacific islands. He is also credited with making the sky a little bit higher and the day a little bit longer. Although he might have spent his time more productively by eliminating greed and hunger, or curing cancer, he did do a pretty good job on the Hawaiian Islands.

In the winter of 2000, Bill Gates quit his job, a new millennium had just begun, and Veronica, ever so subtly, and typically oblique, made a circuitous but implied suggestion. While reading a newspaper and gazing out the window at the murky, grey Vancouver drizzle, she oh-so-casually remarked, "It's thirty degrees in Maui today." I immediately picked up on her sub-subtle-micro-inference and galvanized into action. I immediately booked two return tickets to Maui and rented a red convertible.

We both agreed it was too risky to smuggle MDMA so I packed my usual stash of undetectable LSD and we headed off to the airport. After a mercifully short, three-hour flight, we touched down in Maui and presented ourselves to customs. While our bags were being X-rayed, Veronica caught my eye and flashed me a suggestive glance while applying some lip-gloss. Was this a secret signal too subtle to detect? Had she eschewed the spoken word altogether, resorting instead to imperceptible gestures? Or was this an acknowledgement of my irresistible sexual prowess? At the passport check, the lip-gloss came out again and was applied with exaggerated panache and a puckish grin. A single eyebrow was raised and lowered like a titillating wave. Was Veronica slipping a gear, or merely overcome by the tropical heat?

After clearing the airport, we picked up the red convertible and sped off. I asked about the lip-gloss and with that, Veronica disassembled the container and emptied out a dozen caps of MDMA.

Before arriving in Maui, I had done my usual extensive pre-travel research. I scoured the internet for websites pertaining to DJs, clubs and parties. The name of a DJ trance collective named The Archetechs kept popping up. It was run by DJ Lemondog, DJ Akido, and DJ Jackramit. They were running club nights and beach parties, and they all played progressive house and trance music.

I contacted them by email and introduced myself as a famous Canadian rave promoter and author. They were duly impressed and I mailed them a copy of my book. On arrival, we were treated like visiting dignitaries. The Archetechs had organized a beach party and a club night in our honour.

Lemondog, Akido and Jackramit were dedicated ravers of the highest order, deeply involved in the music and culture. They wore candy bracelets and beaded necklaces and had extensive record collections from the latest producers. In true raver-style, they wore short, blond crops and tight fitting, neon sportswear. And they were all enlisted as career sailors in the United States Navy.

I was curious as to how they incorporated rave culture into what seemed an incongruous military lifestyle. At their club night the following evening, they explained how they were subject to regular drug tests so MDMA was out of the question. They could, however, indulge in LSD because it wasn't detectable with a drug test. They lamented the fact that they had not seen any for a long while. I was only too happy to inform them that the shortage was over.

One of the events the Archetechs had orchestrated for us involved humping a sound system down a precarious, rocky path leading to a secluded beach. We set up decks and speakers and before long, a few locals began to trickle in. I passed out free LSD to anyone who wanted it. Lemondog, Akido and Jackramit eagerly devoured the acid and took turns tag-teaming at the turntables. It was a beautiful, tropical starlit night. We danced barefoot in the sand, paddled in the surf, and marveled at the moon.

Veronica got into a lengthy conversation with Lemondog about his relationship. He was on the fence about marriage and was wrestling with the pros and cons of commitment. LSD is well known for its ability to offer new perspectives on intractable problems. It can focus your mind in new and surprising ways, enabling an objective viewpoint and a fresh take on an old problem. Just as LSD can reprocess visual and audio information where familiar objects and scenes can be experienced with new eyes and ears, thoughts and ideas can also be amplified and illuminated for a fresh perspective.

Without the input of novel experiences and new ideas, our minds become rigid in both perception and analysis, limiting our responses and reactions. We become anchored to well-worn mind-sets which are never re-evaluated or questioned. Like the wheels of a train, our intractable world-view is stuck on a fixed rail, unable to correct course or deviate from its inevitable destination. LSD enables us to jump the tracks and go off-roading. DJ Lemondog plotted a new course that night. He decided to ask his girlfriend to marry him.

At about 1 a.m., the wind began to pick up and the sky darkened. The slip mats were blowing off the decks and a tropical storm was brewing on the horizon. Everyone knew the drill. With military naval precision, the equipment was quickly and efficiently packed up, carried up the bluff, and loaded into cars. Veronica and I jumped into our red convertible and followed Lemondog back to his house.

He lived in an open-plan, rancher-style bungalow in a coconut grove. We set up the decks in his living room and settled in to some deep, soulful, melodic, progressive house grooves. A look of resigned determination spread across Lemondog's face as his eyes intensified with inner focus. The obsessive-compulsive DJ gene was fully activated and there was nothing he could do about it. He played without a break for the next five hours.

Floor to ceiling windows gave us a stunning view of the coconut grove outside. For the first couple of hours, we watched in awe as the willowy palms outside thrashed about in the wind. Rain lashed the side of the house making beautiful, intricate patterns on the windows. Later, the storm slowly subsided and gave way to a typically perfect Hawaiian day. The sun came up and the whole garden took on a purple hue. As the light filled the morning sky, the whole world glowed orange.

After a round of heart-felt alohas, Veronica and I hopped in the red convertible and drove back across the island to our rented cabin. The sun was hot and high, and so were we. The humidity hit us like a warm, wet blanket but with the top down, the effect was nicely mitigated by the wind in our hair.

Nothing is very far on Maui so we took a longer scenic route across the island and detoured through miles of pineapple plantations. Veronica spotted a rainbow, then another. One was short and fat, another long and thin. Then a massive one from horizon to horizon followed by a double, and then a triple. In all, we counted over a dozen different kinds of rainbows, some we'd never seen before.

Several days later, we were exploring the North Shore, driving the winding, mountainous roads, looking for Willie Nelson's house.

Our plan was to visit The Pools of Ohe'o, also known as the Seven Sacred Pools, but we heard that Willie's house was on the way. We had no intention of bothering him, but if he were, say, hanging out in his front yard as we passed by, we might stop and say hi, and he might ask us where we were from? After formal introductions, I might offer him a copy of my book and ask if he knew where we could find some good weed. Being a friendly sort and a famous connoisseur of marijuana, he might invite us in for a joint and a game of poker with Woody Harrelson.

We did drive past Willie's house but the place looked deserted. No sign of Willie, or Woody. But the Pools of Ohe'o were spectacular and, after a careful count, we were able to confirm that there were indeed seven.

Cruising back, we were discussing our options for acquiring some pot when we rounded a bend and spotted a young, native Hawaiian fellow on the side of the road. He raised two pinched fingers to his mouth and flashed the internationally recognised hand signal for dope smoking. I hit the brakes and pulled over.

Most Hawaiian natives are happy, friendly, jolly people. They enjoy life, love a good pig roast, and can't get enough ukulele music. But there are some, who, to this day, have a chip on their shoulder when it comes to westerners. This is understandable, given their checkered history with invaders.

Here's a snippet of that scandalous history:

In 1778, the same year that Britain abolished the slave trade, Captain Cook landed in Hawaii and claimed ownership of the entire island. The Hawaiians, who'd already been there for fifteen-hundred years took exception. If that wasn't enough to piss off the Hawaiians, Cook was later caught red-handed burning Hawaiian temple idols for fire-wood. The angry natives took a dim view and stole one of his boats. Cook responded by kidnapping the king and hold-ing him as ransom for the boat. This strategy had previously worked in Tahiti, but it didn't work in Hawaii. The Hawai-ians attacked, freed their king, and murdered Captain Cook. The British retaliated with cannon fire, killing thirty Hawai-ians.

This is exactly the kind of foreign policy that leaves a bad taste. It's no wonder that some Hawaiians feel justified in ripping off tourists, although to be clear, I do not support or condone the actions of the British and was completely unaware of Captain Cook's bad behaviour which I now wholeheartedly and unreservedly condemn.

Accordingly, in the spirit of international cooperation and reconciliation, I approached this local entrepreneur and enquired about his wares. He showed me a small bag of sticks and stems and demanded three times the going rate. Obviously an opportunist, he was gambling on the fact I had no idea about local pricing and was unable to tell the differ-ence between real buds and scragweed.

I pointed out the obvious problems with quality and pric-ing and, adding insult to injury, he attempted to make the case that there was nothing amiss with either. I assured him of my credentials as a veteran cultivator and connois-seur of fine marijuana. I asked him if he'd ever heard of a book called, *Rave Culture; An Insider's Overview.* He had not. I reminded him of the international reputation held by BC Bud and hammered home the point by asking if he was aware that BC Bud romps the Cannabis Cup in Amster-dam almost every year. He capitulated and put his scrag-weed away. I then asked if he had any real bud. Without a word, he walked over to a bush on the side of the road and retrieved another small bag of weed. This time it was decent-looking product but still overpriced. After a thorough inspection and a brief haggle, we shook hands, the deal was done, and we sped off.

As ambassadors of our respective nations, we had proved that international trade could be conducted with civility and mutual respect, without firing a shot.

43

Here's a mystery: in thirty years of chopping up sheets of acid, I never once experienced a contact high—until I did.

LSD comes in sheets of blotting paper containing one-thousand doses and has to be cut up into smaller batches. This entails a lot of touching and holding and pinching and fondling. Conventional wisdom dictates that with all that handling, some of the substance might be absorbed through the skin. Given that LSD is active in microscopic amounts—a single hit is one-hundred-thousandths of a gram—you might reasonably conclude that carving up several sheets in a row might result in getting totally zonked. This is a reasonable assumption to make, except for the fact that in all the years of chopping and slicing and dicing, I had never once caught a buzz—until I did.

LSD comes from the lab in the form of a white crystal. It is typically diluted in vodka but any alcohol will do. The diluted mixture can be put into a dropper bottle to be dispensed in single drops or, more commonly, soaked onto blotting paper. One gram of crystal is enough to make ten sheets, each containing one thousand hits. These sheets become the canvas for fantastical designs and art-work. There is even an art gallery in San Francisco that is dedicated to blotter art.

If the acid has been freshly laid, the sheets can be slightly damp and the residue can easily transfer onto your skin.

My attitude towards this hazard was always somewhat cavalier. Many times over the years I've gotten the liquid on my hands and have never known it to penetrate through the skin into my bloodstream—until it did.

One time, after cutting up a couple of thousand sheets, I detected the familiar twinkle of lysergic acid diethylamide bubbling up in my brain. I concluded that I must have accidentally picked up a sliver on my finger and ingested a small dose. This had happened once before with an incident involving vegetable soup. I frequently used the chopping board in the kitchen for cutting up acid. I had accidentally left a few fragments on the board and later made some soup. Some of the acid had found its way into the soup and an hour or so later, our dinner guests were well snookered.

Surprise.

This time, and given my past history, the cause was not so obvious.

The next time I cut up some LSD, I was extremely careful not to touch my face, mouth, or any other mucus membrane. I waited for the results and sure enough, an hour later, felt the unmistakable trippy flutter of LSD. This was far from a full dose and so not enough to induce hallucinations. I guessed I'd absorbed about thirty micrograms, or a third of a dose, just enough to brighten up the day and make me unreasonably optimistic about the future. But I was baffled as to why, after decades of contact, I had apparently become hypersensitive? Had my physiology been altered? Had my skin thinned? Was this a manifestation of quantum entanglement?

After that first absorption event, I experienced some degree of contact high every time I handled LSD. Consequently, I either accepted the reality of a trippy day, or snapped on the surgical gloves.

44

In 2006, Saddam Hussein was sentenced to death by hanging while Veronica and I were planning our next international adventure.

Donovan and Nolan had already done a fair bit of travelling of their own. When they came of age, we bought them both one-year return tickets to Australia. They left as dependent children and returned a year later as independent adults. While they were away, their bedrooms were converted into an art studio and an office, thus further encouraging their ongoing independence. My status as a British subject made them both eligible for EU passports and they took full advantage of being able to live and work in various European countries. We had successfully passed on our travel genes.

Donovan was an avid footbagger and competed in The World Footbag Championships five years in a row. Footbag, or Hacky Sack to the layman, is a demanding sport involving the acrobatic kicking of a small cloth ball. Donovan competed at competitions in Prague, Berlin, Montreal, Florida, France and Denmark. He also won the Australian Open twice and eventually became the ninth best footbagger in the world.

As their lives were becoming more and more divergent with ours, we decided to go on, what we thought might be, one last family vacation. It had been a quarter century since Veronica and I had been to India so we decided on another raving holiday. We planned to spend a month in Goa over Christmas and the New Year.

Since we were last there, Goa had become one of the undisputed rave capitols of the world. The psychedelic, all-night rock music parties we had experienced during our previous visit had morphed into the Goa Trance scene.

House music migrated to the beaches of Goa in 1990, the year the World Wide Web was invented. DJs in Goa embraced the new musical genre and remixed it into a frenetic blend of what became known as Goa Trance or Psytrance. It incorporated hypnotic sounds, Indian sitar samples, pixie dust, and cosmic background radiation. With its 140-150 beats per minute and jackhammer tempo, Psytrance is not for the faint of heart.

MDMA had largely replaced LSD as the drug of choice on the beaches of Goa. But as Psytrance is the most psychedelic of all the electronic dance music genres, its followers, and the music, is still heavily influenced by LSD and magic mushrooms. The preferred high of the psy-trancer is a mixture of LSD and MDMA known as a Candy Flip, or a blend of mushrooms and MDMA which is known as a Hippy Flip.

Generally, I find LSD and Magic Mushrooms are best enjoyed alone. They both have unique properties that can be diluted and mitigated by the empathetic qualities of MDMA. Getting the right blend takes practice and awareness. Some drugs are more dose-specific than others but all drugs, psychedelic or otherwise, are subject to the native chemistry of the user's brain. The goal is always to achieve the maximum positive benefits while minimising any unwanted side-effects. The general rule is, start with a low dose and gradually increase until you reach the optimal dose for you.

Our outgoing flights to Delhi were relativity uneventful, just the usual quota of abuse, torture and neglect that we have all come to accept as perfectly normal. We may have been charged a little extra for the neglect. The airline had also successfully shaved another two inches off the legroom. I'm an impressive six-foot-four, so I spent most of the trip with my knees jammed up next to my ears. But the pain and suffering of the outbound flight would pale in comparison to the nightmare of our return flight.

Delhi is an abstract masterpiece of chaos and confusion. Too many of its seventeen million inhabitants live in slums and unauthorised colonies with no plumbing or running water. In 2014, it was rated by the World Health Organization as the most polluted city in the world. In the twenty-five years since our last visit, we expected great changes; a new and thriving middle class, less poverty. We were expecting to see a new modern, affluent India but it all looked much the same to me. It was just as impenetrable and perplexing and fabulous as ever.

On the overnight sleeper train to Bombay, we shared a carriage with an Indian family. Offering hospitality to strangers is a fundamental tenet of Hindu culture so, at dinnertime, when the family pulled out numerous Styrofoam containers of food, they offered to share their meal with us.

The father's name was Milan. He was a Hindu and a chemical engineer who worshipped the monkey god, Hanuman. A lively conversation ensued about religion in general and specifically, the improbability of a monkey god and its incompatibility with the worldview of a scientist who might value the importance of evidence. Milan had no problem with these obvious and overlapping magisteria. In fact, he claimed that unlike the other Hindu gods who had all been killed or transformed, Hanuman was the only one who was still alive. I asked where he might be found. With a wave of a hand and a sideways nod of the head, Milan pointed out the window indicating the jungle.

It's hard for me to accept that anyone, especially a university educated scientist, can sincerely believe in a god who's a monkey. But perhaps it's no more far-fetched than a virgin birth or resurrecting the dead. Fact is, our all too human tendency to create and invest in fantasies is as tenacious as ever. No fiction is too great. No story too outrageous. Human beings will quite literally believe anything. Despite the exceedingly unlikely possibility of an afterlife, the Ancient Greeks are probably not spinning in their graves.

After sharing a meal with Milan and his family, we were left with a mountain of soiled Styrofoam containers. I began to collect them up with the intention of finding a garbage can. Milan laughed at my foolish western ways, grabbed the whole pile, and tossed it out the window of the moving train. Veronica and I were horrified. Milan assured us that the jungle had the capability to absorb and neutralise any amount of garbage. I wondered about the courses taught in the chemical engineering department of the University of Delhi. They might want to consider adding a little more ecology, and a lot less Hanuman.

After a hectic, noisy, dusty, chaotic, thirteen-hour journey, our train rattled to a halt in Panjim, the capitol of Goa. For some inscrutable reason, Indian cities often have two, or even three names. This is partly due to the fact that the British have an aversion to foreign languages and an elevated opinion of their own. Apparently, the original name, Panaji, proved a bit of a tongue twister for the British stiff upper lip. The locals called it Ponnjé but that was even more difficult for the linguistically impaired British. It also sounded suspiciously French, and that would never do. Finally, despite the fact that Goans form an ethno-linguistic group resulting from the assimilation of Indo-Aryan, Dra-

vidian, Indo-Portuguese and Austro-Asiatic linguistic ances-
tries, they settled on Panjim.

A common form of transportation in Goa is the motorcycle taxi. These motorcycles are not specifically modified
for passengers so have only the regular pillion seat designed
to support a driver and one passenger. Luckily, the Goans
are generally diminutive people so, if the driver slides up and
crams himself against the front handlebars, eliminating any
unnecessary steering capacity; you can easily fit up to thirteen passengers, a bucket of ducks, and a goat.

No longer the budget travellers of yore, we elected to take
one motorcycle taxi each. The four of us roared off like a
motorcycle gang past the pristine beaches and palm groves
of Goa.

Our old haunt, Baga Beach, once the epicenter of hip-
piedom, had been infiltrated by more conventional visitors.
Travellers had mostly been replaced by tourists. Tourists
come to observe the culture. Travellers come to immerse
themselves in it. The Goa Trance scene, we were told, was
still active on the northern beaches so we ended up further
north on Vagator beach with its soft, creamy sand, jet black
rocks, and impossibly tall, spindly palm trees. Planning to
stay a month on Vagator, we wanted to rent a house. If you
want anything in India, you just ask anyone in the street.
They are only too happy to help, even if they haven't got a
clue where to find want you want.

For the rest of the day we were directed, chaperoned,
guided, and escorted from place to place by various locals in
search of someone's brother or uncle or cousin. Most turned
out to be dead ends but, by the end of the day, we had found
a suitable house next to the beach, paid a month's rent, and
moved in.

The next order of business was renting our own motor
scooters. Once again, we asked around and were directed to

someone's uncle, or was it a brother? One quickly realizes that everyone in Goa is related.

Ravichandran was an enterprising Goan whose sole business was renting out ten motor scooters. Donovan and Nolan picked out one each and Veronica and I rented one to share. After the customary haggle (he went high, I went low, we settled in the middle) he took our money and handed us the keys. There was no paperwork or rental agreement. No insurance policy or deposit. No license or helmet was required. He simply flashed us a big, toothy smile and said he'd see us in a month. He didn't even know our names, or where we were staying. Later, we discovered this level of trust from the locals was typical. After decades of being overrun by tourists and travellers alike, I'd expected a certain level of cynicism, but far from being jaded, the Goans were surprisingly and invariably open, friendly, and welcoming. This relaxed attitude also extended to buying drugs.

There were several large raves planned over Christmas and New Year so a supply of high quality MDMA was of paramount importance. I asked around and was quickly referred to someone's cousin, who referred me to their brother, who knew a guy. We met in a café on the beach. He was a handsome, affable, young Goan with a thick mop of black curly hair. He introduced himself with a wink and a big smile and said, "Code name Didi." I replied, "Code name Jimi."

I told him I sold ecstasy in Canada, promoted raves, and gave him a copy of my book. Duly impressed, he produced a solid, single MDMA crystal wrapped in tissue paper. It looked like a terminated quartz crystal about three inches long but was ruby red. I'd never seen anything quite like it. In Canada, I usually bought MDMA in crystal form from the lab. Unlike pressed pills, this ensured there were no cuts. The crystals varied in colour and could be clear, white, grey, brown or purple depending on the final reaction and degree of washing. All these colours could produce excellent E. But I'd never seen it bright red before. Didi picked up on my trepidation but assured me I had nothing to worry about. Disarmed by his infectious smile, I bought the red crystal and Didi disappeared into the street.

Back at our rented house, we prepared for our first authentic, bona-fide, Goa Trance party. Normally MDMA crystal is ground up in a coffee grinder and then put through a fine sieve. The powder is then packed into #4 gel caps, which hold an average dose of about a hundred and twenty-five milligrams. Since we had neither a grinder nor a sieve, we used the parachute method. This entails crushing the crystal with the back of a spoon and twisting up the doses in a small square of toilet paper resembling tiny parachutes. The pre-party at our house attracted an enthusiastic group of newly acquired friends and I passed out free E to everyone.

By the time we arrived at the party, our assembled crew were all in an extremely good mood. It was an outdoor event surrounded by palm trees painted with multi-coloured, fluorescent paint. Huge fluorescent banners depicting Hindu gods hung between the trees and a barrage of black lights created a surreal Technicolor glow. The DJ booth was a giant, white sphere which glowed with an ethereal purple radiance under the ultraviolet lights. The DJs were Japanese and Russian and played some of the hardest, fastest music I'd ever heard.

I'd already given out about twenty doses of the red crystal and had now run out. The results were in. It was some of the best E we'd ever done. The group of people we were with all agreed it was exceptional and a couple of hours later were asking for more. We were discussing the next course of action when I noticed someone coming through the crowd.

It was Didi. We met on the dance floor and I asked him if he had any more. He pulled out another fat, shiny, red crystal and handed it to me. I explained I didn't have enough cash on me but could go and get it. I could be back in a jiff. "No problem," he said, "You meet me tomorrow on Anjuna Beach. Bring money. Later, later. No problem." With that he disappeared into the crowd and was gone again.

The MDMA was worth about a hundred dollars which translated to a month's wages in Goa. I was impressed at the level of trust given to a complete stranger. He had no idea where I was staying, or if he'd ever see me again. That night we partied until dawn and walked back to our house accompanied by a herd of cows who were heading down for a day at the beach.

The next day, I grabbed our scooter and drove down the coast road to Anjuna Beach. I asked random strangers if they knew Didi and was incrementally directed to a restaurant on the beach. Didi appeared, smiling from ear to ear. I thanked him for his confidence in me and paid up. We were now officially blood brothers in the international, underground cabal of ethical drug dealers.

The return trip to Vancouver was torture and would test our patience and endurance to the highest degree. The route was straight forward enough: Delhi to Vancouver, with a stop in Singapore. What could go wrong?

On arrival at Delhi airport, we were informed our flight had been delayed by two hours. No matter. We went for a chai. On our return to the check-in desk, we learned there would be a further two-hour delay. The departure lounge at Delhi airport is not, strictly speaking, a lounge. A lounge implies lounging, and lounging requires seating, with a minimum requirement for upholstery, carpeted floors, and perhaps some tasteful accent lighting.

Delhi's departure lounge woefully lacks any of the prerequisites associated with relaxation or comfort. It is a giant, floodlit, concrete and steel bunker with wooden seats. Its cement walls and floors are painted gun metal grey. Its only amenities are a snack bar and a chai stand. It was now 11 p.m. and the snack bar was closed for the night. Back at the airline desk we were told that our delayed flight was now cancelled. We'd been rescheduled for a 9 a.m. flight. We asked about a hotel or meal vouchers or compensation but were told we were entitled to nothing, and don't bother asking again.

This is one of the dirty tricks airlines like to play. All they have to do is claim the cancelation is due to 'mechanical failure,' and they can leave you for dead. You can demand to see a mechanic's report all you want, but you will surely be disappointed. With ten hours to kill, we headed back to the chai stand to formulate a plan. It was closed. We decided to stick it out at the airport and made improvised nests with towels and coats on the dirty concrete floor. After a restless sleep, we made the morning flight. Eight hours later, dishevelled and bleary, we arrived in Singapore.

The flight delay of twelve hours meant our connecting flight was long gone and we found ourselves stranded with dozens of other forsaken passengers who were clamouring for attention at the flight desk. The harried and confused flight attendants desperately tried to deal with the situation. At one point, the staff simply walked away and left the angry mob to argue amongst themselves. We killed some time in a restaurant.

Later, when the mob had dispersed, we made our case to an airline employee and were told all flights to Vancouver were fully booked for the next two weeks. We could try to fly stand-by but we were told it didn't look good. Feeling lucky, we waited three hours for the next flight and stood by. We were still standing by when the plane took off without us. We could try some more standing by in eight hours but were once again told the plane was over-booked and our chances were slim to none. With the horrific prospect of being stranded in Singapore for the next two weeks, we decided to buy new tickets to anywhere in North America and then make our way back to Vancouver.

The four of us gathered up our belongings and took the subway downtown. In most cities, subways are grimy, bustling hubs of humanity that reflect the beating heart of the city. But Singapore is not like most cities. Everywhere is squeaky clean and perfectly ordered. The streets and subway are spotless and it has a reputation as one of the most oppressive and intolerant societies on earth. People move about like automatons, avoiding eye contact. Outwardly, Singapore wears the cheery, superficial smile of western capitalism, but beneath that pseudo-sophisticated surface lays the beating black heart of a North Korean-style totalitarian state.

The laws are some of the most stringent and heavy handed anywhere. Minor offences are punishable by the lash. The importation and possession of chewing gum is illegal and punishable by a thousand-dollar fine or two years in prison. Skateboarding or spitting in the street will get you a good caning. Feeding pigeons carries a five-hundred dollar fine, and Singaporean officials have the right to conduct anonymous and random drug tests without a warrant to anyone, anywhere, anytime. Drug charges carry twenty-thousand-dollar fines, ten years in prison, or even a death sentence.

A sense of civic outrage stirred in my breast. I felt the need to push back against this tyrannical regime, to make a statement, to represent and give a voice to subjugated proletariats everywhere.

Littering, I learned from a public sign, was punishable

with a large fine and a public shaming. I took out a wad of paper from my pocket, screwed it up into a ball and palmed it. This would be a teachable moment for Donovan and Nolan. I attracted their attention as I bent down on one knee and pretended to tie my shoe. I then ejected the ball of paper into the spotless street, stood up and walked away. This was no ordinary littering. This was a revolutionary, political act, striking at the heart of autocratic, totalitarian regimes everywhere, a blow struck for the common man.

We finally found a travel agent in a booth at an antiseptic, pristine, orderly street market. An hour later we had arranged new tickets back to Vancouver via San Francisco and Seattle for a mere eight-thousand dollars. It was a long route but the first flight left Singapore in a few hours. The sooner the better.

As we were just about to swipe our credit card, Veronica received some sort of psychic message and was convinced we could make the next stand-by flight. Given the expense, we decided to give it one last chance. We put the new tickets on hold and returned to the airport.

We watched patiently as the flight boarded, secretly hoping that some terrible fate might have befallen at least four of the scheduled passengers, perhaps not fatal but serious enough to disrupt their travel plans and open up a few seats. When the final boarding call was made, our hearts sank and what little faith I had in Veronica's, or anybody else's psychic abilities, quickly evaporated.

Moments later, however, we were called up to the flight desk, hastily assigned four seats in a row and, with seconds to spare, four tired but happy travellers made it on to the plane. By the time we arrived back in Vancouver, we had been in transit for sixty-two hours.

45

U sing cash to buy gold bullion was another solution to the money storage problem.

Paper money is periodically redesigned and updated. New bills are released and old bills become obsolete. It became increasingly inconvenient to convert larger amounts of paper money, so alternatives had to be found. Gold that is 99.95% pure requires no tax or paper trail. It's not recommended for a short-term investment but for a long-term storage option, it has certain advantages.

I began buying gold bars in the early nineties at four-hundred dollars an ounce, then five-hundred, then six, etc. Unlike money in the stock market, gold, the most noble of all the noble metals, does not disappear. It is produced in supernova nucleosynthesis during the collision of neutron stars and is delivered to Earth in asteroids. Until our own sun goes nova in five billion years, it's not going anywhere.

A one-ounce bar of gold bullion is now worth about two and half thousand Canadian dollars. Long after the inevitable collapse of the global economy, the lustre of gold will continue to shine in a sea of pecuniary darkness. As the global financial system teeters on collapse, I like to imagine myself trudging through the rubble of a post-apocalyptic world clutching a heavy satchel full of gold bullion while feasting on the flesh of investment brokers.

We all have our fantasies.

Those who work in the dubious field of selling investments to starry-eyed suckers will invariably advise putting as much money as possible into a retirement savings plan. This money is invested in stocks and bonds and other figments of the imagination.

Investment counselors recommend diversifying your funds into low, medium, and high-risk categories to ameliorate exposure to loss. When your account loses money, their advice is to 'dollar cost average,' which means putting in more money to replace the losses. As your money evaporates into the ether, they will advise to stay the course, keep to the plan, and increase contributions.

It all sounds feasible until you realise the only ones making any money are the money managers, the fund managers, and the banks. Everyone gets paid, regardless of whether the invertor makes any money or not. Between the losses, the management fees, annual marketing fees, distribution fees, custodian fees, expense ratios, commissions, and broker fees; there is nothing left for the unwitting investor. When the market crashes—and sooner or later it surely will—your money is locked in, trapped in a downward death spiral. There's nothing you can do but sit back and watch helplessly as your life savings disappear forever. When you confront your financial advisor and threaten his life, he will smile sweetly and recommend waiting for the market to recover. He will nonchalantly throw around terms like, stand firm and hold on, and stick it out. Yes, the market may recover eventually, but this could take years.

In the last crash of 2008, I was forced to watch in shocked disbelief as over two hundred thousand dollars evaporated into thin air. Against the advice of my financial advisor, I withdrew what was left of my money and hit the road. I later calculated that if I'd stayed the course, it would have taken another six years to eventually break even. Some investment.

Fact is, the markets are a rigged casino run by criminals. The whole system is a colossal con-job designed to make profits for everyone, except the poor sap throwing in good money after bad. Conventional investments are a lost highway of broken dreams, paved with lies and deceit. Consequently, I have vowed to never again put another dime anywhere near the stock market.

There are only three investment classes worth having: real estate, gold, and drugs.

46

During the first two decades of the twenty-first century, Veronica and I revisited our favourite places and made numerous trips to Mexico, Venice, Hawaii, Guatemala and the US. It was our greatest hits world tour. We returned to places we had been twenty or thirty years before to see how they had changed. Panajachel in Guatemala, the sleepy town we'd lived in and conceived our first born, was unrecognizable.

It is said that tourism destroys that which it seeks to find. Once a critical mass of tourism is achieved, the local ambience and charm becomes a backdrop rather than the main event. The unique flavour and colour of a place becomes overpowered by crowds of gawkers and gongoozlers moving from store to store and bar to bar, in search of a culture that only exists to service themselves.

There are still magical, cultural experiences to be had, but they are more difficult to find. You have to look a little harder, go a little farther.

Occasionally, there are pleasant surprises.

After receiving Canadian immigration status, I vowed I would never again set foot in England. I spent the next twenty-five years slagging off Old Blighty as a backward, stagnant, racist, ignorant, violent cesspit of antiquated ideas. I told anyone who would listen to avoid it like a pandemic.

After my parents immigrated to Canada and my estranged and adversarial sister moved to South Africa, the only relatives I had left in England were a coterie of crackpot, half-wit cousins in whom I had no interest. I had severed all emotional ties to my motherland. Or so I thought.

In 2005, Facebook was launched. Within the first few months, like so many other fickle and treacherous punters, I dumped MySpace like a discarded piece of soiled garbage, and opened a Facebook account.

In recent years there's been a lot of criticism about the platform. I'll be the first to admit it is not without problems, but let's not forget that Facebook is probably the greatest communication tool ever invented. Like any tool, it can be used for good or ill. It's profound effects on global culture, economics, and politics are undeniable and its failings are largely due to its user's inability to parse information, engage in meaningful communication, or maintain a civil discourse. These problems are the fatal flaw in any system involving human beings. Humans are notoriously unreliable, unpredictable, and can rarely be trusted. On Facebook, our inherent shortcomings are magnified on a global scale heretofore unimagined.

It is exponential stupidity squared at light speed.

I'd like to think that with such amplification comes clarity. With our defects so clearly exposed and publicly aired, one would think that self-reflection might lead to such glaring and obvious mistakes being corrected. But then you'd be putting your faith in human nature. Such folly will inexorably lead to disillusionment.

The most frustrating aspect of our current global predicament is the fact we have perfectly good solutions to all of our problems. If we all thought reasonably and rationally, all our most pressing problems including pollution, income inequality, poverty, war, and climate change could theoretically be solved. If we had all taken Stoicism 101 and Critical Thinking in grade school, we would find ourselves living in a very different world. If the same facts or data are evaluated by any group using the basic skills of critical thinking, reason, and logic, they will inevitably arrive at similar conclusions. But when we cease to be persuaded by sound evidence, facts, and reasoned argument, we quickly shed the veneer of civilization and descend into what increasingly looks like today's chaotic and combative world. Can Facebook save us? Probably not, but it did change my mind about England.

As my friends list swelled, I began to see some old, familiar names and faces. Royston Trinidad, whom I hadn't seen in almost thirty years, showed up in my feed. So did Byron Thomas, and Stanley Cartesian, and Dr. Bob Bagshot, my old surgeon friend and immigration guarantor. We messaged back and forth for a while and it quickly became apparent that the old connections were still very much alive. I decided to go back one last time to visit some very old friends and take a victory lap.

That first trip back to England was a revelation. The country I had left for good in the early eighties had transformed itself into a modern, affluent, and cosmopolitan nation. People had money and cars and telephones. They took vacations, bought luxury goods, and foolishly invested in RRSPs.

In my day, the only food available in a pub was a pork pie, a pickled egg, or a packet of cheese and onion crisps. Now, thanks to the European Union allowing the freedom to travel and work in twenty-six countries, talented chefs from all over Europe had flooded into the country, elevating pub menus to a whole new level. The past culinary crimes of deep-fried Mars Bars and jellied eels had been erased and forgiven. There were even vegetarian options for old favorites like bangers and mash, shepherd's pie, and even fish and chips.

Here's a confession that has little or nothing to do with

the intent of this book, although it may provide an additional ethical or moral dimension to my account. I have been a vegetarian for the past four and a half decades. My children, now approaching forty, have never eaten meat.

There are many good reasons for being a vegetarian. It is more economical, more ecological, more protein-efficient, better for our health and the environment and so on. But the main reason for my dietary choice was a moral one.

As a young lad, I became suspicious that it might be immoral to torture and slaughter animals for our culinary pleasure. I credit this realization to my relationships with various animals as a child. I had a dog, seven cats, twenty-seven guinea pigs, three rabbits, seven gerbils, numerous mice, rats, hamsters, turtles, snakes, lizards, a hedgehog, a horse, and a duck. Anyone who has had a close, personal relationship with a duck will attest to their affectionate, flirty nature and wry sense of humour. It's not long before duck à l'orange gets permanently struck from the menu.

This is why we are squeamish about killing the animals close to us, like dogs and cats. When we get to know an animal, it quickly becomes obvious they share many of our human qualities. Animals have lungs and livers and arteries. They have little hearts that beat. They have families and friends and mourn their dead. They defend their land, go to war, and steal and cheat, just like us. The more we study them, the more sentient they appear to be.

Recent research has shown that even fish are more intelligent than first thought. They can recognize individual human faces and exchange information about them. Fish can even eavesdrop on the conversations of other fish and use that information to their advantage. Never underestimate a fish. They are as devious and conniving as the rest of us.

I believe that in the not so distant future, we will no

longer find it morally acceptable to kill animals for food. Meat-eating will go the way of cannibalism, human sacrifice, and slavery, all of which were socially acceptable at one time. Slaves were once considered to be a renewable resource. Think about that. A hundred years ago, animal rights would have been unthinkable. Now we love our pets. They have their own hotels and cemeteries and doctors and psychiatrists. We accept them as family members. I have never understood how people can have so much love and compassion for dogs and cats, but none at all for cows and pigs and sheep.

Food for thought.

Duly impressed by the moral, social, and culinary progress made by my native land, Veronica and I zigzagged across the country looking up my long-lost pals. They were all present and correct. We laughed, we drank, we reminisced, we drank some more, we had a ball and made some whoopee, we kicked up our heels and let down what was left of our hair. We got nostalgic and retrospective and sentimental and drunk. We had such a good time that we ended up going back five years in a row. On the second trip back, we all met up on Stanley Cartesian's canal barge and went on an LSD cruise.

Since I last saw him, Royston Trinidad had become a music teacher at Hazelwick, our old alma mater and where we first met as teenagers. His specialty was teaching students to play the guitar like Jimi Hendrix. Doctor Bob Bagshot had become a senior colorectal surgeon and proctologist at a leading London hospital. Byron Thomas, my old Hazelwick hero and staunch ally in the Brighton squatting campaign of '73 still lived in Brighton. Lastly, I had re-established contact with my earliest childhood friend, Cullum Hewitt, a career flight attendant who claimed to have a clear memory of my fifth birthday party. As teenagers we had made a solemn pact to attend each other's funerals. Of course, only one of us could keep the promise, while the other would be powerless to confirm that the oath had been honoured.

Stanley's sister, Lindy, lived in Warwick, a historic city in the heart of southern England. Veronica and I had arranged to meet up with Stanley and the barge there and then make the seven-day journey to Stratford-upon-Avon.

The canal barge, also known as a narrow boat, was fifty-five feet long and only seven-foot wide. The canal system in England has three thousand miles of canals. Formerly used for transporting heavy goods around the country, they are now solely designated for recreational use only.

If you have never travelled on a narrow boat, you have missed out on one of life's greatest pleasures. Cruising through the English countryside at three miles an hour leaves a unique and lasting impression. The constantly changing landscape reveals rolling green fields, grazing sheep and cows, ancient hamlets, thousand-year-old Saxon churches, quaint villages and Tudor pubs, all passing by in dreamy slow motion. These Shires were the very ones that inspired Tolkien. This was hobbit country.

After seven days and nights, and what felt like an epic, Homeric odyssey, we finally arrived in Stratford-upon-Avon, home of the Bard. Stanley called his sister, Lindy, to inform her of our safe arrival and invite her to dinner that evening. Proving that time is indeed relative, she hopped in her car and took twenty-five minutes to make the same journey.

The following day, my other old school friends arrived and we passed through a lock and transferred the boat from the canal to the River Avon. Then we all dropped acid. It was the first time in a long time for most, but they were all game for an adventure.

Dr. Bob Bagshot, proctologist extraordinaire, got very

chatty and regaled us with stories of patients with objects lodged up their anuses. At least twice a month he had to remove a shampoo bottle or a hair brush or children's toys from that place where no sun should shine. Embarrassed patients came up with elaborate stories of how these objects came to be where they were. They claimed to have slipped in the shower and accidentally fallen onto them. They reported trying to scratch an itch or cure constipation, or that it happened unbeknownst to them whilst they were asleep. Dr. Bagshot listened intently, smiled and nodded, and then got to work.

Byron Thomas, a veteran psychonaut and antiestablishment thrill-seeker, became deeply involved in a surrealistic, stand-up comedy routine. Lost in his own world and gesticulating wildly, he riffed in a stream of consciousness about the day's events and interspersed his manic diatribe with outlandish impersonations. I laughed so hard I spat out half a scone through my nose and fell off my chair.

Suddenly, the impulsive Dr. Bagshot decided to go for a swim. With a great flourish, he stripped down to his underwear and leapt into the murky waters of the River Avon. Cullum donned a head band and pulled out a nerf rocket launcher modified to fire bottle rockets. Like a scene from *Apocalypse Now*, he fired smoky missiles off the bow of the boat towards Bagshot who dodged the flaming projectiles repeatedly by ducking under the water. The smoke lingered in the air and left a shimmering mist on the surface of the water. Jim Morrison crooned in the background; something about the end.

And then the boat got stuck.

Stanley had decided to try and turn the boat around but, because a narrow boat is not only narrow but very long, this has to be done at a winding hole, which is a part of the canal, or in this case, the river, which has been widened to allow a very long and narrow boat enough room to turn around.

Stanley, whose judgment was clearly impaired, mistakenly identified the muddy banks on either side of the river as a winding hole. While trying to turn the boat around, he jammed the bow firmly into the muddy bank. We were now stuck sideways across the river, forming an impenetrable barrier to any boaters travelling in either direction. Stanley revved the engine and cranked on the tiller but the boat wouldn't budge. He slammed the engine into reverse, churning up a violent maelstrom of muddy water. Everyone instinctively moved towards the bow of the boat to see if they might help push it off the bank. This only served to force the front of the boat deeper into the soft mud.

Despite our predicament, morale remained high.

In a largely symbolic gesture, Cullum fired off a couple of rockets directly into the mud to no avail. Byron was in the middle of a Second World War fantasy. He had assumed the personality and thick German accent of Baron von Richter, the Red Baron. He was deep in the throes of a mid-air, life and death dog fight. I had just taken a swig of beer and laughed so hard, a cloud of fine British ale exploded into the air. Dr. Bagshot, still in his Y-fronts, leaned over the bow of the barge to survey the situation. After a quick diagnosis, he leapt into the waist-deep water and attempted to push the boat free of the bank, a valiant effort that proved completely ineffective. This is why there are warnings against the operation of heavy machinery while under the influence of certain drugs. It rarely goes well.

Cullum fired another bottle rocket in Bagshot's direction, narrowly missing his head. Stanley gunned the engine back and forth once again but was getting nowhere. Finally, Stanley figured out that the weight of everyone on the front of the boat was making matters worse. Asserting his authority as the captain, he gave the command for everyone to move to the stern to act as ballast. This lifted the bow slightly and with a final, mighty thrust of the reverse engine, we were free of the bank and on our way.

47

While I have rarely crossed an international border without some sort of illicit substance, this cannot entirely be chalked up to reckless bravado.

My seemingly flagrant disregard for customs and immigration laws has more to do with practical matters. Also, from an ethical standpoint, I refuse to believe I am doing anything wrong. If a law is contrary to common sense then it is, indeed, an ass. And needs must when the devil drives.

As a free-thinking, sovereign human being, I claim the right to put whatever I want in my body, when I choose, and wherever I choose. This I hold as a basic human right and should not be included in the business of the state.

It's hard to gauge the quality of LSD or MDMA from an unfamiliar or anonymous source. LSD is undetectable to the eye or nose and impossible to evaluate on the spot. Any clear liquid or piece of coloured paper could, or could not, be acid. MDMA also comes in a myriad of forms. It can come as a pressed pill of any size, shape or colour. In powder form, it comes in a whole range of colours, textures and tastes. Apart from mass spectrometry, the only way to properly evaluate MDMA is by ingesting it. This is impractical when dealing with a stranger in a strange land. For these reasons, when I travel, I usually prefer to take my own supply. Pot is another matter altogether.

Pot is stinky and bulky and hard to smuggle. Dogs can smell it from a hundred feet away and it lights up X-ray scans like a pin-ball machine. Luckily, if you know how, it is easy to find anywhere in the world. With a practiced and expert eye, it can be easily assessed on the spot. After a five-second examination and a quick sniff, I am able to tell the exact quality and strength of any marijuana or hashish. This is an essential skill when regularly buying pounds of pot. If you sample every batch you will be perpetually stoned. Buying pot is a test I set myself when travelling. It's an international sport in which I'm a world-class contestant.

There is a sense of connection amongst pot smokers and psychedelic drug users, a common understanding of a shared experience. Once you discover a stranger uses recreational drugs, an instant bond is created. You are part of a shared reality. You have something in common.

Pot smokers are the easiest to spot. Anyone who looks remotely like a hippie or a surfer or a raver is likely to either smoke pot or will know where to find some. The danger of asking complete strangers where to score is the possibility they might be an undercover cop, but this is extremely unlikely as undercover cops are easier to spot than pot smokers. Another hazard is being mistaken for an undercover cop. I usually allay fears by introducing myself as a rave promoter, a talented musician, and an eminent author. This invariably does the trick.

If all else fails, find a Rasta. A real one. They will find you some marijuana faster than anyone. Ganja is their holy sacrament and never far from their minds. It's like asking an Englishman where to find a good cup of tea.

Like the sadhus of India, Rastas believe that smoking dope provides a direct hot-line to god (small, disrespectful g intended). Of course, any serious, thinking person will have no problem rejecting this dubious claim.

By now, an alert reader will have suspected correctly that I'm an atheist. But, like the feisty polemicist and writer,

Christopher Hitchens, I would go one step further and describe myself as an antitheist. That is, even if the biblical account of the great god Yahweh were true, I would count myself as a loyal member of the resistance. I would work tirelessly to overthrow that tyrannical despot described in that so-called 'good book.' If you've ever read the Bible, you'll know what I mean.

Like many people I was brought up to believe the Bible was an encoded manual of morality, the unerring, infallible word of god instructing us miserable, puny mortals on how to live a good life. After reading it from cover to cover, I was shocked to find it filled with gruesome murders, sex slavery, genocide, gang rapes, and unspeakable acts of cruelty. It is replete with one pointless violent act after another. Most of these crimes are committed or commanded by the jealous, petty, psychopathic, Yahweh himself. I was genuinely shocked.

How did this awful book ever become known as a source of morality? Next to RRSPs, it is one of the greatest con jobs in human history. If you don't believe me, read it. You can be sure that most Christians have not.

My scepticism of religion extends to all aspects of the supernatural and paranormal. I place gods and devils in the same category as ghosts and mermaids and zombies.

The Amazing Randi, a stage magician and entertainer who spent much of his long life debunking supernatural and paranormal claims, recently died. By his own admission, he harboured no illusions of going to a better place. In the seventies, Randi established a million-dollar prize for anyone able to demonstrate any supernatural ability under scientific testing criteria agreed to by Randi's team and whoever took the challenge. Over the next fifty years, thousands of people took him up on the offer. They were mostly psychics, clairvoyants, and a whole lot of dowsers. All they had to do was prove the ability they claimed to have. Not one person was ever able to claim the prize.

Once again, I'll leave the conclusion to your good judgement.

48

Continuing our greatest hits world tour at the beginning of the second decade of the twenty-first century, Veronica and I decided to revisit Amsterdam. Queen's Day is a really big deal in Amsterdam. When we booked the flights, we had no idea how big the deal was. This would be my fourth visit and the first time back in almost thirty years. Prior to planning the trip, I had sent a copy of my book, *Rave Culture; An Insider's Overview*, to my old comrade and bum surgeon, Dr. Bob Bagshot. A novice in the arena of rave, he was energised by the book and keen to try out a real rave and sample MDMA for the first time. At that time, he was living in England, teaching bum-hole surgery. Or was it key-hole surgery? In any event, when he found out we'd be in Amsterdam, he suggested meeting up for what he described as, "a good old rave up." As ever, the intrepid Doc was up for anything. He also planned to bring along two associates, Dr. Don, his anesthesiologist, and Dr. Dan, a Ph.D. psychologist specializing in addiction counseling. With three doctors on the team, we'd be in good hands if anything went sideways.

While we were booking the tickets and hotel, Rush-the-Fish-Stick stopped by. He'd just gotten fired from his restaurant job for selling magic mushrooms to the kitchen staff. Since I had sold him the mushrooms, I felt somewhat culpable. To cheer him up, we added another passenger to our itinerary.

After booking the trip, I scoured the internet to see what events might be happening. To my surprise, I discovered that we'd be arriving on Queen's Day, the biggest festival in Holland and a celebration of Queen Beatrix's birthday.

Once a year, one and a half million people take to the streets dressed in orange, the symbolic colour of the Dutch royal family. Every public square hosts DJs and other musical events. The canals are chock-full of barges and other types of boats with live bands and crowds of partiers. All traffic comes to a standstill as legions of merrymakers flood into every part of the city.

There was one event that particularly caught my eye. It was a large, underground rave called, Club 11, located on the eleventh floor of an old, abandoned post office in the center of Amsterdam. This would do nicely to introduce our triumvirate of doctors to the wonderful world of raving.

Paramount to the success of this mission was to ensure a guaranteed source of MDMA; uncut, unadulterated, and pure as the driven snow. I could trust no one but my Fairy Godfather. And the only option was to take it with us. We considered a variety of smuggling methods and finally settled on Veronica's vagina.

It's extremely unlikely that a grey-haired, sixty-year-old woman would be pulled aside for a random cavity search. This level of security generally requires some prior intelligence and/or probable cause. The demure and unflappable Veronica could sail through a Nazi checkpoint with a menorah under her arm. We unfurled an extra-strength condom and packed it with a forty hits of world-class ecstasy.

Before leaving for Vancouver airport, I briefed Veronica on the plan. She was to keep the package inside her until we left Schiphol Airport. Under no circumstances was she to remove the package until we were well clear of the airport. She nodded in agreement. No matter what, it stays in. Right? Right. We were good to go. Rush-the-Fish-Stick bleached his hair and packed his orange jump suit. Veronica implanted the slippery torpedo and we were locked, loaded, and lubricated.

The flight was largely uneventful, as long as you classify agony, abuse and indifference as non-events. On flights to Europe, we often preferred to knock ourselves out with Xanax and wake up on arrival. This works well most of the time, despite the relentless efforts of flight attendants determined to thwart the plan with constant interruptions.

We landed on time at a bustling Schiphol Airport and made our way to customs. Rush-the-Fish-Stick loaded all of our bags onto a trolley with Veronica's handbag on top of the pile. He was a short distance in front of us when I asked Veronica about the package. "Are we good?"

"Sure," she said.

"All secure?"

"Yep."

I didn't like the sound of that yep. It carried an ever-so-slight undertone of something unstated, the merest whiff of ambiguity. "It's still inside you, right?"

"No. I took it out on the plane."

"You what? Where is it?"

"In my hand-bag."

Up ahead, Rush-the-Fish-Stick was about to roll the trolley through the controlled doors into the customs area. Veronica's hand-bag sat on top of our luggage like a flashing beacon on top of a lighthouse. I called to Rush-the-Fish-Stick and frantically beckoned him to come back. Recognising something had gone wrong, he turned the trolley around but was too late. He had already crossed the barrier into the high security area and passed the point of no return. The sensors had sensed that he was now going in the wrong direction. The trolley tripped the alarm, sirens went off, multiple flashing yellow lights spun around and security personnel rushed to the area. Rush-the-Fish-Stick froze on the spot and awaited his fate. We stood helpless on the other side of the barrier, unable to help.

A security guard ran up and yelled at Rush-the-Fish-Stick to keep going and clear the area. The distressed guard waved his arms hysterically, indicating the correct direction. Rush-the-Fish-Stick sheepishly turned the trolley around once more and continued on to the customs area. Veronica and I followed close behind and soon caught up to him. The three of us stood in front of a customs officer who asked a few routine questions. While we were talking, Veronica retrieved her hand-bag from the pile of luggage and swung it casually over her shoulder. After checking our passports, the customs officer looked us over, and waved us through.

Outside in the car park, I opened Veronica's hand-bag. There, on the top, in full view, completely unobstructed, lay a very suspicious looking object resembling a wrinkly, white, rubber banana.

After checking in at our hotel, near our old stomping ground on the Leidseplein, Rush-the-Fish-Stick, Veronica and I went to meet up with our medical trio, Dr. Bagshot, Dr. Dan, and Dr. Don, who had all just arrived from the airport.

That evening, we sat in a café and discussed a carefully coordinated plan for the evening. Bagshot, fresh off the plane from England, made the faux pas of ordering a cup of tea. This proved to be a big mistake. The Dutch are masters of the pancake, champions of cheese, and leaders in licorice. But they are sadly and sorely lacking in acumen when it comes to making a proper cup of tea. I knew better and ordered a round of blond, gassy, sweet beer. After several more beers, a plan of action was fully developed and ready to execute. The plan went something like this: go to Club 11 and gobble some Es. The doctors were all in.

Over the years, both as customers and friends, there is something I have noticed about doctors. They are not skittish around drugs. More than most, they appreciate that drugs can improve the quality of our lives. They are also aware of the risk benefit analysis common to all drugs. Let's face it, the average general practitioner is ostensibly a drug dealer or, more accurately, an ethical drug dealer.

Our route to Club 11 took us across downtown, past multiple public squares, each crammed with an orange sea of hedonistic libertines dancing to live bands or DJs. Rush-the-Fish-Stick with his pasty countenance, wiry frame, and bleached hair was constantly mistaken for a junkie and propositioned to either buy or sell heroin.

Night had fallen by the time we'd covered the three kilometers to the old post office. The entire building was empty and derelict except for the eleventh floor, which had been transformed into an underground nightclub, complete with computer controlled lighting and lasers. The walls were covered with wild hallucinatory graffiti resembling an explosion in a paint factory. The sound system would have turned Pink Floyd green with envy. Windows which wrapped around three sides of the room gave a spectacular panoramic view of the city ablaze with twinkling lights and alive with a million and a half people.

We all bought drinks and I handed out the ecstasy. Before long, Rush-the-Fish-Stick was giving a master class in disco moves in his bright orange jump-suit. Our trifecta of physicians were warming up to the music as well.

It's always a particular pleasure to watch people experience the effects of MDMA for the first time. Any experienced ecstasy user will tell you that their first time was the most memorable. It's not that subsequent experiences are deficient, although excessive or prolonged use can result in diminishing returns. It's just that the first flush, that initial rush, is so deliciously surprising, so pleasant, that just the memory of it can bring a smile to your face. The smiles that were stretching across the faces of Drs. Bagshot, Don, and Dan were giving me as much pleasure as it was them.

The triad of doctors danced like teenagers that night, their movements becoming more fluid and their bodies more lithe and supple with each passing hour. By the end of the night, they were tousled and tickled, exhausted and exhilarated. The sun was turning a sea of orange into a panorama of pale pink as the six of us experienced the camaraderie of freedom fighters sharing the sweet victory of a triumphant campaign. Our triptych of medical professionals, like so many before them, had been profoundly and thoroughly converted to the religion of rave.

49

After a forty-year battle of lobbying lawmakers and marching in the streets, on October 17th, 2018, the recreational use of marijuana was finally legalised in Canada.

Medical cannabis had been available in Canada for a number of years before this under a confusing patchwork of regulations. With a doctor's note, a medical user could be licensed under the MMPR program or Marijuana for Medical Purposes Regulations. MMPR license holders were able to possess and grow small amounts for a specific medical condition. This was replaced with the Access to Cannabis for Medical Purposes Regulation or ACMPR. But the MMPR licenses were grandfathered in, resulting in two systems with conflicting rules.

Medical marijuana stores were tolerated everywhere but were technically illegal. The only legal supply available was from government sources, but they grew abysmal pot that no one wanted to smoke. The problem was, the government had no clue how to grow pot and eventually gave up and got out of the cultivation business altogether.

Bent doctors were writing prescriptions with unbridled zeal. I got a license to grow sixty-nine plants for a sore thumb. Everyone I knew had a license to grow pot. The police eventually threw up their hands and walked away. The resulting chaos led the Canadian government to legalise recreational cannabis, only the second country in the world to do so. You'd think that would have been an end to all the confusion, but you'd be wrong.

The whole mess was supposed to be replaced by the Cannabis Act, a national program regulating both medical and recreational cannabis. The only legal growers are now those lucky enough to be issued a production license from the federal government. The production license holders in turn sell to the liquor board who then sell to licensed stores. The requirements for a production license are so prohibitive that only big corporations can afford to participate. Legal growing is now exclusively controlled by big business.

Forty years of growing expertise by dedicated cultivators was kicked to the curb. Also, excessive taxes, fees, and other expenses incurred by this bloated system sucks out all the profits. After a year of legalisation, growers and stores alike are going broke and closing their doors.

For the past half-century, the BC pot industry has worked with the precision of a well-oiled machine. Everyone made money and the consumer enjoyed the finest marijuana in the world. Communities in pot growing areas have prospered and flourished and the BC economy has been the beneficiary of a stable, thriving, and profitable industry. The problem lies in the fact that those now in charge of the industry know very little about it. They are approaching the regulations as if dealing with a highly toxic, radioactive substance.

Cannabis must be grown in sterile laboratory conditions and handled with surgical gloves. At many stores, it cannot be gazed upon by the naked eye or touched by a human hand. The 'product' is hidden away in secret vaults while the customer can only look at pictures and chooses from a menu. Some stores have pot samples sealed in plexiglass boxes with a sniffing tube. Problems with storage and supply chains have resulted in substandard quality. By the time the pot gets to the store, it is often old and dry and tasteless. The result of all this foolishness is a robust and resurgent underground market. Due to the lack of stifling regulations, illegal pot is still better and cheaper than the legal market.

Throughout the medical marijuana era, everyone was growing pot in their houses. Anybody with a sore thumb could get a medical note and fire up a grow room. Growers sold their wares to the myriad of quasi-legal compassion clubs masquerading as members-only, medical marijuana outlets. You could get a membership card by flashing your ID and a big smile.

Growers who sold to these illegal stores found a huge market with competitive prices. Anyone with a pound of pot could walk in off the street and sell it to a medical marijuana store. But when legalisation kicked in, these outlets could only buy from government-approved sources, leaving a glut of unsold pot on the black market. Pot dealers had a huge choice of reasonably-priced pot on offer. Business for the underground dealer was better than ever.

As of 2020, thirteen US states have legalised both the medical and recreational use of marijuana. Another eighteen states have legalised it for medical use only. Around the world, forty-four counties have legalised medical marijuana while only two countries have completely legalised recreational use on a national level, Uruguay and Canada.

It's not hard to see where this is going. As the dominos fall, we are heading for a world where cannabis is no more taboo than alcohol. This is a trend we are also beginning to see with psychedelics.

50

In the year 2000, Paul B. Rothman, Dean of the Johns Hopkins University School of Medicine opened a new department called, The Center for Psychedelic and Consciousness Research. In a statement, he said this of the new center, "Johns Hopkins is deeply committed to exploring innovative treatments for our patients. Our scientists have shown that psychedelics have real potential as medicine, and this new center will help us explore that potential."

This research group was the first to obtain regulatory approval in the United States to reinitiate research into the therapeutic uses of psychedelics. In 2006, their landmark study of psilocybin sparked a revival of psychedelic research around the world. Since that time, Johns Hopkins has published over sixty peer-reviewed articles in respected scientific journals. These studies cover a wide variety of potential therapeutic uses, including addiction, end of life distress, depression, Alzheimer's disease, post-traumatic stress disorder (PTSD) and anorexia nervosa.

In 2016, Imperial College in London, England, launched its center for psychedelic research and was the first to investigate the effects of LSD on the brain using modern neuroimaging. They are also researching the use of psilocybin for treating depression. These types of studies are now cropping up all over the world. China, Israel, Switzerland, Brazil, and others are discovering the potential of psychedelics as medicine. We are on the cusp of a revolution in psychedelic psychotherapy.

One of the most effective organisations working in this field is the Multidisciplinary Association for Psychedelic Studies or MAPS. Its founder, Rick Doblin, has been working tirelessly to legitimise the therapeutic use of psychedelics for the past thirty years. MAPS recently completed the first double-blind, placebo-controlled study of LSD in human beings since the sixties, and is currently funding studies in Mexico and New Zealand into the potential uses of ibogaine, a psychedelic used in addiction recovery. Rick Doblin has done more to legitimize the use of psychedelics than anyone alive. The vision statement on their website at MAPS.org states, "We envision a world where psychedelics and marijuana are safely and legally available for beneficial uses, and where research is governed by rigorous scientific evaluation of their risks and benefits."

MAPS have been especially focused on MDMA-assisted therapy. They have funded and conducted numerous studies looking into healing emotional and psychological damage caused by sexual assault, war, violent crime, and other traumas. The most promising results have come with their treatment of patients with PTSD. The results have been so dramatic that in 2017, the FDA granted MDMA a rare "breakthrough therapy designation," which means MDMA is now fast-tracked to become a prescription medication for PTSD in the very near future. I've been a proud member and donor of MAPS for over twenty years. If you want to find out more or better still, donate, go to MAPS.org.

Another organisation worthy of your attention and money is Erowid.org. This is the most comprehensive and credible site on the internet for extensive information on mind-altering substances. Erowid's vision statement reads, "We imagine a world where people treat psychoactives with respect and awareness; where people work together to collect and share knowledge in ways that strengthen their understanding of themselves and provide insight into the complex choices faced by individuals and societies alike. We believe that truth, accuracy, and integrity in publishing information about psychoactives will lead to healthier and more balanced choices, behaviours, and policies around all psychoactive medications, entheogens, herbs, and recreational drugs." If you want comprehensive and sound information on any psychoactive substance, you can spend weeks getting lost in the Vaults of Erowid.

And the dominoes continue to tumble and fall at record speed.

In 2019, Denver, Colorado decriminalised magic mushrooms and soon after, Oakland and Santa Cruz followed suit. Psilocybin has also been approved by the Canadian government for use in end of life care.

During the US 2020 election several more states legalized recreational cannabis and Oregon voted to decriminalise personal amounts of all drugs. Portugal did this some years ago with great success. Vancouver is considering the same.

We've come a long way since that dimwit, Nancy Reagan, told us to just say no. Let's update that trite and simplistic slogan to: just say *know*. The more we know, the more we find new ways to benefit from psychedelics.

We are at the beginning of a new era of psychedelic research which is already reaping rewards. As with cannabis, medical applications will lead the way, but I look forward to a time when psychedelics will be available to responsible adults for recreational use.

Let's not forget that, apart from their medical applications, what psychedelics do best is stimulate perception and creativity, allowing us to see the world in new ways. When we experience the world through our senses, we map our impressions with neural networks in our brains. Each unique experience produces a neural net, or pattern of neural activity unique to that particular event. In the future, when we encounter the same set of stimuli, the same neural net is produced, giving us a sense of familiarity. The world, as experienced through our senses becomes recognisable, understandable, and manageable.

When we recalibrate the brain with psychedelics, new neural networks are mapped, creating a novel experience from a familiar one. The ordinary potted plant on your kitchen table, seen through a new psychedelic filter, becomes a swirling mass of vibrating filaments. You can see and feel it breathing. You can see it growing. Colours appear fresh and new. You see it for the first time. And this goes for thought processes as well.

Our intellects follow familiar patterns and can get stuck in a rut, in what William Blake referred to as "mind-forged manacles." We react to the world in rehearsed, predictable ways. But conventional thinking does not produce innovation, or promote creativity, or provide inspired solutions.

It's no surprise that Steve Jobs, one of the great innovators of our time, credited LSD with stimulating his creative mind. He claimed LSD was one of the most profound and important experiences of his life, enabling him to think about, and solve problems from a brand new perspective.

Mark Pesce, the inventor of the computer language used for virtual reality claimed that the idea to write the complex code came to him during an LSD trip. The idea came fully formed. It took another three years to write the code.

You can thank LSD for your iPhone and your video games.

Veteran Silicon Valley engineer Kevin Herbert drops acid regularly as a way to hack the limits of his natural thought patterns and claims to have solved many tough problems with this method. Tim Ferris, a Silicon Valley investor and author of *The 4-Hour Workweek*, says he knows many successful entrepreneurs who dabble in psychedelics. "The billionaires I know, almost without exception, use psychedelics on a regular basis. They're trying to be disruptive and ask completely new questions," Ferris said.

A few years ago, an edition of the MAPS newsletter featured interviews with scientists who revealed that many of their major breakthroughs had been inspired by LSD and psilocybin. These advances mostly took place in the sixties and seventies. Now retired, the scientists involved feel free to reveal the truth about their discoveries.

One of the most famous is Francis Crick, the Nobel Prize winner who first identified the structure of DNA. Crick was a well-known acid head and says he saw that beautiful double-helix spinning in space during an LSD trip.

The list goes on.

Dr. Kary Banks Mullis, a biochemist, invented a more efficient way to isolate DNA with an innovative procedure called PCR. When asked how important LSD was to his discovery, he said, "Would I have invented PCR if I hadn't taken LSD? I seriously doubt it. I could sit on a DNA molecule and watch the polymers go by. I learnt that on psychedelic drugs."

There are hundreds of examples of mathematicians, chemists, biologists, and scientists of all stripes who have harnessed the problem solving, mind-bending power of psychedelics. The same goes for the world of art and culture.

The influence of psychedelics in music and the arts has been nothing short of transformative. From Jimi Hendrix to Philip K. Dick, and from Pink Floyd to Hunter S. Thompson, mind expanding drugs have left an indelible stamp on modern culture. Without them, there would be no *Sergeant Pepper* or *Easy Rider*, or *Alice in Wonderland*. In a few short years, LSD catapulted song-writing from, *How Much is that Doggy in the Window*, to *Purple Haze*. Even Ray Charles was an acid head. He once said that LSD was the closest he ever came to seeing.

Notwithstanding the promising developments in psychedelic research, the road to total acceptance remains long and winding. Despite decades of experimentation and investigation, we are still making a lot of the same mistakes and jumping to the same flawed conclusions. Psychedelics continue to be largely relegated to an underground sub-culture and remain illegal. It is still taboo to talk about these drugs in polite society. We have a long way to go before we can openly divulge the details of our last DMT trip at a Thanksgiving dinner with the extended family.

51

Heading into the first quarter of the third decade of the twenty-first century, I find myself looking down the double-barrels of old age and declining health. I am doing more and more things for the last time and less and less things for the first. Fortunately, nature has a few built-in defenses to guard against the unpleasant consequences of advancing age.

The decline creeps up slowly and incrementally. This gradual, almost imperceptible, deterioration gives us time to adapt, like a frog coming to boil on the stove. Abilities decrease at the same rate as our interest in new activities. It's true we can no longer engage in the more rigorous recreations of our younger years, but equally true that we no longer care. Ambition and motivation wane at the same rate as faculties fade. On some days, under the right conditions, and if I pay particularly close attention, I can actually feel the life force draining from my body.

But I'm ok with this. Had I a less fulfilling and rewarding life, I may have had regrets, but this is certainly not the case. If I dropped dead tomorrow, I would count myself as a satisfied customer of Planet Earth and be happy to give up my spot to the next punter.

I gave up celebrating birthdays decades ago. I no longer support the notion there is something special about the arbitrary and accidental date of my birth. The idea that being born on a particular day makes me somehow exceptional seems egotistical and disconnected from reality. Birthdays, once a metric for increased opportunities and privileges, become no more than a countdown to the grave.

The secret to living, a theosophist once told me, is learning how to die. Theosophists invariably wear black. They enjoy being dramatic and mysterious and spooky. It sounded ominous at the time but has subsequently made more and more sense. The truth is, once we conquer our fear of death, nothing else can rattle us to the same degree. Our petty, daily problems become insignificant in the face of our impending and certain death. As humans, we are unique in the animal kingdom in our ability to contemplate our own mortality. We know we are going to die. Everyone we know will also die. No one gets out alive. We have only to gracefully accept our slow decay to the sweet peace of death—unless we're lucky enough to get run over by a bus.

Rush-the-Fish-Stick and I once developed a series of maxims describing our code of life. One of them was, "If you don't care, it doesn't matter." Another was, "No brain, no headache."

Words to live by.

It's no surprise that one of the first therapeutic applications of psychedelics is with end of life issues. With the objective perspective provided by the psychedelic experience, even the fear of death can be conquered. These drugs can fundamentally change the way we think. By creating new neural pathways in the brain, they literally and figuratively expand our consciousness.

To regular psychedelic drug users, this account of mine will seem all too familiar. To me, of course, it has all been perfectly normal and, if you believe the latest research into free will, I could not have lived any other life.

Almost everyone I have ever known has been a recreational drug user. If you include alcohol, the same is true for almost everyone. But the unique qualities of psychedelics put them in a class of their own. If used responsibly, they are truly smart drugs that can increase our perception and awareness and improve the quality of our lives. To paraphrase the prayer used at AA meetings: may you have the serenity to be a smart person doing smart drugs, the courage to not be a dumb person doing dumb drugs, and the wisdom to know the difference.

Psychedelics have done nothing but improved and enhanced the quality of my life. This, I believe, is more the rule than the exception. Have I shaved a few years off my life? Perhaps. But those last few years are surely some of the worst. I might be better off without them.

After four and a half decades together, Veronica remains my soul-mate, lover, trusted confidant, and closest friend. It feels like we've lived several lifetimes together, although I acknowledge the proposition of past lives is both implausible and extremely far-fetched. The fact that we only have one life is all the more reason to count myself lucky to have shared with Veronica the precious singularity of this one.

She left me a note yesterday. It read simply, 'Hummingbird Feeder?'

To the untrained mind, this may seem like an innocuous or mundane comment. But the truth is more nuanced, more beguiling. The question mark was a masterpiece of allusion, a delicate suggestion of inferred meaning. Without the question mark, it becomes at the least, a mundane statement or, at most, a subtle command. The question mark changes everything. It does not direct or dictate but merely invites the reader to contemplate the hummingbird feeder and come to their own conclusion. It says, gently, "What do you think about the hummingbird feeder? What *is* there to think about the hummingbird feeder? And what will you now do, having thought about that hummingbird feeder?"

I looked out the window across the frosted lawn, spotted the empty feeder, and knew that I would soon be filling it.

By the way, if you're thinking about dropping by to pick up a fun-pack for the weekend, prepare to be disappointed. I now make my final confession: after fifty years as an ethical, psychedelic drug dealer and connoisseur of all things mind-altering and consciousness expanding, I have finally and permanently hung up the scales, stashed the baggies, and officially retired. My freezer, once home to bags of magic mushrooms and marijuana, is now the sole domain of bags of French fries and frozen pizza. Lately, I am more inclined to appreciate the subtle pleasures and warm glow of Canadian rye whisky. A couple of times a year, I might indulge in a refresher course of LSD to lubricate the synapses or heighten a walk in the woods. Apart from that, I smoke the occasional legal joint and grow a couple of equally legal plants in my garden as ornamentals. The pot they produce is smokable but not saleable. I give it away to those less fortunate. I sometimes miss the social aspects of dealing, but without the constant interruptions, I now have time for other pursuits, like writing this book. Perhaps I'll make an album of piano songs for my next project?

My brain chemistry no longer seems to respond to MDMA and I have learned all I can from DMT. Like old lovers, we have only fond memories and past glories. My neural networks have thrown in the towel and run out of novel configurations with which to amaze me. The unfamiliar has become familiar. So be it. All things have their cycles and seasons. But the ability of psychedelics to permanently rewire the brain means the changes stay long after the drugs have left your system. Like flashbacks, this is added value for your psychedelic dollar.

Not a week goes by without reminders of my lawless legacy. People I no longer recognise stop me in the street and thank me for their first MDMA experience decades ago. Old customers sometimes approach me in restaurants and thank me for an LSD trip that changed the course of their lives. Sometimes a smile and a nod from across the room says it all.

I am often reminded about past successes with depression or migraines or anxiety. I get emails from friends of diseased cancer patients who tell me the DMT vape pen I mailed across the country had made their last days of life bearable. I am reminded of the times I wandered around parties serving free E and mushrooms on a silver platter. Those days are long gone.

I repeat, psychedelic drugs are not for everybody. Not everyone is ready to step outside of their well-developed belief systems and comfortable mind-sets. Many people will never be ready. But let's not be too quick to judge those who are. Most importantly, we should be wary of condemning an experience we have never had ourselves. People who have learned to use psychedelics responsibly will, without exception, extol their virtues. Whenever someone begins a tirade against the dangers of psychedelic drugs, you can almost guarantee they have never tried them.

The benefits of recreational drugs have been intrinsically woven into the fabric of my life. They have coloured every aspect of my psychology and made the world a more interesting, creative, and rewarding place. I cannot imagine what my life might have been like without them.

In the final analysis, I have lived a charmed existence, enjoyed creative satisfaction, meaningful relationships, and financial fulfillment. My bucket list has been exhausted and I've had more than my fair share of peak experiences.

In retrospect, I would change nothing.

Not too shabby for a brown-shoed boy.

—FIN

Extra Supplementary Bonus Chapter:
How to Make a Cup of Tea

O ne last thing.

As much as I may be acculturated and ensconced in the culture of North America, I feel compelled to correct a glaring and ubiquitous cultural deficiency.

I cannot count the times I've seen a waitress reach for a Pyrex coffee pot containing insipid, brown water from the warming plate on top of a coffee machine, and then pour that wretched dreck into a cheap metal tea pot and place a tea bag on top of the pot. I repeat: on top, and outside of the tea pot.

I have watched in horror as these inept attempts are brought to the table, without milk, barely warm, served with a shriveled slice of lemon on the side in what can best be described in biblical terms as an abomination unto the lord. (small l intentional). While I acknowledge the lack of training and cultural depravation in this field, I cannot forgive the continued and seemingly cavalier abuses to the fine art of tea-making.

Consequently, I offer a few invaluable tips on making a decent cuppa.

Let's start with the water. It must be fresh and cold. Pouring hot water into the kettle may save you a little boiling time but the sacrifices to taste are far too great. It should be noted that water from the hot tap has often been sitting in a tank for too long and will have lost its zest, its will to live. It is flat and lifeless and will ultimately disappoint. Let the cold tap run for a minute or two to clear out the pipes and possible residues. There are bacteria and various dubious elements in tap water known to be harmful. More importantly, they can adversely affect the palate.

Now fill the kettle and bring it to a glorious, rolling boil.

While a bag in a cup will suffice, loose tea in a pot is preferable. Which brings us to the most important and critical factor—the tea itself. Despite the dizzying array of teas on offer, one should not be fooled by faddist collections of herbal, fruited, flowered and scented atrocities available. These concoctions may have their time and place but, rest assured; they will not deliver an authentic cup of British tea. If one is to achieve the characteristic flavour, texture and fragrance of a traditional English cuppa, then Ceylon tea is a must. If you insist on dabbling with a blend, choose one with a maximum of 30 percent Darjeeling. But be warned, this will give you a slightly more full-bodied tea but you will sacrifice some of the sweetness, the velvet texture, and the taste of pure Ceylon.

Next—and this is key to proper infusion—the water must hit the tea at a rolling boil. This is a common mistake and cannot be emphasized enough. Any delay or distraction in marrying the boiling water with the bag or leaf may result in inferior infusion, rendering the finished product substandard, fit only to be poured down the toilet. Concentration, timing, and a steady hand are essential tools of the serious tea-maker.

Next, the brew must be allowed to infuse properly and for the correct amount of time. A clock will be of no use here. Instructions on packages that claim specific amounts of brewing time, two, four, or even six minutes, are misleading and irresponsible. Tea left too long will release tannins and be rendered acidic or bitter. Too short a brew will result in an insipid and flavourless product, surely destined for the toilet bowl.

It is the strength and amount of tea that will dictate timing. Let go of all temporal considerations. Trust yourself. Let
colour, and not the clock be your guide. Tastes may vary
but a middle ground is often best. Not too light. Not too
dark. In time, and with committed practice, you will come
to recognise the perfect colour. We are looking for a mid-
golden brown with a bronze patina.

The cup, too, is of paramount importance. To assess the
correct shade, one must use a cup with a white interior.
A dark interior, black or red, will render it impossible to
ascertain anything useful. Any ceramic or fine china will suffice. Never plastic, paper or, perish the thought, Styrofoam.
There is no sweeter sound than the gentle clink of bone
china against a spoon or saucer. It is a bell of freedom, a
clarion call to a brighter, better world.

The size of the cup is also vital. Large mugs should be
avoided at all cost. Too large a cup can leave the last quarter of the brew cold, dull, and undrinkable, leaving you with
an unhappy memory of the experience, a feeling of loss or
sadness. One should be left with a feeling of completion and
fulfillment.

A good cup of tea should make you optimistic about the
future.

When the perfect colour has been achieved, waste no
time in removing the tea from the teapot. Do not, under any
circumstances, squash or bruise the tea at this stage. Pressing the bag between two spoons is a barbaric practice and
to be avoided at all costs. Gently remove the bag with the
utmost care. The separation must be swift and decisive to
avoid over-steeping. Hesitation is the enemy of the committed tea connoisseur. No less when it comes to adding the
milk. A steady hand and a keen eye are of the essence when
pouring milk. Dribbling should be avoided and an over-pour

can be catastrophic. Take charge. Pour with confidence and control.

Milk must be whole and no less than 3.5 percent fat. Skimmed will not work, and don't even think about milk substitutes. This will inevitably end badly. Once again, colour is your guide. Too little and the tea ends up too strong; too much, and you are left with a milky mess and a hopeless situation. Disposal in the lavatory will be your only option.

If you have done everything right, you should now be in proud possession of a hot, deep-brown beverage bursting with flavour and fragrance. Act quickly. This is not the time to get distracted.

It's time to enjoy a nice cup of tea.

As for the thorny issue of sugar, it is not recommended. Instead, learn to adjust your taste buds to the natural sweetness inherent in the tea. It may take some time to fine-tune your palate, but with determination and resolve, the rewards can be substantial.

We are now ready to drink this marvelous creation. Tea must be sipped vigorously until completely consumed. Any unnecessary delays can result in a loss of both heat and flavour. Halfway through, a moderate gulp is acceptable but never a swig.

Now enjoy to the last satiating drop. Savour the moment. Breathe in the dulcet fumes. Time will stand still and life, for a few precious moments, will be imbued with meaning and purpose.

CPSIA information can be obtained
at www.ICGtesting.com
Printed in the USA
LVHW091517110122
708305LV00005B/68